W9-CCB-908

# THE WOLF'S HEAD

## Also by Peter Unwin

*The Rock Farmers*

*Nine Bells for a Man*

# THE WOLF'S HEAD

## *Writing Lake Superior*

## PETER UNWIN

VIKING
CANADA

VIKING CANADA
Penguin Group (Canada), a division of Pearson Penguin Canada Inc.,
10 Alcorn Avenue, Toronto, Ontario M4V 3B2

Penguin Group (U.K.), 80 Strand, London WC2R 0RL, England
Penguin Group (U.S.), 375 Hudson Street, New York, New York 10014, U.S.A.
Penguin Group (Australia) Inc., 250 Camberwell Road, Camberwell, Victoria 3124,
Australia
Penguin Group (Ireland), 25 St. Stephen's Green, Dublin 2, Ireland
Penguin Books India (P) Ltd, 11, Community Centre, Panchsheel Park,
New Delhi – 110 017, India
Penguin Group (New Zealand), cnr Rosedale and Airborne Roads, Albany, Auckland 1310,
New Zealand
Penguin Books (South Africa) (Pty) Ltd, 24 Sturdee Avenue, Rosebank 2196, South Africa

Penguin Group, Registered Offices: 80 Strand, London WC2R 0RL, England

First published 2003

1 2 3 4 5 6 7 8 9 10   (FR)

Author representation: Westwood Creative Artists
94 Harbord Street, Toronto, Ontario M5S 1G6

NATIONAL LIBRARY OF CANADA CATALOGUING IN PUBLICATION

Unwin, Peter, 1956–
The wolf's head : writing Lake Superior / Peter Unwin.

Includes bibliographical references and index.
ISBN 0-670-04390-7

1. Superior, Lake, Region—History. I. Title.

FC3095.S86U58   2003        977.4'9        C2003-902901-8
F1059.S9U58 2003

Visit the Penguin Group (Canada) website at **www.penguin.ca**

*This book is dedicated to the diarists, letter writers, history buffs, historical society and museum volunteers, authors of self-published chapbooks, storytellers, old-timers, and all the crucial enthusiasts who keep the past from giving up on us.*

*Then I commenced: "Kagagengs, I hear that thy head is full of old stories, as an egg is of meat, and as I am so eagerly collecting the stories of the old time, as thou dost the herbs, I have come to thee to beg thee and to ask thee if thou art disposed to tell me some tradition of thy tribe?"*

*Naturally enough, such a request, which startled the old man like a gun-shot at his ear, rendered him quite silent and confused. He wrapped himself more closely in his blanket . . . At length he said that he was not conscious of knowing any stories, and if he did, they were not worth hearing; and, besides, there were so many stories in the world, that he did not know where to begin.*

—JOHANN GEORG KOHL
*KITCHI-GAMI: LIFE AMONG THE LAKE SUPERIOR OJIBWAY,* 1860

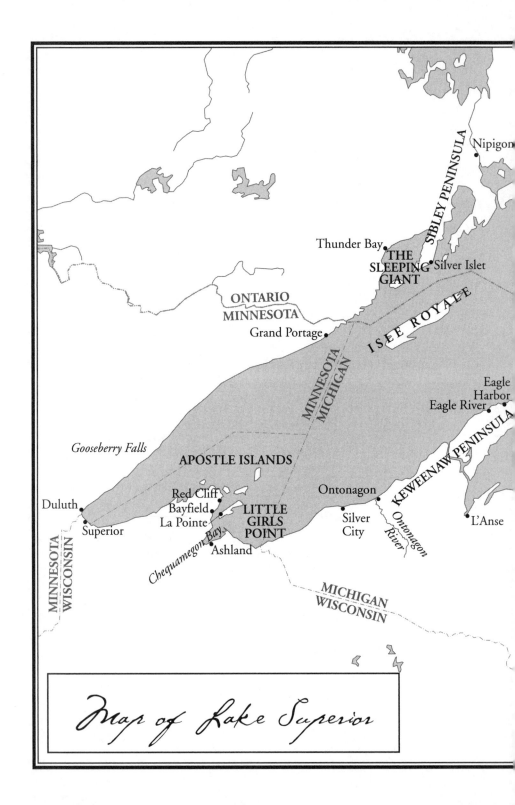

Map of Lake Superior

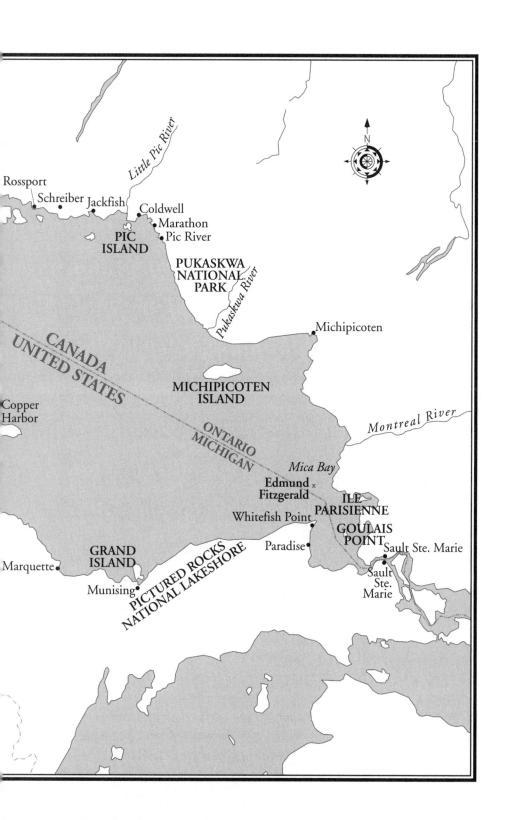

Rossport

Schreiber
Jackfish
Coldwell
Marathon
Pic River

*Little Pic River*

**PIC ISLAND**

**PUKASKWA NATIONAL PARK**

*Pukaskwa River*

Michipicoten

**CANADA UNITED STATES**

**MICHIPICOTEN ISLAND**

Copper Harbor

**ONTARIO MICHIGAN**

*Montreal River*

*Mica Bay*

**Edmund Fitzgerald** x

Whitefish Point

**ILE PARISIENNE**

**GOULAIS POINT**

Sault Ste. Marie

Paradise

Sault Ste. Marie

Marquette

**GRAND ISLAND**

Munising

**PICTURED ROCKS NATIONAL LAKESHORE**

# Contents

*Prologue* xiii

[ 1 ]   The Superior North   1

[ 2 ]   We Weare Cesars   8

[ 3 ]   Mishipizheu   16

[ 4 ]   Standing on Ceremony   25

[ 5 ]   The Water Dogs   34

[ 6 ]   Temperature Rising   45

[ 7 ]   The Ontonagon Boulder   56

[ 8 ]   High Society and the White Indian   67

[ 9 ]   The Snowshoe Priest   83

[ 10 ]   Silver Islet   102

[ 11 ]   Superior Piscine   119

[ 12 ]   South of Superior   135

[ 13 ]   Neys: Captives North   151

[ 14 ]   The North Shore   161

[ 15 ]   Ships Passing   180

[ 16 ]    Big Fitz    198

[ 17 ]    Calling the Wolf by Name    218

*Bibliography*    233

*Acknowledgments*    240

*Source Notes*    242

*Illustration Credits*    243

*Index*    244

# *Prologue*

# *Approaching the Wolf*

**Superior, Lake,** *the most N.W. of the five Great Lakes,*
*and the largest body of fresh water in the world.*

—*GROLIER'S ENCYCLOPEDIA CANADIANA,* 1958

*F*rom the first map it resembled a wolf's head, with an island standing in for an eye and a peninsula for a grinning mouth. As small students we found this helpful. What could be easier to memorize than a wolf's head? For hundreds of years that's how Lake Superior came to be recognized. Soon we would know the rest of the lakes too: Erie, Ontario, Michigan, Huron, the watery guts of where we lived, held together by a swift melody of Algonkian, English, and French. Indian words were as genuine on our immigrant tongues as *baseball*—words such as *totem, Winona, moose, moccasins,* and even *whisky-jack*—words that exist beneath the skin now and will never be foreign again.

We memorized the names of the provinces first. The provinces, the prime ministers, the capital cities, and best of all the five compelling bodies of blue ink that clung together on the pull-down maps that a teacher made appear before us with a swoop of her mighty arm—the

Great Lakes. Five of them, not counting Georgian Bay, which no one counted, probably because of its ridiculous and un-Indian-sounding name.

These were the greatest lakes in the world, and I was enormously proud of them for being so big and for belonging to *us*. Exactly how big was drilled into us every day. Entire countries could fit into them. Scotland, Belgium, England . . . I imagined these paltry nations heaved out the side of an airplane and sinking quickly beneath the hugeness of the Great Lakes—our Great Lakes.

To children all lakes must abound with fish, and so it was that the Great Lakes were filled with great fish. Back then, in our innocence, there could be no gill nets or lamprey, no Port Coldwell or Jackfish, no heavy metal contaminants. Back then, Rossport was a thriving town, home of the world's most famous fishing derby. Sturgeon grew to the size of train cars. Mysterious garfish sawed through nets with their evil noses, and quivering trout were eager to be caught by men who wore overalls and whistled, who opened and shut enormous jackknives, and packed fresh fish into cracked ice—one pound of ice for every pound of fish. For some reason these men looked like our dads.

We sat obediently beneath the gods of Transportation, Commerce, Mining, and Forestry, reciting the names of the Great Lakes on command. From encyclopedias we memorized patriotic, mind-numbing facts that led nowhere: "The Great Lakes are the largest body of fresh water in the world. They have a total of 95,000 square miles. They are of great importance to trade. They are bordered by two countries . . ."

In this way we came to know something alarming about the Great Lakes, that other people lived on them besides us. These people were different from "Indians." Indians were an acceptable and necessary part of the story. We barely knew it, but the story was couched in their language. It blew through everything, in words such as *Keewatin,* the north wind, such as *Canada* and *Chicago*. The story could not be spoken, it could not even begin without Indians. They were the audience—to us. Their purpose was to witness our arrival and brilliant growth. We sat at wooden desks and spent hours, weeks, a half decade of grade school "studying" Indians: how they possessed strange legends, paddled birchbark canoes, scalped people, and suffered forever from the slightest diseases. We were told over and over again in salacious, hypnotic detail how they cut out Father Brébeuf's righteous heart and ate it. We also learned that that sort of thing didn't happen anymore; that Indians had generously disappeared into the woods to make room for *us*.

But these people in that other bordering country were not "Indians," and they were not us either. They were called "Americans" and they were not making room for anyone. They invented spaceships and hot dogs, television and iron-ore freighters that unloaded themselves and stretched a fifth of a mile in length. For unknown reasons they had been given half of the Great Lakes. *Our* Great Lakes. The arrangement wasn't fair, and it made it considerably more difficult to memorize this enormous continent with Americans living all about. What was Lake Michigan to us, with its unknown and countless shipwrecks? There was something un-Canadian about Lake Michigan. On July 24, 1915, the *Eastland* had rolled over in this lake, killing more than eight hundred people in several minutes. We lived in towns of that size.

Lake Erie, at least, we could grasp. My mother had a friend who owned a cottage on Lake Erie, and each summer we went there to swim and eat fresh perch and fried potatoes. Our skin turned crimson, we lived an outdoor life. We shrieked in the white foam of crashing waves while our fathers stood around the barbecue with shirts off, holding brown bottles of beer in one hand and spatulas in the other.

These were the Great Lakes, the *lower* great lakes, a flat, blue-and-amber landscape composed of sand and soda pop. Clapboard cottages leaned against the sky. A dog, struck by a car, bravely hauled itself home on three legs. One memorable twilight a shining rainbow trout was hauled out in a net. Attached to it, like a bad conscience, was a lamprey releasing its life-sucking grip on the trout and slithering, like the coward it was, back into the water. These were the things that made Lake Erie possible.

"Lake Ontario" had a comforting sound to it, but was strangely removed though we lived less than two miles away. Toronto sprawled on its shore. To the small, sunny towns of southern Ontario, Toronto was farther away than imperial Rome. Lake Ontario was the Skyway Bridge, a dredging scandal, the packed steelyards of Stelco and Dofasco. Steel and mountains of purple slag rose from this lake. Black freighters were moored against concrete docks like enormous adventures about to happen. At the sound of a whistle, men emerged from gates holding lunch buckets. Only later when I was an adult did Lake Ontario begin to make some sort of sense. A line of smelt washed like rinsewater against the shore; the gulls wading through the fish devoured their eyes with a quick poke of the beak, leaving the rest to flop in the sand.

One lake in particular stood out—Lake Superior, mounted highest on the pull-down map. The biggest of them all, it also looked undeniably like a wolf's head. In case we had any doubt about this, it was there in the crowded margins of *Paddle-to-the-Sea,* by Holling Clancy Holling. Lake Erie, that remarkable book informed us, was a lump of coal; Lake Ontario was shaped like a carrot. As children we knew better than to eat either one. But Superior: "Lake Superior's outline makes a wolf's head." So it was written. Four increasingly wolf-like drawings followed the lake's outline and drove the point home. After that came a blueprint of a sawmill, and then a few sentences explaining to very young children that a "bull chain" was no different from a "jack chain." The next page offered a detailed schematic on how to build a breeches buoy in case our ship sank. The assumption was that every child at some point would find it necessary to cable off the bow of a sinking Great Lakes freighter. I could hardly wait for my turn.

We didn't know it would never come; the last documented breeches-buoy rescue on Lake Superior had already taken place in 1953 when the freighter *Armstrong* ran aground off the American town of Marquette. We didn't understand the physics of these things and would not have believed them, that a man could be too cold and tired to reach out and seize the rope that could save his life.

How to build a sawmill, how to escape a sinking freighter, and how to see the wolf's head in Lake Superior. These were the essentials of a Canadian education, and like many things we learned them through an American book. First published in 1941, *Paddle-to-the-Sea,* with its stunning illustrations, was the Bible of Lake Superior, turning a faraway body of water into schoolyard discussion. Sixty-five years later nearly every children's library in North America owns a copy.

"The Canadian wilderness was white with snow." With those strangely comforting words a carved miniature canoe is set loose upon Superior, where even the waves themselves "rushed . . . like packs of wolves." It did not yet seem significant that this canoe, so heavily freighted with pathos and symbolism, carried a wooden, miniaturized facsimile of an "Indian" instead of a real one.

Unknown to us, this great body of water had looked like a wolf's head since at least 1672, when the vigorous and dour Jesuit Father Claude-Jean Allouez completed a faithful map. That map, *La Carte de Jesuits,* published in France to accompany the *Jesuit Relations* for 1671, made Superior the first Great Lake to be accurately mapped.

Intensely disliked by the Natives and reputed to be a dreadful canoeist, Allouez eventually paddled the entire shoreline of Superior. He built a chapel out of bark, which was the only Christian institution on the continent beyond Montreal. Without assistance he carried two years' worth of mass wine, a small library, and a portable altar across thirty-six portages. He seems to have been so unpleasant that no one would help him.

Crammed into that head that Allouez drew was all the knowledge of a wolf. In there was the looming adventure of a child's life, the immense distances that must be crossed, the fears, the loneliness and yawning future that lie in wait for a person and a country. We didn't know that this lake was inhabited by a cruel, spindly backed monster named Mishipizheu, who eagerly sucked children down to their deaths, swamped canoes, and hurled enormous bulk carriers to the bottom.

We had not heard of a man named Selwyn Dewdney, who after a lifetime tramping the bush, suggested that "the impact of aboriginal beliefs and attitudes has shaped us more than we know." With this simple suggestion, North America was no longer the faithful story of near extinction and marginalization of Natives, but a subtle and complex tale of how Native culture has penetrated our own, and changed us.

For children this is not a difficult concept. We accepted that a moose was a moose, and a whisky-jack a whisky-jack. We did not doubt that gods lived in the woods who could lasso the moon with a willow switch. Little hairy-faced men who paddled stone canoes into the rock walls of Lake Superior posed no difficulty.

Seated in irrefutable rows on solid land beneath a portrait of Queen Elizabeth, we were ready for anything. We could accept that the Great Lakes were created more than a million years ago during the Pleistocene epoch, and that the land around Superior, freed of the heavy burden of the Wisconsin glacier, was rising straight up at the rate of eighteen inches every century. We would have accepted just as willingly that this lake was formed by a beaver slapping its tail, or that it contained three quadrillion gallons of water, 10 percent of the fresh water on the planet, enough to flood North and South America up to our knees.

We were ready for the truth that children know in their hearts, that magic lives in the dark and bottomless promise of water, and that the greatest water of all was mysterious, clad in a necklace of rock, surrounded by "Indians," and shaped in the head of a wolf. From our desks we saw it crouched low, preparing to lunge westward across the prairies and up snowy mountains.

We knew its name was Lake Superior.

# The Superior North

*"I live down there," said the Indian.*
*"Will you be free tomorrow?"*
*"I'm always free," he said.*

—T. MORRIS LONGSTRETH, *LAKE SUPERIOR COUNTRY,* 1924

Lake Superior: "the lonely, the original, the unspoiled"

In the spring of 1922 a verbose American travel writer of extremely purple prose set out on what he called the "intriguing operation of minding other people's business." To accomplish this, he planned to spend a half year drifting about the Lake Superior shores, convinced like so many before him and since that the landscape would prove compelling and that the "Indian" was still an exotic enough subject for a book.

T. Morris Longstreth set out with a considerable amount of baggage. Perhaps his heaviest portmanteau was his belief in the North as a spiritual forge where boys became men, where "empty-headed, pretty mouthfuls of caviar" became women, and where city dwellers found the "purification which Plato preached and Christ practiced."

Embedded deep in his faith is the unassailable belief that exposure to the North improves human character and that cities are decadent and corrosive. It seems not to matter that four out of five North Americans live in them. What matters is the perception of the North as a region of grace in whose woods and waters we anoint ourselves and are born again.

The North is more than a stretch of earth extending beyond Latitude 42. It is a place that manufactures heroes and heroic narrative. By the 1930s the Soviet Union was officially turning the Russian hinterland into a crucible for the production of heroism. Ships such as the *Cheluyskin* were packed with scientists, soldiers, poets, and painters, and sent on missions deep into the Arctic Ocean. With their ship frozen in the ice, Soviet women gave birth to heroic babies while the other men and women of the *Cheluyskin* formed literary societies and discussed, fittingly, a Russian translation of Henry Wadsworth Longfellow's *The Song of Hiawatha*. These missions were so successful that their participants were deemed untouchable during the purges. A northern apprenticeship could protect a person against even Stalinism.

Not much earlier than this, an American historian and newspaper writer, Guy M. Burnham, sang the praises of Lake Superior. While it went without saying that a great and bottomless wealth was to be found in the American North, Burnham wanted it known that this was "no mere commercial supremacy," but something more sublime. Here was the "actual atmosphere that inspired the most luxuriant thought of American literature." By this he meant Longfellow, John Greenleaf Whittier, and Walt Whitman, "America's great poetical triumvirate." Here, writes Burnham, "amid the gentle swish of Gitchee Gumee, Ascendentalism bursts forth—a new star that marks an epoch in

American progress. Ascendentalism," he croons, "is the watchword of the New Northland."

From such comments it's clear the North is as much a spiritual birthing ground as it is a cold, rocky place covered with snow. "Up North," we say, as though the North were an anteroom to rest in before entering Heaven. "I'm going up North," even though most journeys from south to north are necessarily a journey down—to sea level.

T. Morris Longstreth and his windy accounts of Superior are blunt examples of romancing things northern. To Longstreth it is part of the Anglo-Saxon's racial instinct to travel there. Throughout his 1924 book, *The Lake Superior Country,* the North, almost overnight, cures corrosion of character caused by cities, South, and sophistication. On the shores of Superior "the simple soul of man can burn clear again."

A century earlier, during those moments when she was not tending to her opiated and beautiful husband, Mary Shelley managed to muster similar sentiments in a hastily written book. *Frankenstein* offers one of the first stabs at understanding North as spiritual landscape. When her young Captain Walton recognizes "there is something at work in my soul that I do not understand," he instinctively heads to the polar Arctic to find out what it is. Drifting farther and farther north, he is "wafted to a land surpassing in wonders and in beauty every region hitherto discovered on the habitable globe."

By 1818 the North, to Mary Shelley and her readers, had become a duelling ground between good and evil. In it a scientist scurries about the ice floes pursuing a monster that he himself has created from the flesh of the dead—an eerie echo of the Native Windigo, or the white interpretation of such—cannibals dressed in dead flesh, harbingers of dread and starvation. Such a creature was encountered near Sault Ste. Marie in the deadly winter of 1767. A spectre of a man, reeking of an unapproachable stench, fled into the bush before Alexander Henry, a fur trader. Giving chase, Henry came upon a human hand, half cooked and staked beside a campfire.

This tension is how the North is comprehended. It is a dumping ground for garbage, radioactive and otherwise. It is also the last unspoiled wilderness. Like Frankenstein's monster our darkest psychology thrives there, rutting and howling with wolves. So do our deepest aspirations and noblest humanity. The North exists not only as a place, but as an inspiration that is pristine, beautiful, and redemptive. It seems not to matter if the pickerel are sometimes contaminated with mercury or that posted signs advise pregnant women not to eat them. Nor is it affected by heavy metals poured into Lake Superior by the thousands of tons annually. The North is where we go to live without pavement separating the heartbeat of the earth from our feet. We go there like so many before us, to re-encounter the primitive within ourselves—to become Native.

In the mind of Antoine Denis Raudot, a co-intendant of New France, even the Indians had been made better by the North. In 1705 he wrote, "As these savages of the Northern regions are deprived of the convenience of growing wheat . . . So God for compensation has given them the skill of being better hunters than those . . . in whom abundance renders indolent and lazy."

Here is heard an early and equally ingrained assumption regarding "South," a place that breeds indolence and laziness—character flaws caused by too much to eat and not enough suffering. By 1897 the *Fort William Journal* was confident that the "more torrid parts" of the world produced a "distemper that sometimes gnaws the soul."

That the air of the North or even the North itself cured sicknesses of all kinds was considered a matter of fact by author and Michigan booster C. S. Osborn: "This pure atmosphere, laden with ozone and with balsamic odors; supplemented by the delicious drinking water, fresh from the cool depths of Lake Superior, are never failing restoratives to the victims of catarrh, asthma, hay-fever, sunstroke, fever and ague, and the kindred diseases so prevalent in the heated cities and miasma-burdened country farther south."

Today it is widely granted that the North can take sick, cynical, and complicated people and turn them into healthy, honest, and simple ones. It was not always so. In the 1690s, Hudson's Bay Company factor James

Knight confided to his journal, "This is a Misserable barren Place . . . I never knowd no place so troublesom as this is here." James Knight did not journey north to have his soul cleansed. He came, like his employers, out of naked greed. First for furs, then gold—a mad, doomed pursuit that killed him and all of his men in one of the grimmest tragedies in the history of exploration.

The ennobling effects of the North did not take hold of everyone. Antoine Raudot's father, who was also co-intendant of New France, once wrote an ordinance restricting the amount of *baking* allowed in Montreal, and assessed stiff fines on anyone who sang songs he didn't like. In the 1850s John Ryerson, a Methodist missionary, declared the Superior coast "one barren waste of rocks rising above the other . . . A more sterile, dreary-looking region I never saw." As late as 1900 a Lakehead settler boasted that "the monster trees of the forest are now being hewn down and cast to the fire. The forest," he pronounced, "is surrendering to a prosperous and civilized people."

Settler Susanna Moodie, tourist and author Anna Jameson, explorer and gold-seeker James Knight, the Methodist and Catholic ministers, La Salle, Daniel Greysolon Duluth, Father Claude-Jean Allouez, Father Jacques Marquette, even the latecomer T. Morris Longstreth (though he would not admit it): these people did not come to learn and be changed by the North. They did not view Natives as people to be learned *from,* but as an ignorant, sometimes charming race in desperate need of teaching *to.* The forest was to be tamed, not appreciated. Early *arrivistes* to the North viewed even the great virgin pines with horror. In 1855, the settler John Sheridan Hogan wrote an ambitious piece, *Canada: An Essay,* in which he postulated that the axe was the "only hope against the forest shutting him in forever." Others remarked on the foreboding melancholy, the surpassing loneliness of the woods.

Trees were to be cut down, lakes traversed, wolves annihilated, and the savage made Christian. The summer migration of the monarch butterflies, the sough of pine branches, or the clatter of grasshoppers across boiling July rocks did not elucidate spiritual matters. The North was not yet viewed as a cure for the domesticating effects of modern society, nor was Native spirituality being sought as a panacea for Anglo-Saxon boredom and disaffection.

The moment was not far off. Pauline Johnson, Mohawk poet and stage performer, and no slouch when it came to the North, once suggested to a friend that she go out. "It is the only way to chase the glooms away—go out no matter what the weather." To Go Out was to be cured. To Go Out into the North was to be cured more deeply. To Go Out on to the shores of Superior was the most profound cure that a century of travellers and writers could think of.

Longstreth, who characterized urban Americans as "dandies living in an era of chatter and snappy cynicism," could envision no greater purgative than Superior, a place where people might "become Indian in their virtue" and men—Canadian men in particular—were men "before they were merchants." Longstreth sought the finest incarnation of Anglo-Saxon manhood, and not surprisingly he found it in the red-coated Mountie, or any other man who could "hustle the languorous redskin and yet hug the delicacy of the forest to his heart."

Stopping briefly at Longlac, Ontario, on the north shore of Superior, Longstreth wrote approvingly of the local Ojibwa for not having too many children, as did "our grosser immigrants." Despite his romantic and predictable attitude toward the Natives, he concluded without too much grief that their fate was inevitable, the "higher must succeed the gross."

This process of pruning away the gross and unessential is, for Longstreth, one of the prime virtues of the North. Here there is "no nourishment for parasites." Never at a loss for words, he almost chokes while attempting to describe his subject, the "purest fountain of water in the world, the lonely, the original, the unspoiled."

From the beginning Lake Superior has produced a mythical significance in the eyes and words of the people who have encountered it. The trader, poet, patriarch, and grandfather of Sault Ste. Marie, Michigan, John Johnston, states, "There is not perhaps on the globe a body of water so pure and so light as that of Lake Superior." He adds intriguingly: "It appears as if conscious of its innate excellence." This attribution of self-awareness to a body of fresh water is Native in its thrust, suggesting the thing that lives within the other, the spirit inside the visible form. In the early 1760s Jonathan Carver, one of the first English-speakers to encounter Superior, looked out across its waters and reported that soon "your eyes were no longer able to behold the dazzling scene." Here are echoes of the face that cannot be looked upon.

Ruminations like this are prevalent enough that in 1985 a Canadian Christian travel writer, Reverend T. S. H. Baxter, wrote his book *Quiet Coves and Rocky Highlands* to set the matter straight. "The power you see in Lake Superior," he warns, "is only a small fraction of the power and ability of God."

Religious, mythic, Christian, pagan, serene, and then suddenly ferocious, the world's deadliest inland sea: this was the European comprehension of Superior from the start. Over the centuries that perception has produced a symbol of wildness and purity, perhaps the most dangerous body of water on the planet. "The ocean in its greatest fury," wrote the Jesuit explorer Father Charlevoix, "is not more agitated."

The reputation of this mythical and massive lake was assured on November 10, 1975. At 7:10 that evening Captain Ernest Michael McSorley sent a radio message. His radar had been swept away. Boarding seas crashed across his deck. In command of a badly listing freighter, taking water above and perhaps below, ripped by winds that topped ninety miles an hour, McSorley spoke five curt and impenetrable words: "We are holding our own." Moments later the S.S. *Edmund Fitzgerald* was gone. The waters of Superior closed overtop and the freighter began its terrifying five-hundred-foot plunge to the bottom.

Lake Superior had claimed its most celebrated victim. A mystique of power and violence, more than three centuries in the making, was now irrefutable.

# We Weare Cesars

*Nothing but death could make men doe what wee did.*

—PIERRE ESPRIT RADISSON

*Radisson and Groseilliers,* painted by Frederic Remington, 1905

The first European to reach Lake Superior is thought to be the young Étienne Brûlé, who had a penchant for doing such things. In 1610, as a teenager, he sought permission from the explorer Samuel de Champlain to live among the Natives and learn their language. In doing so he became the first *truchement*—translator, the first white man capable of speaking fluently to a member of the Algonkian language group, and the first to cross over, however blindly, into the "Native."

Brûlé was also the first Christian and first European to shoot the Lachine Rapids by himself, a feat that certainly caught the attention of the local people. He was the first non-Native to penetrate into Huron country and the first European to see lakes Huron, Ontario, and Erie; the first to paddle down the Humber River and stand at what is now Toronto, first to set foot in today's Pennsylvania. He was also perhaps the first European to have his face scarred and his fingers mutilated by the Iroquois.

From Brûlé Europeans learned of Lake Superior, a vast body of water beyond Lake Huron. Champlain, like many others, assumed it led directly to the Kingdom of China and the East Indies, and expected custom duties from Chinese silks and spices to be collected at Quebec and to fill the coffers of the grateful Bourbons. Today we understand that Superior leads more directly to Duluth, Minnesota, a place where Brûlé was the first European to land, probably in 1622.

In the official pages of history Brûlé has been described as "a striking example of the fascination that the free life of the Indians held for young Frenchmen." He was also one of the first of many Europeans who would deliberately cross over and lose themselves in a "savage" civilization. There seems little doubt about his eagerness to live, to travel, to eat with the Native people of the New World, in particular to lie with Native women, to dress like Natives, and to learn their language, which is the deepest penetration of all.

In doing so he donned and shed three civilizations. When the English Kirke brothers captured Quebec in 1629, he simply put aside his French heritage, betrayed Champlain, and joined the conquerors, earning history's contempt as a man "much addicted to women and very vicious in character."

Like most things about Brûlé, the circumstances of his death are mysterious. He is thought to be the first European to be murdered "in a Huron brawl," the first to be eaten by Native North Americans. Of the many plaques and signs scattered around Lake Superior commemorating

Brûlé, none fails to recount the salacious details of his death. According to the Shipwreck Museum at Whitefish Bay he was turned on by the Hurons, who had him "bound, tortured, quartered and eaten." The Historical Society of Sault Ste. Marie has him "killed, quartered and boiled by his blood brothers." His first biographer, Consul Willshire Butterfield, has "his lifeless remains . . . feasted on" by horrible and ferocious savages. Whether he was boiled, eaten raw, or made into a feast, he was likely the first in a long line of adventurers, profiteers, explorers, and wild young men to reach Superior and come to a bad end.

His killers fared no better. The Bear tribe, among whom he lived, were devastated by epidemics and abandoned their village. They admitted later to Father Jean de Brébeuf that "no satisfaction had been obtained" from Brûlé's death and thought themselves haunted by the vengeful spirit of Brûlé's brother or sister.

The first European to encounter Lake Superior wrote nothing that survived and left nothing behind. Brûlé's spoken words, according to Butterfield, "are not calculated at once to awaken the thought that they border on the marvelous." What he looks like is unknown, though it is not difficult to imagine a shock of wild hair matted with bear grease, a thick body slumped low into a canoe, the snow slanting into his eyes, nervous and ferret-like, glaring from a cruel face already scarred by the Iroquois. He gazes west along the North Shore of Superior, hopeful that the great wealth of Asia waits around the next bend. It is not known whether he noticed the summer monarchs, hugging the southern shore, flitting like gold through the pines. We can barely sense his strange life in the soughing of branches, in the pages of the *Jesuit Relations,* and in the words of a Recollet priest who called him "a transgressor of the laws of God and man." According to Champlain he lived a life of "unrestrained debauchery and libertinism . . . without religion," sinking so low as to eat meat on Friday and Saturday.

As little more than a boy, Brûlé eagerly abandoned a world of elegant and stifling manners to head north, to wear buckskin and eat *sagamite,* a Native staple said to cause a European to urinate more than fifty times a day. He learned the creation myths of another people and memorized the phonetics of a foreign language. He lived twenty years among the Hurons and finally met a very foreign death.

Afterwards it was said among the Bear tribe that "his wounds are still bleeding."

The next restless pale-faced men to reach Superior would be immortalized to a generation of schoolchildren as "Radishes and Gooseberries," a musical handle plucked from the healthier food groups, suggesting two rather flamboyant vegetarians wrapped in furs.

Arriving in 1659, three decades after Brûlé was killed, Pierre Esprit Radisson and his brother-in-law Médard Chouart, sieur des Groseilliers, gave the world its first written account of Lake Superior. A Hudson's Bay clerk translated this document from French to English for the fee of five pounds sterling. Somehow the translation ended up in the possession of the great diarist Samuel Pepys, and remained in manuscript for two hundred years, eventually to be published in 1885. The American historian Francis Parkman said of this work that it is "written in a language which for want of a fitter name, may be called English." A bewildered preface to the publication warns the reader that the writing "conforms to no known standard of English composition."

From this astonishing book, *The Explorations of Pierre Esprit Radisson,* we get a decidedly un-classroom-like picture of "Radishes and Gooseberries" on their journey out of Quebec toward Superior. Defeating a group of Iroquois in battle, Radisson's party chops off ten heads, which are kept in a canoe where they roll back and forth for some time. In the morning with the fogs lifting through the pines, Radisson quickly wolfs down a bowl of human flesh. "We broiled some of it and . . . flung the rest away." He has with him "foure prisoners," kept alive so that they can be brought back and "burned att our own leisures for the more satisfaction of our wives." Unfortunately for the wives, Radisson is later left with no choice but to kill the prisoners "because they embarrassed us."

This scene from three and a half centuries ago is dealt with in two sentences. In the shadows of a primeval forest two French citizens, one of them Radisson, perhaps not yet twenty years old, and a company of Indian allies, are being taunted by four young Iroquois prisoners. The taunts are strategic. Through them the youngsters hope to earn quick deaths, although Radisson and his group were prone to rip out men's fingernails before killing them. A group of Mohawks had already relieved Radisson of his own fingernails. Probably the prisoners' heads were chopped off and added to the collection already knocking about in the canoe. Archeologists believe that such killings were often followed by ritual cannibalism. Flesh was eaten, prayers offered to various gods, including the Christian one.

The party set off and arrived shortly at the eastern entrance of Lake Superior, where the great discoverers gazed out upon a land of incredible beauty. "Indeed it was to us like a terrestrial paradise." Radisson had not lost his eye for scenic landscape.

On the South Shore the group came across nuggets of pure copper weighing a hundred pounds. They saw "sturgeons of a vast biggness" and pike seven feet long. Later Radisson and Groseilliers encountered a nation "not numbering a hundred souls" and shared a "friendly fire" with them. Severed heads were arranged on the ground and "weare danced."

At some point in this region the bushes quivered and a small group of men emerged. They stared intensely at Radisson and his brother-in-law— the first white men and, in Groseilliers' case, the first bearded man the Sioux had ever laid eyes on. Groseilliers was also the first known epileptic to reach Superior. So occurred the remarkable moment of "contact" when the representatives of an alien race arrived on a foreign shore, dressed in a foreign skin.

They also arrived heavily armed. Both Radisson and Groseilliers landed on the South Shore of Superior packing "five guns, 2 musqueton, 3 fowling peeces, 3 pairs of pistoles, 2 pairs of pocket pistols," plus the obligatory sword and dagger. Radisson developed a neat trick with his gunpowder, tossing pinches of it into the Natives' ceremonial fires, where it produced a much more dramatic effect than traditional Indian tobacco.

Radisson also reports giving away two simple tools as gifts. It is conceivable that in giving away these "hatchetts" he changed forever the social and strategic balances existing in this region. In his own words, he distributed these gifts to "encourage the young people . . . to preserve their wives and shew themselves men by knocking the heads of their enemyes wth the said hatchetts."

Shewing themselves to be men was of some concern to Radisson, although there were times when he could not live up to the standards set by his companions. Confronted with a five-day portage into the interior of the Wisconsin woods, Radisson frankly excused himself. "Brethren," he said, "we resolve to stay here, being not accustomed to make any carriage on our backs as ye are wont." On other overland journeys he had no qualms about hoisting his luggage onto the backs of the Native women. In his opinion, the "poore misserables" were "happy to carry our Equipage."

When their companions left for the interior, he and Groseilliers became the first white men to build on the shores of Superior, erecting a triangular pole palisade not much bigger than a tent, surrounded by an alarm system of strung bells—a basic protection against sudden death— at the end of Chequamegon Bay, somewhere near today's Ashland, Wisconsin. His Native companions were much intrigued by it. "We weare Cesars," observed Radisson. "There being nobody to contradicte us." When the Indians returned, they discovered these Caesars lying in their little fort "in a starving condition," having already eaten their woollens.

In writing history's first descriptions of the people of Lake Superior, Radisson displayed few of the assumptions that characterize European observations over the next three centuries. He did not come to collect souls, or to stop young women from dancing naked. His contact with the Native inhabitants was intimate in a way that would rarely, if ever, be recorded again. He praises the "subtilty of the wildmen" who "shewed themselves far gratfuller than many Christians," probably a reference to the notorious officials of Quebec. Radisson pays particular tribute to a young Native who hurled himself out of the canoe and resurfaced from the water grasping a live beaver. "By this," states Radisson, "we see that hunger can do much."

Here is first sounded the grand Northern theme of hunger, a scarcity of food, the regular onslaught of famine, starvation, and death—the familiar stench of the Windigo. On the southern shore of Lake Superior, hunger came heralded by deep snow that stuck to trees so that it "caused yt darknesse upon ye earth," eclipsing the sun for two months. Hunters could not wear snowshoes, as they made too much noise and scared off the game.

"Everyone," Radisson wrote, "cries out for hunger, the women become barren and drie like wood." In two weeks the group ate their dogs. Wood was tried next. The Natives ate the strings of their bows, as they no longer had the strength to draw them. They returned to the carcasses of their eaten dogs and pulverized the bones, mixing the powder with dirt, and ate that. They ate the beaver-skin diapers of their infants "where the children beshit them above a hundred times." They ate the skins of their tents, "going so eagerly to it that our gums did bleede like one newly wounded." Radisson and Groseilliers ate their stockings. Two travelling Indians managed to arrive with a dog, "the dog was very leane, and as hungry as we weare." Radisson, with a degree of shame, sneaked out into the dark and stabbed it. "He was broyled like a pigge and cut in peeces, gutts and all." Later he went back to where the dog was stabbed, scooped up a few drops of the animal's blood in the snow, and used it to season the kettles.

With the spring came warmth and a softening of the snow crust. This snow surface often determined whether a people lived or died. Radisson reports that he and the Indians were able to tramp out into the woods and simply cut the throats of the deer they found sunk and immobile, trapped in the snow. The famine had passed, leaving "above 500 dead, men women and children."

In 1661, after spending two years in the Superior region, Radisson, Groseilliers, and a party of seven hundred Natives in four hundred canoes departed from the lake after a send-off by the women. "It was a pleasure," wrote Radisson, "for all the young women went in stark naked, their hairs hanging down . . . they are not altogether ashamed to show us all, to entice us and animate the men." This remarkable flotilla headed to Quebec with a legendary cargo of furs garnered from the shores of

Superior. These furs, valued at somewhere between $70,000 and $400,000, are said to have saved New France from complete ruin. Upon arrival the whole cargo was impounded, confiscated, and stolen by officials. Radisson received a stiff fine, and Groseilliers was tossed into jail for trading without a licence and travelling without a Jesuit.

Not surprisingly, Radisson ended up on a far-flung adventure to kill Dutchmen on the coast of Africa. At the conclusion of this affair his fleet was broken up on a Caribbean reef and, in a phrase that seems invented for him, we are told "he barely escaped with his life."

Today, by virtue of Radisson's writing, he and Groseilliers stand out above the handful of young seventeenth-century French adventurers who were drawn to a mythical place called Superior. A French youth, once captured by the Iroquois, Radisson devoted his life to continual attempts to be wild and entirely free, to exist in the remotest seams between two different worlds. Of his companion it was said, "He is a man capable of anything . . . who has been everywhere." Together they said prayers, baptized children, and ate human flesh. They spoke French, English, Latin, Huron, proto-Ojibwa, and some Iroquois. They witnessed and recorded in detail the Feast of the Dead on the southern shore of Superior, founded the Hudson's Bay Company, and conversed with kings. They lived through the plague and the Great Fire of London. Groseilliers eventually vanished into the crevices of history. Some speculate that he died at Sorel, Quebec, in 1696, although Radisson claimed that he "died in the Bay," in 1683.

Radisson himself, while little more than a child, had killed at least one man in his sleep by driving his hatchet so deep into his skull that he had difficulty removing it. Eventually he married three times and is said to have died in abject poverty. His third wife survived him by many years and also died in poverty. He crossed the Atlantic Ocean twenty-four times, and travelled thousands of miles through the great pineries of the North. Too young to even grow a beard, he swashbuckled his way to the shores of Lake Superior, where he danced in a circle around human heads.

"We knowed what we were," he wrote later. "Discoverers before governors."

# [ 3 ]

*Mishipizheu*

*I am wildcat. I come up from below, I come down from above . . .*
—"SONG OF MISHIPIZHEU," RECORDED BY EDWIN JAMES, 1830

Sketches of Mishipizheu, based on rock art at the Agawa site,
Lake Superior Provincial Park

Pukaskwa National Park encompasses nearly eight hundred square miles of intensely rugged landscape, all of it fronting the eastern shoreline of Lake Superior. It is rugged enough that the builders of Canada's first national railroad, the Canadian Pacific Railway, decided to bypass the region when they came through in the early 1880s. A half-century later, engineers for the Trans-Canada Highway reached the same decision.

Despite the rock and the wilderness, several stunning, bone-white beaches also grace the area. Park literature strongly urges people not to swim off them. A sign bolted to the rock on one of these beaches states that a boy drowned here several years ago and urges extreme caution. Like everything close to Superior's North Shore, the sign is eroding markedly and will exist perhaps another few years.

"That was quite a day," offers the warden, a modest man with a face given to easy creases that run from east to west. His glasses rest uncomfortably on the bridge of his nose, and require frequent adjustments. He attempts a dry laugh entirely unrelated to humour; the tense exhalation of a man trained to attach radio collars to wolves and contain the spruce budworm, not to stand next to parents white with shock and grief on the shores of a beach.

"Something happened." He waves his hands to indicate the tug of an undertow, a sudden hole in the sand not there an hour or a moment ago, the deadly appearance of an ancient monster known for its predilection for children. In one or two feet of treacherous water, a child drowned in Lake Superior, joining several thousand other people who have drowned here, plus an unknown number of their Native brothers and sisters, all made equal in the black depths of the frigid water that slowly bleached the colour from their clothing. "This is a *wilderness* park," he repeats, as though the word explains everything, and perhaps it does. At the height of summer, campers are advised not to swim. Backpackers are told to expect no speedy rescue. Sometimes even the wolves here starve to death. The warden is more comfortable dealing with such matters. Talk of a drowned child fills the room with silence and the inadequacy of words, the spectre of the very worst thing that can happen.

It is beyond both of us to attribute this tragedy to an aboriginal entity. We have no way to start, no way of knowing whether this spirit actually killed the boy, or whether attaching such blame would be symbolic only, a means of bridging and withstanding intolerable grief.

To confront this spirit, which is not just a killer but also a benefactor, is to be confronted by a world of "transformations," "shape-shifting," and "in-dwelling," where nothing is merely what it seems, but contains within it something else, and within that something else again. Even the basic terminology warns of the difficulty that lies ahead.

According to brochures on the table in front of us, Pukaskwa National Park is "Where Earth Meets Superior's Spirit!" or, in the Anishnabe translation, *"Aki-Ezhi-Nagishkang Manido Zaagigan!"* Anishnabe is usually translated as "the first" or "original people," sometimes as "good person" or "one who came down from the sky." The term is widely used now instead of *Ojibwa,* sometimes spelt *Ojibwe,* a modernization of *Ojibway,* although Bishop Frederic Baraga, the author of an Ojibwa dictionary, insisted on *Otchipwe.*

To Edmund Danzinger, a scholar at the University of Oklahoma, *Ojibwa* means "Those Who Make the Pictographs." But it might mean "puckered voice" from *bwa* (voice), though another American historian, William Warren, whose mother was Ojibwa, insisted those who speak the language do not pucker up when doing so. A century and a half ago elders insisted it meant "puckered seam," referring to stitching on the Ojibwa moccasin. Warren was adamant that the term means the flesh that "puckers up" when roasting an enemy of the Ojibwa (from *ubway,* "to roast"). Paul Kane, the nineteenth-century Canadian painter, had no doubt that "Ojjibeway" means "the jumpers and derives . . . from their expertness in leaping their canoes over numerous rapids." Canadian historian Pauline Dean is confident Ojibwa stems from *Od-chip-way* and means "the Eater of Cooked Meat," distinguishing themselves from *Eskimo,* "the Eaters of Raw Meat," which she notes is also an Ojibwa word.

Over the years the word evolved, at least in the United States, to *Chippewa,* which is a corruption of *Ojibwa,* although some argue that *Ojibwa* is a corruption of *Chippewa.* The word *Chippewa* should not be confused with *Chippeway,* a different nation now known as the Dene, which also may mean the First People. (Similarly, the Sioux, who reached the southern shore of Superior, should not be confused with the Sault, and consequently the Saulteurs on the eastern end, though both Sault and Sioux are pronounced "Soo.")

These complexities are apparent early when trying to flush out Mishipizheu, a creature whose name is rarely spelled the same way twice. The word *creature* is problematic, for the thing isn't so much a creature as a spirit, and not so much a spirit as a composite entity. Selwyn Dewdney, the Canadian author, painter, and Native rock art scholar who spent several years paddling Superior in the hope of finding this beast painted on a rock, has stated that "a bird is a loon is an eagle is a man is a manitou," referring to the multiplicity of aboriginal narrative, the absolute refusal of anything to sit still.

What is known for sure about this thing is that it controls the waters of the Great Lakes, and of Lake Superior in particular. In this capacity, it brought down the *Edmund Fitzgerald* in 1975 and an estimated four hundred other vessels that have sunk in Superior's waters. It also has a reputation for killing children. To Christopher Vecsey, an American anthropologist, this underwater manitou (which he spells *manito*) was not one being but two, a horned serpent and an underwater lion. In the creation myth of the Ojibwa, Nanabozho fought with it to secure hunting rights for Natives in the future. Like repressed memory, Mishipizheu appears at any moment, and always from beneath something. It resides underwater, and also underground.

Some of the first Europeans to encounter it included the Jesuit Claude-Jean Allouez, who came to the shores of a mysterious lake waving a cross and attempting to baptize everyone in sight. He had little use for such complications. In his contribution to the *Jesuit Relations,* written in 1667, he referred to it as "Missibizi," noting that sacrifices were made to it to bring the sturgeon and to quiet the deadly waters. A contemporary, trader, explorer, and translator, Nicolas Perrot, called it *Michipissy,* adding "he has a large tail [and] when he wiggles it lively it causes great tempests." Raudot called it *Michapoux* and said it was born on a turtle-shaped island off the South Shore of the lake, where it taught the people to fish. Bishop Baraga spelt the word *Mishibiji* and defined it as "a lion."

This difficult entity has caused men trouble for four hundred years. In 1985 the Reverend T. S. H. Baxter angrily demanded, "Why do people who consider themselves thinking people . . . go to such great lengths to deny the living Christ and yet get caught up in the fantasy of Misshepzhieu?"

Mishipizheu, like Lake Superior itself, is inextricably associated with copper, providing it to the local inhabitants, who cut it from its horns as it raises them above the surface of the water. Mishipizheu's power resides in that of copper, which itself can bring good luck. Étienne Brûlé carried a nugget with him wherever he went, for what little good it did him.

According to a Native story, the enormous copper pieces once plucked from the shores of Superior were called both the cradles and the toys of Mishipizheu's children. In the late 1660s four Natives attempted to carry off a canoe-load of these nuggets from Michipicoten Island. As they paddled away, the great underwater manitou spoke to them. All four died soon after, and by 1669, according to the *Jesuit Relations,* the Natives refused to land on the island at all. Other writers have claimed with confidence that Natives refused to land on any of the islands in Lake Superior. There are an estimated sixteen hundred of these islands, although no one seems to know for sure. Apparently some of them float, like Michipicoten.

The island of Michipicoten was Mishipizheu's home, as was Michamakila, and so were the depths of Superior and the deep caves beneath the rocks of Superior's shore. Mishipizheu's wigwam was a mountain. The Thunderbirds threw lightning bolts at it to try to kill it. It was a beach stalker and a child stealer, capable of claiming a seven-year-old boy in two feet of water.

Some speculate that Mishipizheu protects those it looks directly upon, which may explain why it is sometimes painted with its face staring straight out from the rocks, an unusual pose for manitous. We can glimpse the ancient horror of death by water in this detail, the monster that stares into the face of a drowning man during his final, thrashing moments.

In 1838 a Wesleyan preacher, James Evans, embarked on a harrowing canoe trip up the eastern shore of Superior. He described the view as "the most barren imaginable, nothing but dreary mountains." During the course of this lengthy trip, he and his Native companion frequently had to put down their paddles and knock the ice off their legs with an axe handle. Evans later wrote of his companion that "the poor fellow laid his face in his hands in the bow of the canoe, he has since told me, that he might not see himself drown."

Perhaps what Evans describes was not a man refusing to see himself drown, but a man attempting to stare directly into the eyes of a manitou and somehow stay alive. This was something Evans knew a great deal about. In 1844 during a brutal canoe journey into the Athabasca region, he reached behind to pick up a rifle and accidentally blew a hole through the head of his best friend and assistant, Thomas Hassell, a Chippeway. Today Evans is remembered as the man who invented Cree syllabics, a written form for the recording and exchange of Native speech. He built a printing press from a stamping vise used for pressing pelts and fabricated ink out of dirt mixed with animal blood. He collapsed dead in a chair on November 23, 1846, in Hull, Scotland, after delivering his first lecture on the missionary life in the Canadian North.

The first European to actually see Mishipizheu was Father Paul Le Jeune, the renowned editor of the *Jesuit Relations*. In 1636 he watched a young man catch a fish, which he described as resembling a great lizard with four feet and a long tail. The young man quickly returned the creature to the water, explaining to the Jesuit that it would be a mistake to keep it, since it caused enormous winds on the water.

Almost twenty years later, a young Pierre Esprit Radisson was taken on a spring expedition by his Iroquois captors near what is now Schenectady, New York. What he saw there confirms the Le Jeune sighting: "there layd on one of the trees a snake with foure feete, her head very bigg like a Turtle, the nose very small att the end."

More than a century later, between Thunder Bay and Grand Portage, while searching for a new passage between Lake Superior and Lake

Winnipeg, Vincent St. Germain, a trader and shareholder in the North
West Company, saw something that haunted him for the rest of his life.
On May 3, 1782, involved in the increasingly tense fur trade, he looked
out from the North Shore of Superior and saw an object in the water
"about the size of a child . . . seven or eight year[s] of age, the eyes were
extremely brilliant, the nose small . . . the animal looked the deponent
in the face, with an aspect of indicating uneasiness."

This "uneasiness," which is not apparent in either the Radisson or Le
Jeune sighting, could indicate 150 years of immigrant penetration, an
echo of an Ojibwa dispersal legend in which Nanabozho moves his people
to the end of Lake Superior to protect them from impending catastrophe.
St. Germain goes on to suggest that "the frequent appearance of this
extraordinary animal in the spot has given rise to the superstitious belief
among the Natives that the God of the Waters had fixed upon this for
his residence."

It appears the Natives were quite willing to accept that this extraordinary entity lived in different places at the same time. According to early
researchers, the Ojibwa saw Mishipizheu in the sudden squalls of Lake
Superior. The most astonishing aspect of this shape-shifting was put
forward by Francis Kellog in 1917, who stated that Mishipizheu was
often depicted "in the shape of Lake Superior itself"!

Here is encountered one of those jolting lateral shifts that represents
the challenge of New World thought; a creature lives in Lake Superior. It
is a cat, and a catfish, a lynx, a horned serpent, always with horns. Ancient
pictographs show it with power lines radiating from its torso. Longer than
it is wide, pointed at one end and stickle-backed like a rocky shoreline, it
forms a basic map of Lake Superior. It *is* Lake Superior.

Today the old image of Mishipizheu painted on the Agawa Rock is a
tourist destination provided with parking spots and designated with
signs. Experts have been hired to write thoughtful and culturally sensitive texts. Park officials gamely tried to erect a steel walkway, bolting it
to the rocks so that people could come and examine the images. Superior
ripped the rails down within a year. Now to see Mishipizheu, visitors
must flatten themselves face-first against the ancient rock, holding on to

a chain. The pictograms themselves are fading; enormous chunks of rock have dropped into the water. Some visitors come with cans of spray paint. The stories written in stone, unknown to us in the first place, are fast disappearing.

In the early 1970s, the captain of the freighter S.S. *Edmund Fitzgerald* observed the harrowing buckling of metal as the great bulk carrier pulsated on rough waters. In his words, the vessel was doing "that wiggly thing." Here in that wiggle it is possible to get one more glimpse of Mishipizheu as it slithers in through the hatches. In a world in which shapes do not hold fast and one thing "in-dwells" effortlessly within another, it is easy to posit an elusive Ojibwa manitou among the massive mounds of taconite pellets that filled the belly of the *Big Fitz*. In one manifestation it is merely four feet long, thrashing wildly in the great storm of November 10, 1975. Its tail clangs against the bottom of the hull, its head extends seventy-five feet upward and pounds against those troublesome hatches until they bend and break.

The water races in now from above and from below. This is fresh water, not so much water as melted ice, a cliché of Lake Superior—that it has two temperatures: one of ice, the other melted ice. The massive iron plates that make up the *Edmund Fitzgerald* extend the length of two and a half football fields. They wiggle like a snake, or lynx, a sinewy catfish. Mishipizheu is in the hold of the *Edmund Fitzgerald*. Searching for children.

It finds only taconite, the red stone that made the tools and spear tips of the ancient Superior people, and helped them bring down mastodons. The taconite is pelletized now, fired in a kiln at 2,200 degrees Fahrenheit. Mishipizheu finds taconite pellets and men. It slithers below the pellets and below consciousness, raises its tail made of copper and thrashes hard. Mishipizheu is in the creaming waves of Lake Superior. It *is* Lake Superior. A sailor watches 730 feet of metal plates wiggle in front of him like the tail of a beast and for a moment this ancient manitou is dwelling in the *Edmund Fitzgerald;* it *is* the *Edmund Fitzgerald*.

Mishipizheu is in its glory, singing full-throated the songs that celebrate itself. An American doctor and writer, Edwin James, wrote down these songs at Sault Ste. Marie in 1830: "I am wildcat. I come up from below, I come down from above. I come to change the appearance of the ground, *this* ground!"

# [ 4 ]

## Standing on Ceremony

*Through all this granite land*
*the sign of the cross*

—LORRAINE NIEDECKER, "LAKE SUPERIOR"

Saint-Lusson claiming the New World for his king

In the spring of 1671 a French regimental officer with a bad reputation arrived at the Jesuit mission at Sault Ste. Marie with a party of fifteen men. He had come under orders primarily to search for copper mines on the shores of Superior. He had also come to take formal possession of the interior of North America, from Mexico to the Pacific Ocean—about one-tenth of the earth's surface.

Daumont, sieur de Saint-Lusson, accomplished this feat to his own satisfaction on June 4 in a ceremony at the village of Sault Ste. Marie. A large cross was raised as the famed rapids, teeming with whitefish, glittered and rushed in the background. The local Jesuit, Claude Dablon, blessed it "in solemn form" and the cross was planted. The Frenchmen removed their hats and sang "Vexilla Regius." A cedar post bearing a plaque engraved with the royal arms of France was pounded into the dirt. Several Frenchmen began to sing the "Exaudiat," and an unnamed Jesuit prayed aloud for the king.

Saint-Lusson, wearing a burnished metal helmet, stepped forward, brandishing a sword in one hand and a clump of dirt in the other. Through his translator, Nicolas Perrot, he told the gathering of fourteen Indian nations that the "Most High, Mighty and Redoubted Monarch, King Louis XIV" had just taken possession of not only Lake Superior, Lake Huron, and Manitoulin Island, but all the lands that had been discovered and "those which may be discovered hereafter."

According to the American scholar Francis Parkman, "a great throng of Indians stood, crouched or reclined at length with eyes and ears intent." That intensity may have slackened as Saint-Lusson droned on about "potentates, princes, sovereign states and republics," before finishing mercifully with an exhortation of *"Vive Le Roi."* The French fired their muskets and, according to Parkman, "the yelps of the astonished Indians mingled with the din."

The "yelps" were premature. The speeches were not yet over. Father Claude-Jean Allouez, one of four Jesuits in attendance, spoke next in the local language. He would spend nearly thirty years on the shores of Superior, and be remembered in United States history as the first European to mention the Mississippi River. He, with Dablon, would paddle the entire 1,700 miles of Lake Superior shoreline, contributing to the *Carte des Jesuites,* the first detailed map of the lake. Allouez despised all Native behaviour, including "improper dances," and set out single-handedly to lead Native girls "who did not blush" toward "the modesty so becoming to their sex."

Allouez found the absence of this modesty incomprehensible. Like the rest of the Jesuits, he was outraged that a Native woman could divorce her husband whenever she felt like it. He was equally horrified by her complete sexual autonomy. The entire lives of Native women, in his view, were directed toward "libertinism," "divorce," and "profligacy." Even more appalling was the fact that Native men often sided with their wives rather than the Jesuits. This caused the mighty Father Le Jeune himself to lose his temper with one unfortunate fellow. "In France," he bellowed, "women do not rule their husbands." That they were no longer in France seems to have escaped the Jesuits, who worked hard to import the gender assumptions of the old country. Even its history was considered transportable; Allouez unilaterally changed the name of Lake Superior to Lake Tracy, in honour of the marquis de Tracy, a professional French soldier who burned four empty Mohawk villages and hanged a prisoner, before returning home a hero.

On that spring day in 1671 Allouez managed to swallow his indignation long enough to give "a solemn harangue," in which he explained to the assembled nations how "Jesus Christ, the Son of God, after making himself a man for the love of men, was nailed to a cross and died to satisfy his Eternal Father for our sins."

Watching approvingly was another black-robed figure, head of the Sault Ste. Marie mission, Father Gabriel Druillettes. This man is said to have learned the Abenaki language in three months and, according to a French historian, was considered "a miraculous being" by Natives everywhere. In 1652, while starving, he ate his shoes, his moose-skin jerkin, and the thongs of his snowshoes. As a younger man he had suffered from serious eye problems, exacerbated by the dense smoke of the Native lodges where he often lived. An unsuccessful cure was provided by an elderly woman who scraped his corneas with a rusty knife. He later assembled the Natives and asked them to pray for him, after which his vision was restored.

Satisfied with his sermon, Allouez directed the audience's attention to the post and to the French coat of arms attached to it. For a man entrusted to bring Christian serenity to the souls of the savages inhabiting the forests of the Northwest, he possessed a decided flair for military rhetoric. With considerable zeal he threatened the assembled nations with the sheer bloodlust of the king of France, "the chief of the greatest chiefs." First he calculated the size of the French army in terms they could understand—"ranged in double file they would reach from here to Mississaquenk." When the king attacks, he warned, "the air and sea are on fire with the discharge of his cannons." The French king does not even bother to count the scalps he has taken, proclaimed Allouez, "but only the streams of blood he has caused to flow."

All of this, according to Dablon, was received with wonder by those "poor people." It seems those poor people were not altogether as passive as Dablon would make out. They had already coined a rather delicious term to describe the Jesuits, *Wametigoshe*—"the people who wave sticks." It was a habit of the Jesuits to march through the woods holding crosses in their outstretched hands. Nor were the Ojibwa entirely lacking in their own spectacular narratives. These stories suggest that they themselves were created out of the foam of Lake Superior, that the rapids before them had once been a beaver dam, kicked apart by Mishipizheu, and that the Great Fisher, straddling both sides of the falls, had held the world together by singing a song.

Saint-Lusson, having no idea how tentative the New World was, resumed, as before, confidently explaining through his translator, that the king of France had just taken possession of the entire region. The ceremony closed with "a fine bonfire which was lighted toward evening, and around which the *Te Deum* was sung."

What is striking about this ceremony is how familiar it all seems. It has been witnessed before, in history books, in half-remembered classrooms, in the engravings of C. W. Jefferys and European artists who tentatively positioned a few palm trees about the North American forest.

Occupying a prominent space in the foreground are the Europeans. They are dressed in luxurious raiments with a faint celestial aura emanating from their heads; the forest has begun to melt in front of them and resembles, already, a cultivated European garden. There stands Saint-

Lusson, sword in one hand, a fist full of native soil in the other. In that symbolic and revealing gesture he demonstrates how North America will be interpreted and treated for the next three and a half centuries. He has come for land and for copper. He has come with a large sword.

In Allouez's words, the Jesuits have come "running after souls." Those souls are visible in the background, always in the background. Barely distinguishable from the trees, these "children of the woods" are rapt, attentive, and anonymous. They have no names, no opinions, and no objections. The blessings they are about to receive are visible, and rendered in oil.

At first glance it looks predictably heroic. On a second look, it is a shade pompous and silly. On a third, it is a tableau of arrogance, hypocrisy, and unimaginable self-deception. Saint-Lusson, he of the sword and soil, would get so drunk at the Soo and engage in such behaviour that he was sent back to France in disgrace. He left with a six-month-old moose and twelve geese, in an attempt to curry favour with the king. In a cryptic remark it was written of Saint-Lusson that "I see no change in his conduct." "I am afraid," wrote the Abbé Dudouyt, "that he will be what he was before."

The man who translated Saint-Lusson's haughty speech, Nicolas Perrot, a former domestic servant, was secretly trading furs. Before he left Lake Superior his personal cache was seized by Saint-Lusson. He spent the next three decades inciting tribes against one another, destroyed five Seneca villages, and was continually harassed by the people to whom he owed money. "I am the dawn of that light that is beginning to appear in your lands," he babbled to any tribe that would listen. Married to a woman described as entirely insane, he undertook to write his memoirs but stopped when he ran out of paper. For many years he was thought to have poisoned La Salle. La Salle, the French fur trader and explorer who built the first masted ship to sail—and sink—on the Great Lakes, would himself be butchered, with cause, in a Texas swamp in 1687.

In the end, this pompous stab at French sovereignty was reduced, in the opinion of Francis Parkman, to the "occasional accents of France on the lips of some straggling boatman or vagabond half breed."

The Jesuit effort, based on strange words written by the order's founder, St. Ignatius of Loyola, in a faraway cave using a lava-stone as a writing table, would also end in misery. Father Brébeuf and Father Isaac Jogues, among the first missionaries to see Lake Superior, would, like Brûlé, die brutal deaths. Jogues, mutilated by the Iroquois, wrote piteously that "our hands and fingers being all in pieces, they had to feed us like children." He was later murdered with a hatchet, his head mounted on a palisade. Brébeuf suffered a lengthy and hideous death while tied to a post.

They were followed by Father Pierre Ménard, the first priest to say mass on what is now Wisconsin soil. Although he was overwhelmingly convinced that God wanted him in these parts, a less driven man might not have been so confident. Arriving at Lake Superior sick, feeble, and more than sixty years old, he was immediately injured by a falling tree— while paddling on the lake.

This elderly Jesuit actually ran from Indian to Indian, barging into their quarters to baptize them. In fairness to Ménard, it might not have been zealotry alone that quickened his pace. A contemporary described the insects in the Lake Superior region as so thick it required three men to take a drink of water, two to keep the flies off the third while he quaffed. Radisson saw men at what is now Sault Ste. Marie bury themselves in the sand to escape them. Astonished travellers to this region report being attacked by mosquitoes while standing knee-deep in snow.

Insects or not, local inhabitants were terrified of Father Ménard and his strange baptismal ceremony, and attempted to hide their infants from him. A statement recorded in the *Jesuit Relations* pits a furious Native woman against her Christianized husband: "Dost thou not see we are all dying since they told us to pray to God? Where are thy relatives? Where are mine? the most of them are dead; it is no longer a time to believe." Father Jacques Marquette, a kinder, less neurotic, and more popular missionary, arrived in the Superior region in 1669 and was faced with people who hid their dying relatives from him in an effort to avoid the dreaded and, in their eyes, fatal ceremonies of the Jesuits.

Ménard was so unpopular with the locals that they refused even to feed him. This is striking behaviour for the Chippewa, whose generosity was renowned. In 1855 the German ethnologist Johann Kohl commented on the largesse of Native hospitality on the South Shore, noting that by his and all other reports, "the [Indian] is always ready to share his last meal with the starving stranger." It is perhaps a tribute to Ménard's unpleasantness that for days on end he ate nothing but wood and moss, the famous *tripe de roche,* or "Windigo cabbage," as Kohl described it, boiled down to a black and sickening paste. While Kohl was being addressed in Ojibwa, his translator interpreted the words into French, Kohl jotted them down in German, and a man named Lascelles Wraxall finally rendered them into English. Nonetheless, in Kohl's opinion, "Windigo cabbage" was eaten "only [by] those driven to Madness by fasting and want." This could easily apply to Ménard, whose writings are tinged with the zealot's madness: "I entered crawling on my belly and found there a treasure . . . two little children in a dying condition." When one of those children died, he happily proclaimed her "the first fruit of this mission."

Located on the west end of Lake Superior, that mission, La Pointe, ended in failure and was abandoned. Less than two centuries later it became a wild and semi-barbarous assembly point for copper prospectors. Ménard, in a stubborn and hopeless journey to baptize a group of starving Hurons, got lost in the woods. His body was never found.

To be saved, Natives first needed to be doomed. To be enlightened, it was essential that they be ignorant. Logic such as this was essential to the Jesuits and has proved extremely useful to the people who came after them. It has influenced nearly four centuries of scholarship and until very recently has shaped the stories and the language that teach us who we are—and who we are not.

In his 1968 book *Jacques Marquette,* Joseph P. Donnelly, an American historian, describes the Native inhabitants of the Lake Superior basin with a telling list of adjectives. They are without exception "poor, hopeless, blind, savage, disheveled, unattractive, fickle, inconstant, devious, vain, gross, revolting, lewd, immoral, uncouth, fetid, licentious, barbaric, addicted, cringing, cowardly," and emit "offensive body odor." The same book describes the Jesuit missionaries in equally telling terms. They are, without exception, "gentle, wonderful, cheerful, willing, physically strong, buoyant, clean, kindly, sympathetic, and understanding."

Language like this defines the "two solitudes" of North America. It is not English and French or United States and Canada, but Us and Them, Native and Immigrant. They are "filthy," we are clean. Their women are "lewd," ours modest. They "squat," we sit. Our babies cry; theirs "screech." While we are blessed by extended families, they are pestered by "hordes of relatives."

These associations have penetrated so deep into language as to be invisible, and not just to hoary old American academics either. E. J. Pratt, one of Canada's more respected if admittedly hoary poets, wrote an epic poem about Brébeuf in which, without blinking, he describes

*Papooses yowling on their mother's back,*
*The squatting hags, suspicion in their eyes . . .*

Even the language of the poet can perpetuate a habit of dehumaniza- tion. The ideal Jesuits, wrote Allouez, were "men dead to themselves and the world." He meant this as a compliment to himself, and to his right- eous and considerable struggles in the lands surrounding Lake Superior. Unfortunately, his words have a literal ring to them. The Jesuit effort, long considered, and taught, as the apotheosis of human heroism and self- lessness, has been re-examined. Today it is hard to ignore the ideological and racial undertones of these "dead men"—obsessed fanatics who roamed the woods of North America, spreading confusion, oppression, and deadly disease. Disliked, abused, and mocked by the people they were so desperate to civilize, the Jesuits were restricted by the English after a few short decades, and finally suppressed by Pope Clement XIV in 1773.

In the end the "idolatrous and heathen" religion they were intent on destroying has not only outlived them, but to many has challenged

Christian Church–based religion as a truer, more connected, and more meaningful form of worship. Today, non-Natives from around the world travel great distances to experience some form of Native spirituality. "Superior by Nature," claim the tourist brochures of Thunder Bay, cleverly linking an ancient Native heritage with the physical power of Superior, presenting it as a region of spirituality and grace. From pow-wows to sweat lodges to historic Native-run retreats where visitors are invited to "discover a way of life that is centred on respect for all things," fascination with Native ceremony has increased as dramatically as interest in Christian ritual has waned.

On June 4, 1671, on the southeastern tip of Lake Superior, this state of affairs was unthinkable. There, a debauched French soldier, swarmed by blackflies, delivered a speech to the representatives of fourteen as-sembled Indian nations. A strange king was eulogized by a strange man. A cross was planted, then a cedar post bearing a metal plaque. One-tenth of the earth was given away. A debauched Frenchman proceeded to get extremely drunk, and was shortly ordered to leave. As soon as he had departed, the Royal Arms of France was stolen off its post and never seen again. Twenty-five years later the mission at Sault Ste. Marie collapsed for good when a tired and elderly Jesuit, Father Abanel, died and was not replaced. Said Antoine Raudot, "It was the first [mission] where the Indians laughed at our religion and so it has now been abandoned."

Today a faded white statue of Jesus stands in downtown Sault Ste. Marie, Ontario, commemorating "the heroic work of the early missionaries." As for Saint-Lusson's historic landing and proclamation, they are indicated by a small metal slab embedded in the Russell Food Equipment building at the corner of Queen and Gore streets. Across the road stands a Wendy's fast-food outlet ("We Open Late") and next door stands the O'Aces RiverRock Bar & Café.

# *The Water Dogs*

*. . . swearers, cheaters, drunkards, etc.*
—BISHOP FREDERIC BARAGA

"Live hard, lie hard, sleep hard"

In 1784, following his first journey to Lake Superior, William McGillivray, founder and shareholder in the North West Company, accompanied a party of men trudging westward out of Grand Portage, a trading settlement on the western shore of Lake Superior and nine-mile path heading up and westward into the hills. At the Height of Land, he was made to kneel. A drenched cedar bough was tapped three times on his head, and the young trader uttered a solemn vow never to kiss a voyageur's wife "without her permission."

A shot was fired, hands were shaken, and drinks were called for. These drinks, some say, were the real reason for the ceremony. Either way, McGillivray had been initiated as one of roughly five hundred white men each summer who reached the tip of Lake Superior and beyond. He had become an *"homme du nord."*

The title was honorary; McGillivray would not be required to carry enormous packs or to paddle canoes. This was left to a group of men known variously as "comers and goers," *"coureurs de bois,"* "pork eaters," *"mangeurs du lard,"* and, most famously, "voyageurs." They were also called simply "Canadians." For two hundred years they provided the numbing work necessary to get to Lake Superior, cross it, and get back home.

As a class of people they originated from the small farms and villages along the rivers near Montreal, villages named Sorel, L'Orignal, and Trois-Rivières, where Radisson had once lived. Quickly their ranks were swelled by Native paddlers, the "half-breeds" and "quarter-breeds" called "quarts" or "quadroons." They spoke French, laced with English and Ojibwa phrases. Charles Penny, an American city man who toured the south of Superior in 1840, noted, "These unlettered half breeds speak three languages fluently." Following a beaching in Whitefish Bay, one of them hoisted him out of the boat, placed him on his back, and carried him to shore. "They are admirable water dogs," he conceded. Passengers, including women, were routinely carried to shore. The voyageurs did not want their boots piercing the bark bottom of the canoe.

For three centuries these "unlettered half-breeds" have been *the* romantic figures of the North. The "savage" Indian, the "heroic" missionary, and the "lusty" voyageur are the trinity in a northern wilderness narrative that has constructed Lake Superior and the frontier itself. For a century they swept around Point au Chapeau, having raced in the lake's dense June fogs some 450 miles along the North Shore, paddling eighteen hours a day, sometimes for weeks on end. They pulled the water at sixty-five strokes a minute, flashing the painted cedar paddles that they carried with them like bohemian guitars through the streets back home.

Finally Grand Portage came into view, a stockaded post rising beneath the shadow of what is now Mount Rose. After docking at a rough timber wharf, the men looked up to see the sharpened palisade walls, the tops pointed to split the rain, put there in the first place to keep *them* out. Outside the walls they saw the wigwams, conical frameworks wrapped in skins with a pole sticking through the top. The grand journey was over. No man, not even a voyageur, was expected to go farther than Superior. Here, new teams were hired to go west along the Grand Portage itself, a nine-mile trek to the interior. By 1800 it was said of this trail that "where it is not rock, it is mud." Here the cost of operating the fur trade doubled.

If certain historians are to be trusted, it was also at Grand Portage that these lusty boatmen were met by "the welcome and pleasant sight of Chippewa girls in their graceful buckskin tunics." When the North West Company threw a party at its inauguration there in 1784, "every Chippewa girl wore her finest beaded tunic, for tonight she would dance with the white men!" These voyageurs were then "initiated into the agreeable ways of Indian girls," following which they "slipped away for a more intimate rendezvous."

This nod-and-wink sexuality, apparent in much early-twentieth-century writing about the voyageur, is provided by Canadian historian Marjorie Wilkins Campbell in her 1957 book, *The North West Company*. For the next twenty-five years any time a Canadian schoolteacher prepared a lesson on the voyageurs, she took her material almost entirely from this book. Campbell in turn took a great deal of her material from American historian Grace Lee Nute, the author of two formidable classics, *Lake Superior* (1944) and *The Voyageur* (1931). Between them these two women taught a half-century of North American schoolchildren almost everything they would know about the voyageurs.

As they paddled Lake Superior, these lusty voyageurs seem to have carried not only rum kegs and trading blankets, but a cargo of erotic baggage. Grace Lee Nute routinely has her voyageurs undressing in the rain as they attempt to keep their clothes dry. Nute, the doyenne of Superior-basin history, cannot help mentioning the "cold rain that coursed down their powerful naked backs." When they weren't paddling naked, they were forever "donning gay sashes and plumes in order to win the favours of dusky maidens." These distinctive sashes were the famous *ceintures flechées* of the voyageurs, the real *ceintures flechées,* woven on the fingers, with the weft thread running perpendicular to the warp. Campbell, writing two decades later, could barely mention a voyageur without slipping breathlessly into bodice-ripper purple. After initiating her boatmen into the "agreeable ways of Chippewa girls" and sending them outdoors for a "more intimate rendezvous," she feels no shame in leaving them out there "until dawn brightened the lead-coloured waters of Lake Superior."

No sooner had Lake Superior been brightened than these exhausted voyageurs had to paddle back to Montreal, where they become "intoxicated by the sight of white girls." Campbell takes it for granted that dusky maidens might prove a pleasant and agreeable distraction for a man far from home—but that only white girls could truly intoxicate him.

The casually sexualized account of the voyageur constitutes a subtext of Lake Superior—that here in "Indian Country" masculinity achieves its most potent manifestation. This manifestation involves the manners and instincts of the Indian merging into those of the white man, making him better, stronger, more potent, a more skilled boatman, more open to the spiritual, and more irresistible to women.

Even before reaching Superior the voyageur had come through thirty-six killing portages to arrive at Georgian Bay. Here he engaged in a ritual that demonstrated how much Native culture had entered his own; he tossed a bit of tobacco over the gunwales, to appease the water. When

William McGillivray set off on his inaugural trip to Grand Portage, he was, Campbell writes, "steadying himself for an ordeal equal to that of a young Indian facing the rites of manhood." In her mind the journey across Lake Superior was one of the most important tests of masculinity. It is also so inextricably mixed with the "Indian" that rites of white male passage and those of the Native blur together and become one.

The transformation of whites into Natives was an intriguing process. It is well exemplified by a young evangelical Christian fur trader, David Harmon, who arrived on the shores of Superior full of typical urban contempt for local ways. He was shocked to find men playing cards on Sunday and disgusted to see white traders marrying Native girls, "a snare," he wrote, "laid no doubt by the devil himself." At a Grand Portage ball he encountered a number of "this Countrie's Ladies" and was surprised to find that they could not only behave themselves, but "danced not amiss."

Under some pressure he eventually accepted a fourteen-year-old "mixed-blood" girl as a wife, or at least a companion. At first he justified the arrangement by promising to "place her into the hands of some good honest Man, with whom she can pass the remainder of her Days in this Country." In his journal he refers to her exclusively as "the Woman." A little later he calls her "the Woman who remains with me." By 1810 she was upgraded to "my Woman," and by 1819 she was promoted to "the mother of my children." A short while later he was "very pleasantly, teaching my little daughter Polly to read and spell words in the English language . . ." Later he took his woman and children east into civilization, found it intolerable, and came directly back. Tempted to write to a friend in the east, he decided against it on the grounds that "I am an Indian, he is a Christian, he will not like such a rough correspondent."

The "Indianization" of the early white travellers included staples such as food. Seventeenth-century *coureurs de bois* proved quite capable of wolfing down the infamous *sagamite,* a mix of grease and Indian corn boiled in lye that tasted like wallpaper paste, and was sometimes flavoured with a little eel skin. A century later the voyageur, up to his arrival on Lake Superior, could count on his pork fat and his ground peas, as well as any local delicacy he may have gleaned from the Chippewa. In 1840 the celebrated, arrogant, and doomed Michigan state geologist Douglass Houghton, while camping on the Keweenaw Peninsula, became fascinated with the culinary skill of one of his voyageurs. Using a technique borrowed from the Natives, the man inserted his pipe into the rectum of a dead porcupine, blew hard into it to inflate the animal, and then cooked it over the fire; the inflation allowed the quills to be scraped off without difficulty. According to the wide-eyed Houghton, "the perfect nonchalance" with which the man removed his pipe from the back end of the porcupine and returned it to his own mouth "was beyond conception."

West of Superior, following the nine-mile "lift" out of Grand Portage, the voyageur fed almost exclusively on pemmican. This staple would play no small part in the rivalry between the Hudson's Bay Company and the Nor' Westers, resulting finally in the massacre at Seven Oaks in 1816. In the 1850s, a young Chicago scientist named Robert Kennicott undertook a study of the fauna of the Canadian Northwest. He observed that pemmican consisted of pressed buffalo meat and hot grease, mixed with liberal amounts of "hair, sticks, bark, spruce leaves, stones, sand, etc." A favourite dish of the northern voyageurs, noted Kennicot, was "rubbaboo," pemmican boiled into a soup. "Those who have no spoons generally eat it in dog fashion, licking it up with their tongues." The fried tail of the beaver had become such a staple that voyageurs sought permission from the Sorbonne to eat it during Lent. The great ecclesiastical thinkers at the Sorbonne pondered and then permitted the request.

By the end of the nineteenth century the notion of a Canadian man as larger, stronger, better with an axe, boat, and horse than his European counterpart was well entrenched. The popular conception of the voyageur lay behind it. When the British troubleshooter and adventurer Chinese Gordon was sent into the Sudan and then refused to come out, Prime Minister William Gladstone called on Canadians to fetch him. Gladstone shared at least one Canadian habit himself—a mania for cutting down trees. A crew of Métis, French-Canadian, and Ottawa Valley boatmen was assembled to pole the British army up the Nile River. By the time the Canadians put the English army ashore, Chinese Gordon's head was on a pole. Nonetheless the voyageurs' exploits, particularly the breathtaking sweep *down* the Nile, helped to cement a conception of Canadian vigour—so much so that when British historian Arnold Toynbee attended Queen Victoria's Silver Jubilee as a boy, he did so mainly to see the Canadians.

Like Lake Superior itself, the voyageurs symbolized something better: a more potent masculinity, a more vigorous love of song, a rough-and-ready physicality that a mechanized world was already beginning to pine for. They could, according to Thomas McKenney, a Superior-bound official with the United States Bureau of Indian Affairs writing in the 1820s, "take a canoe out of water, mend it, reload, cook breakfast, shave, wash, eat and reembarke in fifty seven minutes." McKenney became so fascinated by the voyageurs on Superior that he estimated their daily stroke count: 57,600. "No human being but the Canadian French could stand this." John Jacob Astor, founder of the American Fur Company, said he would take one Canadian voyageur to three of any other kind. Astor himself presumably knew a little something about hard work. A native of "old Heidelberg on the Rhine," he arrived in America with his entire possessions wrapped in a bundle, fiercely determined "to be honest, to be industrious and to avoid gambling."

An agent under Astor's command expressed less sympathetic views toward the Canadians: "Although the body of the Yankee can resist as much hardship as any man, 'tis only in the Canadian we find that temper of mind to render him patient, docile and persevering. In short they are a people harmless in themselves whose habits of submission fit them peculiarly for our business . . ."

When they were not busy unfastening the buckskin tunics of Chippewa maidens, becoming intoxicated by "white girls," or just singing lustily, the voyageurs worked like pack animals. During their killing portages, as much as 480 pounds was loaded on a man's back. One such lift in Wisconsin stretched more than forty miles. They bore cast-iron stoves and live pigs. They took in Chinese vermilion and Brazilian tobacco, and they took out virtually the entire fur-bearing stock of Canada on their backs. As to these backs, Colonel McKenney suggested that they packed on them "what only a horse in our country would be expected to carry."

They were also flamingly colourful. "I have had twelve wives and six running dogs," bragged one of them. "I could carry, paddle, walk and sing with any man I ever saw. No portage was ever too long for me." Dr. John J. Bigsby, who drew the treaty line down the heart of Superior, took a close look at his voyageurs and noted that "one had his nostril bitten off." Another had been slapped in the face by a grizzly bear and consequently "had his features wrenched to the right."

As to their legendary musical skills, David Harmon, the fur trader, engaged in a little debunking when in 1841 he wrote, "This day being Christmas our people have spent it as usual in drinking and fighting . . . music consisted of a very bad performance of one vile, unvarying tune, upon a worse old fiddle, [with] a brilliant accompaniment upon a large tin pan." Harmon, unlike certain female historians of the next century, remained resolutely unsmitten by the voyageur: "The Canadian Voyageurs possess lively and fickle dispositions . . . they are talkative, and extremely thoughtless, and make many resolutions which are almost as soon broken as formed. They never think of providing for future wants . . . They are not brave . . . they are very deceitful . . . and are even gross flatterers to the face of a person, whom they will basely slander behind his back."

Since, in Harmon's opinion, Canadians made such "indifferent companions," he was pleased instead to read his books, "my dead friends," he called them, "who will never abandon me until I first neglect them."

Travellers, traders, officials, and sightseers who managed to reach Lake Superior in the 1800s looked upon the voyageur as one of the highlights of the journey. All who kept a diary wrote about them. What these observers could not have known was that the voyageur was already on the verge of extinction. The glorious rounds of their voices echoing off the rocky shores of Lake Superior, timed to the dip and lift of the paddles called forth by the man sitting in the bow of the canoe, hired specifically to sing, were already dying. The voyageur was disappearing. Decked vessels and the steady elimination of fur-bearing animals had eroded his livelihood. By 1814 a North Shore trader described the bear and deer as extinct in the region.

The glory days of the voyageurs peaked some time after 1763. Thirty years later the explorer Alexander Mackenzie alluded to a voyageur community, a kind of retirement colony near Lake Superior, "a village of about thirty families of the Algonquin nation, who are one half the year starving and the other half intoxicated, and ten to twelve Canadians who have been in the Indian country from an early period of life and inter-married with the natives who have brought them families."

This glimpse suggests a group of white labourers being assimilated into the ways, the woods, and the family structures of the Natives. Perhaps they felt more appreciated there. Mackenzie, who sometimes suffered from terrifying visions of the dead, would coolly note in his journal, "lost two men and eleven pieces of goods." To some extent the problem of the ageing voyageurs was dealt with by allowing them to settle outside the walls of the trading post.

In 1840 when Charles Penny stopped at La Pointe on Madeline Island in present-day Wisconsin, he observed "about 40 lodges [and] about 46 dwellings, most of which are occupied by old voyageurs . . ." From this community can be read a story of exile, usually a willing one, of men who crossed over into another culture and were never comfort-able going back. This is what Lake Superior was, and how it is still commonly conceptualized, a place for vigorous and wild souls to make room for themselves.

When he did not die young—typically of a strangulated hernia or drowning—the voyageur passed his final years here, among the rocks, the water, the trees, the club moss, and the familiar company of Natives. By 1840, the profession was decidedly on the wane. The American Fur Company briefly kept the voyageur working by commercially fishing Lake Superior. But in 1850 the company went bankrupt, and with it went those long, improbable dashes across the world's largest lake by the world's most renowned paddlers.

A hundred years after their disappearance suburban schoolchildren would sit in rows learning their songs, the back-and-forth rounds, the "Alouette, gentile alouette," that mimic the lift and dip of the paddle. They became such a core component of the Canadian school curriculum that many children first experienced the woods, the waters, and the rhythm of the canoe through the songs of these long-dead men.

"His Gallic ancestry was nowhere so evident as in the deferential ease with which he addressed his superiors, the Indians, ladies, or men of his own class," wrote a wistful Grace Lee Nute. His chivalry and his manners are long gone. His renowned obscenity no longer rings a furious blue against the rocks. For all of his singing and his celebrated colour he does not speak in his own voice. Presumably illiterate, he left no letters home, wrote no journals. The companies depended entirely on him, as both labourer and their most reliable customer. It has been estimated that ten years of work often put a voyageur eleven years in debt to the company.

The North West Company itself was composed of driven, single-minded Scotsmen who worked round the clock to duplicate the slash-and-burn madness that had beggared their own homeland and would soon lay waste to the new one. In their spare time they built castles to live in and hung paintings of themselves on the walls of the Great Hall, first at Grand Portage, then Fort William.

In that same hall they developed an intricate hierarchical seating arrangement based on clanship, kinship, prestige, and paternalism, and built themselves an empire of such bureaucratic complexity that it would have confounded Franz Kafka. Here took place the petty intrigues, the backstabbing, and the naked greed that erupted finally in the Seven Oaks massacre. The incident began with braggadocio and insults, a fateful slap, the smooth slipping of the Métis carriers into the tall prairie grass where they knew exactly what they were doing, and then twenty-two dead. Radisson had it right: little men playing at Caesars, with no one around to tell them otherwise.

The voyageurs transported their bosses and their wealth across a continent. They carried both men and women on their vulgar backs, missionaries as well as their disgusted wives. They carried history on these backs as well, and paddled through the heart of it. They arrived on the shores of Superior laden to the gunwales with children born of Ojibwa wives, with dogs, puppies, and falcons in cages. In the end they themselves became historical artifacts, objects to be observed and written about, like the Native, like the Pictured Rocks of the South Shore, and the Ontonagon Boulder. The extent of their homesickness can be read in the number of French-Canadian place names that crowd Superior's shores. Their names can still be found in the phone books of Sault Ste. Marie and other places, the Cadots and Cadottes, and others.

Fortunately the echo of who he was has not disappeared entirely. David Harmon captured at least an essence of it when he wrote down one voyageur's credo as it was told to him: "Live hard, lie hard, sleep hard, eat dogs."

# [ 6 ]

## *Temperature Rising*

*I consider this whole region doomed to perpetual barrenness.*

—THOMAS McKENNEY

Thomas McKenney

In 1825 Thomas McKenney, superintendent of United States Indian Affairs, was sent on an official journey to the western tip of Lake Superior to negotiate a treaty at Fond du Lac, near today's Duluth. This treaty would provide a payment of two thousand dollars annually to the Chippewa nation in exchange for which the United States government would be allowed to "search for, and carry away, any metals or minerals from any part of their country." The party was also to make sure that several Chippewa suspected of murdering four white traders near Lake Pepin and who had recently broken out of jail at Michilimackinac were brought to trial.

McKenney, who described himself as a colonel but was not, was a large man with a conical and bewildering outcrop of white hair. Like many travellers to Lake Superior, he felt obliged to write a book about his experience. This book, published in 1826, bears the onerous title *Sketches of a Tour to the Lakes: of the Character and Customs of the Chippeway Indians and of Incidents connected with the Treaty of Fond du Lac* and consists of a series of self-conscious letters to his young wife. It also provides some insight into the efforts of the United States officialdom to come to terms with Lake Superior.

The title page includes an epigraph of two telling lines from the English poet William Cowper:

> *Thus fare the shiv'ring natives of the north,*
> *And thus the rangers of the western world . . .*

Shivering natives are found in abundance throughout McKenney's journal. Usually they are huddled against the shores of Lake Superior in obvious need of Christian benevolence and the assistance of the United States government. The rangers of the Western world would be McKenney and his party. That party included the Michigan Territory's first governor, Lewis Cass, an extremely rotund man nicknamed "Big Belly" by the Chippewa, a hater of all things English, a loyal supporter of Jeffersonian republicanism, and a massively wealthy land speculator. He was also notably sympathetic toward the Native peoples of the United States.

Along with them was the geologist, travel author, explorer, and Indian agent Henry Rowe Schoolcraft, brought on board at the Soo. Accompanying him were at least eleven more officials. Also attached to the party was a military band with a fondness for playing "Hail Columbia," the first and perhaps last musicians to ever accompany a United States government delegation on a treaty negotiation. Finally, there was a small military contingent, a company of the Sixty-Second Infantry. Its arrival on Superior represented the United States Army's farthest penetration north to that date.

Along with this odd flotilla that stretched for several miles across the lake was an assistant surgeon and Mr. George F. Porter, who was given the task of removing a boulder from the banks of the Ontonagon River. This rock, weighing several tons, was somehow to be dislodged, transported across Lake Superior, and brought back to Washington, D.C.

Not only was Colonel McKenney heavily equipped, he was also heavily laden with science. Lake Superior was now to be squeezed into the formidable vise grips of rational thought. McKenney's journal bristles with measurements, numbers, and observations. Barely a tree, a rock, a fish, a bay, or a Native's head could be passed without being measured. Of Lake Superior itself McKenney writes, "Its width is computed at an average of one hundred and nine miles, and its depth at nine hundred feet, and its elevation above tide water, nearly one thousand and fifty feet." A bay was not a bay but "a curvature, oval in its figure. It is a mile deep, on a line drawn from the centre, extending out to another drawn from its capes; the capes are two miles apart . . ."

Of the landscape, in particular the interplay between water and sky, wind, sun, and sand, McKenney observes, "The elements appear to have nothing else to do but amuse themselves." Nature was like the Natives, lazy, indolent, and in obvious need of discipline. Riding the high swells of Lake Superior he refused to take thermometer readings from inside the canoe, considering that "the reflection of heat from the water and that arising from eleven bodies" would prevent him "from ascertaining the temperature correctly."

Armed with this science, McKenney was able to quickly dispel age-old Native "traditions." When the Natives refused to coast Keweenaw Peninsula in their canoes, insisting on a portage instead, he got straight to the bottom of things. Their reluctance was due, he wrote, to a long tradition in which a group of men approaching Beaver Island witnessed the form of a woman, growing larger "until her size became so overpowering and fearful" that the Natives fled. Because of this apparition, local people refused to hunt the beaver in that area, and by the 1780s the local rivers were said to be brimming with them. According to McKenney the tradition was still intact when his voyageurs paddled him around the peninsula in 1825.

This intriguing Ojibwa "belief" seems to speak of the relationship between hunting, conservation, and the replenishment of stock, at the same time touching on the mysteries of birth and fertility. This fertility is echoed in the cycle of the beaver, its decline and replenishment. The story also probes the parameters of male and female, explores the role of the hunter, and postulates a seemingly female principle, a figure of protection, sustenance, and longevity. McKenney puts it this way: "And believing that this woman held dominion over all the beaver of Keweena point, they never dared disturb these animals here."

Despite the apparent nuances and complexities to the story, McKenney consigned it at once to the ash bin of "Indian beliefs." Of this growing female gliding over the water he writes: "It was doubtless a mirage." In his mind the matter is settled. The Indian is not capable of telling a giantess from a mirage. Twenty-five years later the German ethnologist Johann Kohl, travelling close to this same area, drew a very different picture of the Chippewa understanding of mirages: "That the watchful Indians not only observe this optical delusion, but also form a correct idea of its cause, is proved by the name they give to the mirage. They call it 'ombonitewin,' a word meaning . . . 'something that swells and rises in the air.' They also make of it a very convenient and excellent verb; 'ombanite' ie, 'there is a mirage about,' to express which the French and English require considerable circumlocution."

McKenney, having shed light where before was only darkness, hunkered down in his canoe, timepiece in hand, counting the paddle strokes of the voyageurs, per minute, per hour, per day. That night he closed his journal with another observation, a scientific bookend from which nothing could escape: "Thermometer at sundown, 57 degrees." Sleeping for four hours, he woke up, reached for his journal, and wrote, "Thermometer at sunrise, 63 degrees."

Near the end of his trip ("temperature at sunrise 60 degrees"), McKenney attended a Chippewa ceremony outside the establishment of the American Fur Company at Fond du Lac. He was there not to enjoy or learn from it, but to debunk it. In particular he was out to debunk the mystery of the fire-eaters. The complex ceremony of the *wabana* employed young girls in a kind of choral function, followed by a theatrical interplay between dancing, drumming, singing, fire, darkness, light, and silence. At one point the audience inside the lodge sang in unison with the audience outside the lodge. Elderly male singers in this ceremony could extend their voices over two full octaves. To McKenney it was all "one loud yell of savage confusion." When a fire-eater approached, he reacted like any good scientist—he leaped up, peered into the man's mouth, and "saw in what the deception consisted."

This statement cuts to the heart of McKenney's other agenda—to re-create the Native in an image of ignorance and destitution, sorely in need of the protection of the United States government. His adjectives pound home the message: the land is "doomed and barren," the Indians are "shivering, unfortunate, hapless, unlettered, wretched, uninstructed unfortunate people and poor creatures."

In the end more than adjectives were needed to prove that the Indian was fit only to be a ward of the state. Brave, rational men were required, men willing to look him square in the face, even the mouth if necessary, and see through his crafty deception. "I am convinced," McKenney writes, "that all the accounts we have seen of Indians eating fire, are only exaggerations of attempts of deception." All such attempts fail, of course, before the science that McKenney can call upon.

McKenney was the son of Quakers and a devout man. He had already worked hard on a piece of legislation known as the Indian Civilization Act of 1819, which provided federal support for "Indian education," providing it was conducted in English. His whole career was based on the assumption that "Indian" culture was depraved and dying, and that the Natives themselves desperately needed help. This attitude framed his observations and accounts for his telescopic vision toward the fire-eaters, who were arguably actors in a kind of play. To grant them this degree of sophistication not only would have undermined his own training, but would have challenged the official construction of Native North

Americans as a race of "poor hapless wretches" requiring the benevolence of the president.

Before McKenney's perceptive gaze everything that is Native in origin falls to pieces. "We have all heard a great deal about the skill of Indian doctors," he warns, "but take them as a body and they are utterly ignorant." He mocks practitioners of Native medicine for having no understanding of the *materia medica* and in particular "the Harveynian system of the circulation of the blood."

At one point during the expedition he stood at the bedside of a sick Chippewa girl while the expedition's surgeon cupped blood from her neck. He notes that "the blood was coagulated . . . indicating how languid the circulation is." When the girl complained of pain in her eyes, McKenney, who felt deeply for her, rose on the wings of scientific rapture and suggested, "Possibly the case might be interesting to craniologists, who contend that the optic nerves have their origin in that region of the brain [the *occiput*], whilst others contend they do not extend beyond the *thalami nervorum*."

The triumph of science over superstition plays out on every page of McKenney's account. At Fond du Lac an enormous deer was shot by a Native hunter and brought back to the American Fur Company post, where a local trader had it stuffed and mounted "in the posture of a living deer." Likely this was the first time the Chippewa of Lake Superior had ever been exposed to such a curious procedure. The dead animal stood there immense and frozen, its living eyes replaced by marbles, the scouring winds of Superior lifting the hairs from its back. To McKenney and his party, to the white traders buzzing about the post, it stood as physical proof that nature could be tamed and great animals rendered immobile for the amusement and inspection of their new masters. To the locals, who suspected and even insisted on the living spirit in the living thing, this stuffed facsimile must have appeared as something else entirely. They were not long in interpreting it.

The appearance of the stuffed animal coincided with a lean period for local hunters, who, not surprisingly, attributed their difficulty "to the indignity that the deer on display had suffered." McKenney, in what he imagines to be a comic set piece, describes how Native hunters resolved this problem. A group of men approached the stuffed deer, arranged themselves on the ground around it, and there ceremonially smoked and addressed the spirit of the animal, asking forgiveness and giving assurances that it was not *their* fault that this indignity had taken place. At one point, "they put their pipes into the deer's mouth that it might smoke too." After the ceremony was over, they went away believing, in McKenney's words, "that the spirit of the deer was appeased."

The tableau is carefully constructed to show a group of ignorant Indians caught addressing a dead animal. In a giveaway gesture, one of them puts a smoking pipe into the creature's mouth. All of this is presented as the play of children, whose naïveté should be suffered with a smile.

As soon as the Natives had departed, McKenney leaped up with measuring tape in hand and got to the heart of the matter: "This animal measured eight feet. Its neck was three feet and a half long; its head three feet. Horns near the head measured nine and a half inches round. There are fourteen tips or branches . . ."

Throughout his journal McKenney proved that the inhabitants of the region, like the carcass of a deer, could be reduced to a series of numbers and configurations. Without knowing it, he presented a vignette that summarizes two separate cultures and two distinct and irreconcilable attitudes toward animals. One is based on intuition and darkness; the other is bathed in the truth of science and numbers. He had also brought a new God to the region, and a very demanding one. Each night and morning he paid his respects to it—the ceremonial reading of the thermometer.

By the time it was all over, McKenney had, in his own estimation, acquitted himself well. The Chippewa had surrendered their claim to the copper or other minerals in the ground beneath their feet. In exchange they asked that a school for their children be built at the Soo. The request was denied by the United States Senate, and later struck from the treaty. The chiefs also agreed to give up the men responsible for the murders of the four traders (they didn't) and to cooperate with the federal government. McKenney extracted this promise by using language similar to that used by Father Claude-Jean Allouez at the other end of Superior a century and a half earlier. First he emphasized the devastating power of the "arm" of the Great Father of the United States of America:

> *You know nothing about your father's arm because you have not seen it . . . I will tell you what it is like.*
>
> *You have all seen the sky grow black. You have heard the wind out of the clouds, and seen it tear the leaves off the trees, and scatter them . . . and blow them along the ground. And you have seen the fire struck by the Great Spirit out of the sky. Then you have seen something that is like your great father's arm, when he is stirred, and when he paints himself and goes forth to war.*

"Take care how you stir him," warned McKenney, for when the great father lashes out his arm, "it may fall and kill the innocent too. This will not be his fault, but yours."

In all respects McKenney conducted himself successfully. He oversaw the giving of the gifts at Fond du Lac, the fish hooks and flour, the four-point cherry-red blankets, the vermilion and pork, the government medallions, the knives and the whisky, a commodity McKenney doled out regretfully, the Chippewa having already been reduced by it to a state of wretchedness, in his opinion. In his official capacity he ensured that every Native recipient made the mark of the cross on the corresponding official document. To make matters simple, a government clerk had already inscribed the crosses on the page. All the Indian need do was step forward and touch the clerk's pen, a gesture that both saved time and conferred enough legitimacy to satisfy the government.

The colonel also demonstrated that science could be used to comprehend the Indians, to outwit and to improve them. "A thorough knowledge of the Indian character will enable any person to avoid and elude most of their plans." Besides accomplishing his mission, McKenney came away able to experience that "one pleasure on earth more pure than the rest," that special feeling that comes from "feeding the hungry . . . clothing the naked . . . conferring benefits on the destitute, and making the miserable happy." As to the massive and unfathomable presence of Superior, he stated confidently, "Lake Superior has been coasted—its peculiarities, both in regard to the variables of its surface, and its shores, have been sketched."

With this little note tucked securely into his journal, McKenney had done his job. Lake Superior had been coasted and sketched. Science had rendered it tame and comprehensible. Nothing was left for him to do but float back home and put his mind to more serious matters.

Somewhere off the Huron Islands, sprawled in a canoe festooned with a feather at bow and stern, and supporting an awning to keep the sun off his busy head, McKenney got down to tackling the thorny issue of women. Having already determined how to edify the poor females of the South Shore, he rather subtly began to extend the process to his own wife. Logically enough he began with the Irish playwright Richard Sheridan, or at least Sheridan's wife. "We see in her all that makes woman lovely," he writes to the young woman back home, going on in a similar vein for two full pages of dense text. On the wildest shores of the New World, borne across the surface of an inland ocean by voyageurs, McKenney's mind drifts back to where it is most comfortable—the drawing rooms of polished society.

The contemporary European concern with women and what to do with them was a topic that, not surprisingly, McKenney had some opinions about. In his mind, the surest way to improve the Indian woman was to make her resemble her white sister. This involved a little more pianoforte and needlework on her part and a lot less dancing naked and sleeping with whomever she pleased. Much had changed in the two hundred years since Radisson, somewhere nearby, had unabashedly admired the naked Chippewa women as they danced en masse to ensure that their men hurried back to them.

Charles Penny, the young civilian who followed McKenney's journey a decade later, became hopelessly infatuated with a young Chippewa woman. He admitted rather coyly that he found the local girls, at least the ones with plaited hair and clean faces, "almost good enough to kiss."

It is doubtful that McKenney would go so far as Mr. Penny. His notion of the ideal Native woman was the young Mrs. Jane Schoolcraft. He admired in particular her "mildness of expression," her "softness and delicacy of manners." A modern reader senses that what he really admired was that "you would never judge, either from her complexion, or language . . . that her mother was a Chippeway." That she neither looked nor sounded like a Native woman is accounted for, in McKenney's opinion, by her "highly finished compositions in both prose and poetry." Add these accomplishments to the fact that she was twenty-two and attractive, and she comes very close to becoming what he respectfully describes as "an ornament to any society."

Although he offers no concrete strategies on how to turn Chippewa women into ornaments, he closes his narrative confident that he has met and solved all the problems in his mandate. He has promised the residents of Lake Superior that he will ask their "great father to take pity" on them.

If one issue stuck in his throat, it was the rock, that famous piece of copper called the Ontonagon Boulder. In this he failed miserably. The massive hunk of metal remained resolutely stuck in the side of Lake Superior, a stain on the white pages of science, and proof that the North was not yet ready to be tamed. "How much I regret this failure," he confided to his journal.

For all of his science, his Latin, his medicine, his fondness for Cowper and Sheridan, for all of the modern wisdom and best intentions that Colonel McKenney brought to Lake Superior, he too ended badly. To the extent that his name lives at all, it does so in shame. On returning from Lake Superior he began work on his second major piece of legislation, the Indian Removal Act of 1830. This act, designed to remove the eastern tribes to a region west of the Mississippi, led to the infamous "Trail of Tears," the eight-hundred-mile forced march of the Creek, Cherokee, Choctaw, Chickasaw, and Seminole peoples. The outrages associated with their removal were a burning scandal even in McKenney's time, and the name associated with it is his own.

In fairness to the colonel, he insisted to the end that the policies of President Andrew Jackson were responsible for the travesties of that forced march. Unfortunately for him, President Jackson was in charge of the Indian department, and McKenney was fired for his criticisms. He spent the rest of his life trying unsuccessfully to persuade the government to rehire him.

During his eventful career, Thomas McKenney sounded the confident voice of science. With it he reduced Lake Superior to a series of measurements and readings on a thermometer. He came north bearing gifts for the Natives, accompanied by the army and a brass band. He saw through the superstitions and deceptions perpetrated by an ancient people, and decided after considerable thought that the North American Indian was morally superior, at least, to the European gypsy, whom he had read about in a hateful poem by Cowper. In what little spare time he had left in his busy life, he pondered the improvement of women.

Having outlived his wife and child, he died without friends, penniless and forgotten, in a Brooklyn rooming house in 1859.

# [ 7 ]

## *The Ontonagon Boulder*

*Whoever visits the rock pays well for his curiosity.*
—CHARLES PENNY, 1836

*Mass of Native Copper on the Ontonagon River* by Henry Rowe Schoolcraft

*A*t one time it rested stupendously on the banks of the Ontonagon River, a massive free-standing rock made of 100 percent native copper. It had caught the attention of Europeans since contact and gained a reputation as one of the most singular natural objects on the face of the earth. The crowned heads of Europe were said to talk of nothing else.

For four hundred years it has been known as the Ontonagon Boulder or the fabled Copper Rock of Lake Superior. Father Charlevoix claimed that Native captives were commonly sacrificed on it. By the 1600s the Jesuits were reportedly hacking off pieces for the French king. In 1766 the English fur trader Alexander Henry estimated its weight at five tons. According to him, the copper was so pure and malleable that one-hundred-pound lumps could be lopped off easily with an axe.

From this early celebrity the Ontonagon Boulder fast became a premier tourist destination of Lake Superior, and a wonder of the natural world. Not only Charlevoix, but Jonathan Carver, explorer Alexander Mackenzie, fur trader Alexander Henry, and the indefatigable French officer baron de La Hontan (who sometimes recorded his notes on birchbark) all published their observations on the rock, bringing to the Lake Superior area what Henry Schoolcraft called "a notoriety . . . which it had otherwise certainly lacked."

No trip along the South Shore was complete without a visit or at least a comment on the fabled stone. Reaching the boulder meant paddling southward some twenty miles up the Ontonagon River, then hiking inland along a river fork for six more. "The way to this rock is difficult," notes a mystical-sounding McKenney. In 1820 an Ojibwa guide got lost himself while searching for it. The man was put in charge of guiding Governor Lewis Cass to the rock. Governor "Big Belly" Cass, as the Natives called him, puffing over the treacherous landscape and melting beneath the scorching sun, wandered aimlessly for several hours until he and his guide finally encountered the remainder of the party.

The possibility that Cass's guide was wilfully misleading him cannot be entirely ruled out. Wabishkeepenas (White Pigeon), the Indian who successfully guided the other half of the expedition and received a gold medallion for his efforts, found himself immediately ostracized by the Chippewa. By all accounts his manitou deserted him. When Cass met him again six years later, the man was starving, destitute, and almost naked. The medallion given to him years earlier was his only possession.

Interpretations of Native attitudes toward copper suggest that the mineral played a complex and valuable role in Native ritual trade and tool-making. Five-thousand-year-old copper fish gaffs have been found on Superior's shores, and extensive Native mining of copper is thought to have begun some seven thousand years ago in the region. As American copper prospectors spread over the South Shore in the mid-nineteenth century, they discovered that every productive vein in the region had already been mined.

The Chippewa certainly noticed the enormous interest the mineral held for the white-skinned newcomers, and that interest caused some tension. At the 1825 treaty gathering at Fond du Lac, an old chief chose his words carefully when he told McKenney and Cass, "Fathers, I have no knowledge of any copper in my country." In the next breath he changed course: "There is a rock there," he admitted. "I met some of your people in search of it. I told them if they took it to steal it, and not let me catch them."

The other chiefs jumped in. "Fathers, you have heard of the words of the Plover on the subject of the rock. This, fathers, is the property of no one man. It belongs alike to us all. It was put there by the Great Spirit, and it is ours." The same speaker then summarized the oral history of the local Copper Rock over the preceding hundred years:

> In the life of my father, the British were engaged in working it. It was then about the size of that table. They attempted to raise it to the top of the hill, and they failed. They then said, the copper was not in the rock, but in the banks of the river. They dug for it, and while working under ground by candle light, the earth fell in upon them and killed three of the men. It was then abandoned, and no attempt has been made on it till now.

This fairly accurate description of Mackenzie's assault on the Ontonagon Boulder nearly a century earlier is thought to be the first non-Native attempt to mine copper in North America.

Despite Governor Cass's failure to see the rock for himself, it did not prevent him from later describing how "our chissels broke like glass" against the copper. An amused McKenney added that the Indians attributed Cass's losing his way to "a manito, who they believe, guards that rock, and preserves it from the profane touch of the white man."

It's a measure of the profanity or perhaps the frequency of that touch that no visitor to the rock could leave without first whacking off a hunk to take back home with him. By the time Charles Penny arrived in 1836, he found the corners of the Ontonagon Boulder "to have been so often trimmed before that it required an immense deal of labor to get off even a small bit." By that time the rock was said to weigh approximately 3,500 pounds, which suggests that within less than half a century, relic hunters had chipped away two tons of the boulder! One member of the party did manage to get off about thirty pounds' worth "for the University and other institutions."

The idea that the Copper Rock belonged in a university or other official institution took hold in the early 1800s. The first attempt to put it in one was the Cass-McKenney expedition of 1826. "We must remove the copper rock!" wrote the breathless governor, perhaps still stinging from his earlier failure to so much as lay eyes on it. "Provide such ropes and blocks as may be necessary." McKenney engaged the services of George F. Porter for the sole purpose of bringing out the rock and transporting it back to Washington, D.C.

On August 1, 1826, George Porter set out with twenty men in two boats to rescue the rock. Proceeding up the turbid and sluggish waters of the Ontonagon River, they reached the first rapids, where one of the boats was left behind. For the next two days the expedition dragged the remaining boat up a series of continuous rapids until they reached a fork. Two miles up the right branch they had to leave the second boat behind as well and tramp inland, a torturous five-mile trip through bogs, ravines, and thick underbrush, where finally "we at length with some difficulty, discovered the object of our search, long known by the name of the Copper Rock of Lake Superior."

Although Porter failed to remove the rock, he did succeed in writing a two-page report outlining his mission. Finding his plans "frustrated by unforeseen difficulties," he informed Governor Cass and McKenney that he regretted his failure, but remained, with great respect, their most obedient servant. McKenney was horrified to learn the party had attempted to crack or melt the copper by lighting a fire on the surface of it, then dousing it with cold water. Native copper miners had employed the technique as long as six thousand years ago, but in McKenney's scrupulous opinion, it was possible the fire might be construed as meaning that "the mass" was "a production of human agency," and therefore worthless. Such a rumour, he was sure, "would destroy the interest that is now felt in this wonderful production of nature." Henry Schoolcraft was utterly scandalized, calling the effort a blatant "attempt to mutilate and falsify the noblest specimen of native copper on the globe." This is a far cry from his first impression of the rock in 1820 that left him entirely unimpressed: "The first feeling was that of disappointment. It has been greatly overrated by former travelers."

For McKenney, the vision of himself trekking into the remotest regions of the United States and marching out with a celebrated symbol of pure wilderness must have been a shining one, and it was only with great bitterness that he was able to concede defeat. A morose McKenney confided to his journal, "As I looked into the mouth of this river [Ontonagon] for the last time, I felt the disappointment occasioned by the failure to bring the rock out."

Despite the fact that Superior had, in his words, "yielded before Anglo-Saxon power," the Natives pacified with promises and gifts, and all mineral rights transferred to the United States government, the Ontonagon Boulder was not his. It rested as cheekily as before on a riverbank, an inscrutable and somewhat freakish object of nature sitting there like a slap to the face.

Through the first half of the nineteenth century, the fame of the Ontonagon Boulder continued to grow. Each new description saw the rock swell in size and importance. A sketch published in 1821 by the *American Journal of Science* shows the boulder nestled between the trees, a shining ingot of transcendental beauty, the Ontonagon River lapping at its base.

Although the value of the boulder was never to exceed one thousand U.S. dollars, as a symbol of unspoiled nature it was priceless. Onto the "fabled copper wonder" was foisted all the attitudes by which the North was comprehended. Like the North itself, it symbolized sheer abundance. It also epitomized the astonishing purity of Lake Superior, and of Lake Superior copper in particular. For two hundred years it had been viewed as an object of almost unbelievable untapped wealth, "guarded by surly Indians and impenetrable forests." Its removal would represent the gelding of Superior, the triumph of culture over nature, and of the civilized over the savage. It would also demonstrate that a hunk of native copper, like the Native people themselves, could be probed, studied, written about, then uprooted and transported somewhere else.

Drawn into these complexities was an undistinguished fifty-three-year-old hardware merchant from Detroit. It is thought that Julius Eldred became smitten with the boulder during a conversation at a Detroit dinner party. In 1841 he set out on an implausible journey to transport the rock to Detroit with the solidly American ambition of putting it on display and charging admission to see it. Making his way up the Ontonagon River, he purchased the boulder from a man named Okondokon, a chief of the Ontonagon band of the Chippewa, for $150 down and a promise of more to come. A year later he made a second trip to determine what equipment and manpower he would need to remove the mass. Before leaving, he hoisted it up on skids and re-deposited it on dry land.

By the time he made his final assault, he found the Ontonagon area crawling with copper miners, most if not all of whom were convinced the rock belonged to them. These were decidedly not the sort of men to be pushed around by a Detroit shopkeeper. In the spring of 1842, a mysterious Colonel Hammond sent his own crew overland to claim possession of the boulder. Among that wild and illiterate party was a former Mississippi boatman described as "half horse, half alligator." James Paul was a veteran of the 1832 Black Hawk War—and his commanding officer had been a young man named Abraham Lincoln.

With this party stoutly holding the rock, another crew arrived, led by a certain Colonel White. Arriving in May, the White gang learned that

Colonel Hammond was in firm control of the rock but lacked a permit from the War Department. The latecomer Colonel White sold his own permit to Colonel Hammond, and beat a tactical retreat.

Into this mess landed Julius Eldred with a carpenter, a boatload of custom-made equipment, and a work crew of twenty men, both whites and Natives. At some point negotiations between the various groups became sticky, and as permit orders were waved around, James Paul pulled out two pistols and announced, "I don't give two hoots in hell for your order. I got a couple of orders here that are a lot better." The redoubtable Eldred offered to buy the rock yet again, which he did, paying $1,365 to Colonel Hammond. At this point James Paul quit the scene and hurried off to found the town of Ontonagon, where he would soon be selling 40 Rod Whiskey from behind the bar of his hotel.

Eldred set about hacking a four-mile clearance through the forest, bypassing a span of difficult rapids. "It was no small task," he reported to Congress. By now he was borrowing money from his own children to finance the rock's removal. The rock was then levered, inch by inch, fifty feet to the top of the river bluff and loaded onto a crude flatcar. This part of the operation alone took more than a week. The cart, mounted on two lengths of track, was moved forward by tackle attached to the trees. Workers picked up the tracks from behind, repositioned them in front, and manoeuvred the Ontonagon Boulder through four miles of dense thicket, underbrush, and white cedar swamp. At the river, the rock was shifted onto a raft—only for Eldred to discover that the level of the river was too low to float the boulder out.

In one of the few examples of good luck to come Eldred's way, a providential shower fell, which raised the water level high enough for the men to begin their journey to the river mouth with their cargo. Eldred went ahead, and found an unamused Colonel Hammond waiting for him with news that Eldred's cheque for $1,365 had bounced. The hardware merchant then made a lengthy dash to Detroit and back, and managed to fix things up with Hammond, who agreed on a new price of $1,765 for his trouble. Eldred then chartered the schooner *Algonquin* to pick up his boulder and stopped briefly at Copper Harbor along the way.

In 1843 the town of Copper Harbor, Michigan, consisted of precisely "nine tents, averaging six to a tent." As one inhabitant noted, this "makes for quite a society." Waiting for Eldred and his precious cargo in Copper Harbor was a General Cunningham, the government representative overseeing the distribution of mining permits, and a man whose professional reputation was soon to be tarnished by his inability to tolerate mosquitoes. He had with him a letter written by the secretary of war, who insisted that "the object . . . really [was] one of great importance to the scientific world." The letter also demanded that "the mass" be transported to the city of Washington, D.C., to be placed in the National Institute, and authorized General Cunningham to call out the army at Fort Brady in Sault Ste. Marie if he met resistance.

The exasperated would-be owner then sailed with General Cunningham aboard the *Algonquin* to the mouth of the Ontonagon River, where the boulder floated majestically on its raft. There Chief Okondokon also waited, expecting to collect the remainder of his payment.

The financial implications of the Ontonagon Boulder were something about which the Chippewa were acutely aware. Twenty years earlier at the Fond du Lac treaty gathering, McKenney, Schoolcraft, and Cass were presented with an impassioned plea by a speaker who gave a persuasive summation of the economics of the rock: "Fathers, at the time of which I speak, a great price was paid by the English for our permission [to mine copper]. We expect no less from you. If you take this rock, Fathers, the benefit to be derived from its sale, *must be extended to our children,* who are now but this high [a foot]. For ourselves, we care but little. We are old and nearly worn out. But our children must be provided for."

Eldred paid the chief another $105 in goods, which, along with the previous payment, represented the total benefit the Chippewa nation would ever receive for the removal of the fabled Copper Rock of Lake Superior.

In Washington a poorly informed secretary of war, speaking to the members of the National Institute, said he was pleased to announce that the boulder was on its way to that city. As one writer noted, the secretary "was a long way from Lake Superior," and Eldred in fact was, at that moment, portaging the rock around the St. Marys Rapids and winching it on board a ship downbound for Detroit. In an act of sympathy, General Cunningham had "deputized" Eldred and, for a transportation charge of one hundred dollars, allowed him to transport the boulder to Detroit and keep it there until the government reimbursed him.

On October 11, 1843, the triumphant Julius Eldred landed at Detroit and arranged for his boulder to be pulled through the city by four black stallions. Taken to a room beneath the office of the *Advertiser* newspaper, the rock was put on display for a fee of twenty-five cents per customer. One of the first members of the public to put down his money and gaze on the treasure was Henry Schoolcraft, who had seen the rock twenty years prior, resting on the banks of the Ontonagon River, and had been, at that time, quite disappointed.

As the boulder became *the* symbol for a Lake Superior mining fever and the first mining rush in United States history, Schoolcraft, always quick to side with a winner, revised his earlier estimation of the boulder, calling it "the noblest specimen of native copper on the globe."

By this point there appeared to be no limits as to how the Ontonagon Boulder could be interpreted. It was called "the Mass," ethereal and ubiquitous, usually with a capital *M,* indicating its status as an icon. Like humankind itself, the boulder had once been part of primitive and unknowable Nature, but now was far removed from it. To the secretary of war it was "the object," another all-inclusive term suggesting there was little the rock could not represent. To the traveller Charles Penny it was a "fabled mineral wonder"; Schoolcraft found it "noble"; the American public, on the verge of its first full-blooded mining rush, viewed it as a "siren" calling them to the mythic North, where immense copper nuggets lay on the ground to be scooped up by the common man. As late as 1960, in an attempt to enliven his book *Boom Copper,* a history of Lake Superior copper mining, Angus Murdoch would confidently insist that a naked, writhing fifteen-year-old Chippewa girl had been tied to the boulder and shot through the heart with the arrows of many "braves," who then dipped their arrowheads into her spurting blood to render themselves invincible.

Besides its obvious financial component, the Ontonagon Boulder was also a thing of the spirit, a mystical object. Unfailingly it was described as "native" and "pure," the adjectives used interchangeably, pounding home a particular perception of the North, of Lake Superior, and of the Natives themselves—one that McKenney was desperate to dispel. "Tell me not of the happiness of the Indians, of their freedom from restraint, their independence. It is all fable."

The rock too was now a fable, its meaning shifting and changing in interpretation like a Native story, even as a curious public lined up to pay for the privilege of gazing at it.

Despite confusion as to the boulder's meaning, the United States government had no doubts at all when it came to who owned it. At the height of Julius Eldred's success, the attorney general stepped in and once more seized the "object" in the name of the United States of America. For the second time in two months, the infatuated hardware merchant was told that federal troops were on the verge of being deployed against him. On November 1, 1843, after three summers of exhausting labour, Eldred accompanied the Ontonagon Boulder aboard a United States revenue cutter and sailed for Washington, D.C. There he pleaded with the government for financial compensation. Following a lengthy wait and a special appropriation of the Twenty-Eighth Congress, the War Department presented him with a cheque for $5,664.98. Mr. Eldred died a poor man in Detroit in 1851. He was sixty-three years old.

The Ontonagon Boulder had journeyed more than five hundred miles and was now safely ensconced in the hands of scientists. These sensible men quickly stripped it of its more poetic associations. "The object," after centuries of chipping and hacking, was found to be four feet wide and to weigh slightly more than 3,700 pounds. Its market value at the time was set at six hundred dollars. "Ere long," predicted the Wisconsin *Democrat* newspaper, "copper rocks will cease to be a curiosity." In fact, masses of "native" copper dwarfing the Ontonagon boulder were routinely discovered during the lengthy mining run on the Keweenaw Peninsula. One single mass was recently unearthed weighing 100,000 pounds. As a local scribe noted, "That's a lot of pennies."

This waning interest, at least to one American historian, had a sexual component to it. Robert James Hybels, writing in 1950, suggested that with the arrival of the copper miners the region's "virginity had been violated [and] men lost respect for the Boulder." Whether the boulder was respected or not, the publicity it received kick-started North America's first mining rush and propelled white families in growing numbers to the shores of Lake Superior.

Removed from its natural location, the Ontonagon Wonder almost immediately stopped being of interest to anyone. It languished for many years on the lawn of the War Department, and was finally uncovered by a curious newspaper editor in a dusty storeroom in the Smithsonian Institution. From there it was eventually moved to a spot one floor above the elephant.

# High Society and the White Indian

*. . . a wretched miserable existence.*

—JANE SCHOOLCRAFT

Face to face: John Tanner (left) and Henry Rowe Schoolcraft

*O*n a February evening in 1834, within earshot of the celebrated rapids of Sault Ste. Marie, a young woman named Anne Marie Johnston was having a beating administered to her by her Ojibwa mother. She was being beaten with a pair of fire tongs, and the woman wielding them was not only her mother, but the mother-in-law of the local Anglican missionary. To make sure Anne Marie could not escape, she was restrained by her sister Charlotte, the missionary's wife. One writer has described Charlotte as "a woman of elegance and beauty," and characterized her sister Eliza, who was also on hand, as "a woman of beauty and accomplishment."

These beautiful, elegant, and accomplished women had recently spread the rumour that Anne Marie was the kept mistress of a young man with whom she was desperately in love, James Schoolcraft. In fairness to the rest of the Johnston family, the object of her infatuation was not much good. Known around Sault Ste. Marie, Michigan, for "generally running wild" and for his gambling, drinking, and embezzling, Schoolcraft had recently broken out of the jail at Mackinac (formerly Michilimackinac). Apparently such an escape was not difficult. The only reason he had not been hanged for murder was that the boy he stabbed in the neck did not die. Young Anne Marie's lover was apparently too drunk to remember the incident.

James Schoolcraft was the youngest brother of Henry Rowe Schoolcraft, whose own name hangs over Lake Superior like one of its sudden fogs. In 1822, the United States government appointed Henry Rowe Schoolcraft, a bankrupt glassmaker and geologist, as the first Indian agent at Sault Ste. Marie. A year later he married a daughter of John Johnston.

Johnston, Sault Ste. Marie's first white settler, was a Belfast Irishman by birth, a long-time trader and occasional poet who read Latin and spoke perfect Ojibwa. His wife was the daughter of a former chief at La Pointe, who had watched the young Irishman's courting of his daughter and told him bluntly, "White man, you desire our women. You marry them and when they cease to please your eye, you say they are not your wives." Despite these notions of fidelity, the chief had lately supplanted his own ageing wife with a fourteen-year-old girl. He told Johnston to come back in a year and try again.

A year later the determined Irish trader returned and married Oshawguscodawayqua, Woman of the Green Glade (her name was later changed to Susan in a Christian church service) and set her up in a log house. As a wedding gift he had personally transported a cast-iron stove all the way from Montreal but could not persuade her to use it. He also proudly boasted of this young woman that she could run faster than any girl in Dublin or Montreal.

Their house was elaborate for the region; the gaps between the logs had been chinked with plaster most likely bound together with moose hair, and the logs themselves polished with beeswax. In this house Johnston and his wife proceeded to produce a clan of eight children. Their sons and eligible daughters soon formed the nucleus of Lake Superior high society, their house becoming *the* destination of all distinguished visitors to the region. Here took place the long and entertaining evenings featuring poetry, singing, Ojibwa folk tales, criticisms of the paintings of Correggio, the writings of Goethe, as well as scandalous talk of celebrated actresses such as Anna Kruger. This was followed by a rousing imitation of a drunken "squaw," performed to great effect by Charlotte Johnston, herself the daughter of a full-blooded Ojibwa and the wife of a minister. "The Englishman will give me some of his milk," she sang, dragging a blanket behind her. "I will drink the Englishman's milk." Her performances were illuminated by the oil of the sperm whale—the species was not extinct yet and père Johnston preferred it to tallow.

While visiting this house, Henry Rowe Schoolcraft became smitten with one of the trader's daughters and soon married her. His wife, Obahbahm-wawa-geeezhaqoquay, Woman of the Sound the Stars Make Rushing through the Sky, was called less satisfactorily in English, Jane.

The life of Jane Schoolcraft is one of those calamitous and tragic arcs that seem to describe the intersection of two civilizations. A thin woman with a narrow face and evasive eyes, she was for almost two centuries presented by gushing commentators as a figure comparable to the Virgin Mary, Florence Nightingale, and Pocahontas all in one. In the Osborns' massive tome *Schoolcraft, Longfellow, Hiawatha* (1942), she is canonized as "universally beloved" and a "cultivated and naturally superior woman." She seems also to have been a two-way cultural viaduct "whose unique personality of gentleness and charm carried from the red race to the white a tenuous ray of imagination and spirituality." For carrying this tenuous ray, she received, in return, the Christian faith.

By the late twentieth century she had been reconstructed as a proto-feminist whose humourless and ambitious husband ruthlessly exploited her access to Native folklore. In her own life she made maple sugar and read Plutarch's *Lives*. In childhood she had spent two miserable years as her father's companion in Ireland. There the duchess of Devonshire had sought unsuccessfully to adopt her. There she also learned many lessons of female etiquette, including how to make sponge cake, write verses, and speak with a cultivated Irish accent. These lessons helped her to become what her husband called "early fitted to adorn society."

As the wife of Henry Rowe Schoolcraft, Jane offered hospitality that became legendary. No visitor to their house, Elmwood, at Sault Ste. Marie could pass through without paying a literary tribute to her. It was at this house that the origins of Longfellow's *Hiawatha* are to be found, includ-ing the mistaken linking of the historical Hiawatha, an Onondaga, with the Ojibwa. In 1825 McKenney found Jane Schoolcraft "an ornament to any society," though clearly feeble, chronically ill, and usually hidden behind her shut bedroom door. Twelve years later author Anna Jameson was overcome by Jane's "true lady-like simplicity" and her "choice of language, which was pure and remarkably elegant." Mrs. Jameson also noted "the damp tremulous hand, the soft, plaintive voice, the touching expression of the countenance."

In her eagerness to turn Jane into a paragon of exquisitely fragile European womanhood, Jameson was careful to gloss over her religious fanaticism, a quality with which her wealthy and rational readers back home were increasingly uncomfortable. She also did not notice other realities of Jane Schoolcraft's life: that she was a helpless drug addict, crippled by a morbid and consuming grief over the death of her first son, and married to a cold, absent, and increasingly racist husband who was concerned that his wife's Native blood was proving a hindrance to his career.

At the time of Jameson's flattering remarks, Jane Schoolcraft was, in her own words, "a nervous invalid . . . day after day I drag out a wretched miserable existence." Anna Jameson, who arrived on the shore of the St. Marys River brimming with aristocratic smugness, was herself an unhappily married woman with a weakness for Italian travel and English poets. She was also one of the first in a long line of tourists to aggressively seek "the Indian" as a type of "gazing stock," a source of romanticism and inspiration. Like many travellers who attempted to write the North, she was heavily invested in the literary Indian—as constructed and disseminated by the publishers of New York, Boston, and London.

To some extent this may explain the suffocating flattery that defines the portrayal of the Johnston and Schoolcraft clans. Historically they have been viewed as demigods, living proof of the benefits of white society and values. Visitors, imbued with a generous Victorian optimism, proved reluctant or incapable of seeing anything else, and the descriptions they left behind form a dizzying catalogue of compliments. Of Charlotte Johnston, a cringing Jameson wrote, "Her figure is tall . . . with that indescribable grace and undulation of movement which speaks the perfection of form."

Out of these perfect forms an oasis of elite refinement was established in the rough North, a great improvement on the crude society that existed at the Soo in 1820, consisting entirely of voyageurs, Natives, fur traders, and their mixed-blood children. Here, at long last, were people who could read and write poetry, who possessed a "charming" and "native" taste for literature, who read "chaste" books and dressed with great taste. Their homes "took the place of the opera house in the cities," wrote McKenney. "When I look upon this group of children and reflect that their mother is a native of our wilds, I wish for the sake of the Indians that every representative of the people . . . could see them."

Presumably Colonel McKenney would have preferred them to be seen at moments when they were not smashing each other over the head with fire tongs, consuming vast amounts of opium, embezzling money intended for the local Natives, or "dirking" people with knives. Even a superficial scrutiny of the compliments lavished on these families reveal tantalizing cracks. Eliza, one of Jane Schoolcraft's sisters, said to be the most Ojibwa-looking, was educated at a private school in what is now

Windsor, Ontario. In an act of sullen and mute resistance, she refused to speak English. Jane Schoolcraft herself, despite her sponge cakes and "irreproachable ringlets," never entirely perfected her own white costume. "She dresses with great taste," noted McKenney, "but wears leggings," adding almost hopefully, "I think them ornamental." Perhaps Jane's leggings, a close-fitting Ojibwa garment concealed by a blossoming European skirt, were as symbolic as her sister's refusal to speak English.

Sister Charlotte married a Canadian Anglican minister named William McMurray, who, by 1838, was supplying Jane with her opium. The clergyman, frustrated by the obstinacy of the local Natives, packed up and moved to Dundas, Ontario, where he became archdeacon and had a street named after him. Jane Schoolcraft would die in his house a few years later, alone in a chair, hundreds of miles from home, while her husband was off to England with a collection of "Indian curios."

Upon learning of his wife's death, Henry wrote to his children, reminding them that their mother's "refinement, taste, propriety of manners, purity & delicacy of language, & correctness of sentiment were such as few females . . . possess . . . Her taste in literature was chaste . . . She wrote many pretty pieces."

His own search for a British publisher continued unabated and without success. Within a few days of his wife's death he was in Manchester giving a lecture on the effects of wind erosion on the shores of the Great Lakes. He then embarked on a grand tour of Europe and was dismayed to find so many Catholics there.

Back at the Soo, the ardent Anne Marie Johnston had finally got her way and married Henry Schoolcraft's youngest brother, James. As already noted, James at twenty-two had stabbed a boy in the neck, during a drunken Thanksgiving Day ball. At the time he was serving as the only acting magistrate in town. Sixteen years later, on a summer morning in 1846, James himself was shot dead while standing outside his home at Sault Ste. Marie, Michigan.

His murderer was immediately thought to be a famous and notorious local man, John Tanner. Tanner, from the start, was a storied individual. At the age of nine he had been kidnapped by a band of Shauwnees and eventually fostered by a powerful Ottawa woman, Net-no-kwa, who lived among the Ojibwa south of Lake Superior and had bought the boy for a keg of rum. For the next thirty years he lived as a Native, married a Native woman, and raised Native children. During the last few decades of his life he attempted to reintegrate into white society at the Soo. In this he was unsuccessful and remained, until his end, a tragic and ostracized figure.

In 1827 a sympathetic U.S. Army doctor, Edwin James, recorded Tanner's life story. According to James, the fifty-year-old Tanner possessed "piercing blue eyes" that spoke of the "stern, the violent, and unconquer-able spirit . . . which still . . . disqualifies him for that submissive and compliant manner which his dependent situation among the whites renders necessary." James had the manuscript, *A Narrative of the Captivity and Adventures of John Tanner,* published in New York, and it was criti-cally acclaimed on both sides of the Atlantic. A Paris edition followed in 1835, and another in Leipzig in 1840.

The story has become something of a legend, at once a truth and a complex moral fable that skirts the centre of Us and Them. As a white man robbed of his whiteness by three decades of living with the savages and simultaneously a savage troubled by dim memories of living as a white, John Tanner became a figure of some fascination to the nineteenth-century imagination. Few literary-minded visitors to Lake Superior, including Anna Jameson, could resist jotting down their comments on the man.

Tanner also soon ran afoul of Henry Schoolcraft, who had hired him briefly as a translator. The two had travelled to Detroit together, putting up at Uncle Ben Woodworth's Steamboat Hotel, where the barber appar-ently quoted Greek and Latin to them. When they returned to the Soo, Tanner, to the settlement's general astonishment, brought with him a wife—one of Uncle Ben Woodworth's trusting chambermaids.

The liaison between Tanner and Schoolcraft did not last long. Schoolcraft, a profoundly insecure and vain man, had worked hard to establish himself as the expert on "Indian" matters. He had based his career, his reputation, and his own self-esteem on this presumed expertise. Believing himself superior to other men, he insisted on being treated as such. As for Tanner, thirty years of living as a Native had not made him fluent in this sort of subservience, and not surprisingly, Schoolcraft soon fired him.

Nor did it help that Schoolcraft and the author of Tanner's life story, Edwin James, were slinging insults back and forth, having developed a puckish jealousy of each other. Tanner was helping James become fluent in the Ojibwa language, a skill Schoolcraft nervously claimed to have mastered. In the end, the Ojibwa vocabulary he was painstakingly assembling was eaten by his dog Ponte, and he never did manage to do without the services of a translator. When James and Tanner produced an Ojibwa translation of the New Testament, Schoolcraft peevishly dismissed it as worthless on the grounds that neither Tanner nor James were, like himself, "vital Christians." A local missionary observed, "Mr. S and Dr J are not on friendly terms. Oh the pride, the foolish pride of man."

Although Schoolcraft found the narrative "a mere packhorse of Indian opinions," no one could deny the success of Tanner's story. Nearly everyone at the Soo read it—except John Tanner, who could not read.

The book has been described as a classic Indian narrative, and its realistic portrayal of Native life in the Northeast has ensured its interest not only to literary students but to ethnologists and anthropologists. In the 1880s it was republished and re-marketed as a children's book, *Grey Hawk: Life and Adventures*. In the 1930s in Canada it was distributed as a truncated school reader titled *John Tanner: Captive Boy Wanderer of the Border Lands*. This little book ("endorsed by the Imperial Order Daughters of the Empire") continued the tradition of pitching the Tanner story to children, minus Tanner's observations on Native homosexuality and Chippewa prophet movements. As a school reader it sounds an instructional warning about the savage life and the trouble that awaits little boys who wander from home. In 1956 the original was reprinted in full. An introduction describes the book as a "tragic and age-old story of a man who had no country, no people, no one who understood him . . ."

To the people of Sault Ste. Marie, John Tanner had long been known as "the White Indian," or just "Old Tanner." With the publication of his celebrated book, which Tanner wrongly believed to be full of vicious smears against him, he became known as "the Old Liar." As years passed the townsfolk of the Soo increasingly viewed him as an alarming figure. The vernacular that describes him is one of anxiety and ambivalence; in it is heard the fears of the Immigrant come face to face with the Native. To one historian, Tanner was "fully accepted by neither the white nor the Indian [and became] a man without country [living] in a shadowy half world." Tanner "was not able to distinguish between illusion and reality." According to Schoolcraft, he was "capable of the most foul deed . . . a captive . . . brought up by the Indians, who[m] he exceeds in ferocity, ignorance and evil passions." A contemporary said of him that he had "the most savage, vindictive, suspicious and may I add demoniacal expression I ever saw."

In 1830 the Michigan territorial legislature, at Schoolcraft's prompting, ordered that Tanner's daughter be removed from him and placed under the care of missionaries. Tanner had allegedly threatened the girl in some way, although Schoolcraft believed that more serious improprieties had taken place. The legislation allowing for her removal is a unique piece of U.S. jurisprudence, a law directed at one man, John Tanner: *An Act Authorizing the Sheriff of Chippewa County to Perform Certain Duties Therein Mentioned.* The sheriff of Chippewa County was, of course, Henry Rowe Schoolcraft.

John Tanner responded to his own ostracization with sullen rage. At one point he crept into the home of Abel Bingham, the local Baptist missionary, and "most spitefully" wrung the man's nose. The gesture seems appropriate for a person in Tanner's position, calling forth an image of the Trickster prancing about in a minister's book-lined study, tweaking the nose of pomposity. Bingham failed to see the humour in this, and had the offender thrown in jail.

Abel Bingham has been called a dogmatic, narrow-minded man "of average intelligence . . . personif[ying] many of the traits that contributed to the general lack of success among Protestant missionaries working among the Indians." In twenty-five years of attempting to convert the local inhabitants, he never bothered to learn the local language. Instead he instigated a course of education that proved ruinous to generations of Natives. The residential system has been notably summarized by the Onondogan Olympic athlete Tom Longboat, who said of his own residential school at Brantford, Ontario, "I wouldn't send my dog to that place."

Bingham has the dubious honour of instigating this system at Sault Ste. Marie, Michigan, where he had an expensive full-scale boarding school constructed. In it small numbers of Indian children were taught in isolation from their families and culture. In four years of operation the school took in twenty-four Native students, four of whom died while they were there.

In the end the wringing of Bingham's nose and various other capers might have transformed John Tanner into a tolerated village character had not James Schoolcraft, Henry's younger brother, been shot dead in 1846. Two nights before, in a weird and seemingly unbalanced act, Tanner had set his own house on fire. He then disappeared from sight. According to Abel Bingham's daughter, "Nobody went out of the house in the evening because they were afraid of John Tanner." Whatever happened, John Tanner did it. It was called the "Tanner Summer." Search parties were organized and bloodhounds let loose, but John Tanner was never seen again.

For several years he was the preferred suspect in the James Schoolcraft murder. Later that suspicion shifted to a soldier, Bryand Tilden Jr., a West Point graduate. During the 1840s Tilden had been stationed at Sault Ste. Marie, where he and James Schoolcraft had quarrelled over a French-Canadian girl two days before the murder. Tilden loudly and publicly threatened to kill his rival. Shortly after Schoolcraft's death Tilden was transferred to Mexico, where he was later convicted and sentenced to be hanged for burglary and the murder of another man. His sentence was postponed, and he managed to leave the army alive. On his deathbed, Tilden made a full confession, admitting to the murder of James Schoolcraft. Henry, for his part, never conceded that John Tanner was not his brother's murderer.

The real John Tanner remains obscure, a troublesome figure, seventy years old, picking his way through the balsam and the cedar bush, pursued by tracking dogs and soldiers. In a monstrous irony, the soldiers are led by an officer named Bryan Tilden Jr. John Tanner's feet are clad in the moccasins that he and many white people could not give up, made of moosehide and tanned with oil. By now he has entirely abandoned the costume of the white man; a string of wampum hangs from his hunting shirt. A terrified Indian woman soon reports seeing him on his hands and knees, creeping over the earth with grass attached to his body as camouflage.

The mosquitoes and blackflies torment him. His face is demoniacal and twisted as he flees into the woods, desperate to escape the high society that has infiltrated the North, *his* North. Behind him are the tedious and dogmatic missionaries, the religious zealots, the nepotism, the jealousies of the Johnstons and the Schoolcrafts. He wants away from it all; he wants to return to himself as a boy on the fringes of the woods, as a hunter among the Ojibwa.

For thirty years Tanner lived as a Native until finally the English language, and even his own name, evaporated from his tongue. He would come to know himself only as Shawshawa-benaysee, the Falcon. As a grown man he was forced to speak with his own brother through an interpreter. For some reason he attempted to come back into whiteness, to cross over near the shores of Lake Superior in a sixteen-year effort to resume life as a white man. Nearly murdered by his Native wife, he later married a white woman, only to be quickly divorced by her. His inability to return to "civilization" was so complete that even to sleep in a bed made him physically sick. Eventually he became not a man at all, but a character in a book that he could not read. Townspeople knew him as a bogeyman, and they invoked his name to frighten children into obedience: "You be good, or John Tanner will get you."

He was labelled "the White Indian," and his story became the corner-stone in a burgeoning field of literature known today as the "captivity narrative." In these tales, readers experience the exotic "other" in the safety of their own drawing rooms and feel the predictability of a regimented city life evaporate into a vicarious, primal existence lived on the dirt and the rush mats of Native society. The literary Tanner became part of the general fascination with the literary Native, so much so that when Longfellow came to write *The Song of Hiawatha,* he would consult not only Schoolcraft's ponderous works on Native folklore, but also John Tanner's narrative.

By the 1930s Tanner had entered into both Canadian and American folklore. A Canadian school reader called his life "one of the saddest in all Indian annals . . . His face is that of a baffled man." In the end Tanner's story lies just beyond the reach of interpretation. Here is a man who was neither savage nor civilized, who led the most tactile of lives, one of flesh and physicality, living with the burn of hunger and the smell of animal fat. He watched men crouch at the edge of a pond while a moose sank beneath the water's surface, only to rise up again hours later when it believed the danger had passed. As an elderly man he ran away, wandering across the face of the hinterland, picking his way among the rocks and searching for a home that did not exist. Finally, "gloom engulfed him in its dark billows," and John Tanner, the White Indian, the man who "had no place to lay his head," vanished from the earth.

At the time of Tanner's disappearance, the high society of Sault Ste. Marie was being engulfed in a gloom of its own. By the early 1840s miners and would-be miners spurred on by the much-publicized Ontonagon Boulder were streaming into the South Shore of Lake Superior, turning the Soo into a crowded and drunken frontier town. One observer at the time noted that "the roar of bowling alleys and the click of billiard balls" were heard from morning until late at night. A gallon of Luke's Best whisky could be purchased from the Van Anden house for twenty cents. The whisky, explained a local French Canadian, was needed "to cook our vittles in our stomachs."

About this time, Eliza Johnston, still refusing to speak English, began taking long melancholy walks, wearing a copper-coloured satin bonnet, twirling a sprig of eglantine or wintergreen, and dispensing pieces of warm sponge cake to the children who followed her. She died at eighty-two, in abject poverty, the old Johnston log house having been sold from under her.

John Johnston, the patriarch and virtual founder of the town, had already died after years of pressing fruitless claims against the American and Irish governments. Having eagerly taken up arms against the United States in the 1812 war, he unrealistically sought to be reimbursed for the burning down of his house by an American officer during that conflict. Betrayed by the flesh and by time, Johnston, "a free liver in earlier life," ended his extraordinary existence a feeble and nearly bankrupt man. Toward the end he picked up his goose quill and wrote,

> *Hope, deceiver of my soul,*
> > *Who with lures, from day to day,*
> *Hast permitted years to roll*
> > *Almost unperceived away.*
>
> > *. . .*
> *. . . when thou'rt gone,*
> > *Where shall sorrow lay her head,*
> *Where but on the chilling stone*
> > *That marks the long-forgotten dead.*

After his death his Native wife kept the family going by catching and curing enormous amounts of whitefish and producing, by herself, in a good year, more than two tons of maple sugar.

In the meantime, Henry Schoolcraft had been caught up in the religious revival that swept Sault Ste. Marie and a great deal of the United States in the early 1830s. As councillor he passed an act allowing Natives to testify in court cases providing they believed in Heaven, Hell, and the Christian God. He forbade voyageurs their daily round of grog, and put an end to Sunday travel. When the Wesleyan missionary James Evans tried to pull this stunt in the Canadian North, the Hudson's Bay Company bribed several Cree girls to claim he had "sexually importuned" them. The troublemaker was promptly shipped back to Scotland.

Following Schoolcraft's joyless conversion, he came to view the Indian as an abject savage, which estranged him further from his own wife. Jane Schoolcraft withdrew into self-pity and addiction, convinced of her impending death and writing melancholy letters to her often absent husband. He wrote back, informing her that it was "the domestic conduct of a female that is most continually liable to errors, both of judgement and feeling." In case she should waver, he reminded her that it was still by "order of providence that man should be active & woman quiescent." Jane's sister Anne Marie never forgave Henry for abandoning his wife during her final illness.

As an adult Henry Schoolcraft had earned his living on the back of the Ojibwa. As Indian agent and then superintendent, he had tried to avoid travel into the rigorous woods of Lake Superior. On the few occasions when he did venture forth, he double-billed the government for his efforts. Otherwise he insisted the Natives come to him, often over hundreds of miles of dangerous inland water, to meet with the great man in his stately Federal-style home and intimidating grandeur. Today the house still stands, boarded up, forgotten. His firm belief was that "unless the Indian mind can be purified by gospel truth," all attempts to provide assistance to the Natives would prove futile. Despite the gross mismanagement of Schoolcraft's regime, at least one American historian, Richard Bremer, considers his nineteen years in the Indian service far less unsavoury than those of the "corrupt self-seekers who swarmed into office" after him.

In 1841 Henry Schoolcraft, under investigation for mishandling government funds and for nepotism, was fired from his position. He had put as many as eight members of the Johnston and Schoolcraft families on the government payroll, including his son-in-law George Johnston and the man's wife, hired as government interpreter though she could not speak a word of Ojibwa. He refused to remove his family members from office even when ordered to do so. He was forced to fire brother-in-law William Johnston for stealing. A thirteen-year-old girl living in the James Schoolcraft family was found to be receiving three hundred dollars a year as an official interpreter for the Mackinac Indian Agency.

After losing his job Schoolcraft moved his family to New York, where he found it necessary to sell his furniture to pay the bills. By this time he was entangled in various lawsuits. In 1843 he was arrested on the street in New York when the United States Treasury brought a civil suit against him for the misuse of government funds. Tried and convicted, he was required to make restitution.

A photograph of Henry Rowe Schoolcraft, taken at some point during the 1850s, shows a joyless man; a bare forehead races back to reveal a head that is large, filled with a large brain. The bald brow is broken only by the severity and sternness of his eyes. The mouth does not even hint at the possibility of laughter, the intractable face of a man who suffered and yet commands no sympathy for his suffering. He wears a suffocating collar; the knuckles of his left hand are as fat as sausages and rest on a book, presumably one of his own leaden volumes.

Today his many books, culminating in the impenetrable *Historical and Statistical Information Respecting the History, Condition, and Prospects of the Indian Tribes of the United States* (in six volumes, published by Congress), are an unavoidable starting point for any serious student of the history of the indigenous peoples of North America. In Schoolcraft's own opinion, his books, the folk tales in particular, provided insight "into the dark cave of the Indian mind." Of his own dark cave, it is worth noting that in his official 1837 report to the U.S. government, he intended to give a factual account of Satan's activities in the Mackinac region; both he and Jane were convinced the Prince of Darkness had left Europe and recently taken up residence there.

Schoolcraft lived for years on the shores of Lake Superior, where, in his own words, "the air itself is of the purest and most inspiring kind." But instead of purity and inspiration, he breathed pettiness, jealousy, and worry. He personally devised the treaty that saw more than sixteen million acres of land sold to the United States government for twelve and a half cents an acre. He invented the word "Algic," having decided "Algonquin" was too cumbersome. The National Institute of France awarded him a gold prize for his essay on Ojibwa syntax, translated into French. He served as president of the Society for the Diffusing of Useful Knowledge. All of his life he was haunted by responsibility, gamely, if sometimes illegally, attempting to meet the needs of an extended and demanding family. A fiercely religious man, he was devoted to the denial of all things earthly, including his children, who would lead their own troubled lives. His son Johnston would be killed in action in the Civil War. John Tanner's son would be killed as well, fighting for the other side.

Henry Rowe Schoolcraft died in 1864 in Washington, D.C., following one of the paralytic attacks that had plagued him for most of his adult life.

## [ 9 ]

## *The Snowshoe Priest*

*I am not yet entirely free of the Indian*
*and never will be as long as I live*

—BISHOP FREDERIC BARAGA

Statue of Baraga, L'Anse, Michigan

*A*t five o'clock in the morning on the last day of May 1972, a slow
cavalcade began a forty-mile trek down the Keweenaw Peninsula toward
L'Anse, Michigan. Cradled and strapped to a special truck was a thirty-
five-foot brass statue of Bishop Frederic Baraga. The hand-wrought brass
and the other materials used in the statue originated, as far as possible,
from the Lake Superior area. When assembled, the sculpture would

include clouds made of bronze, concrete teepees, and immense snowshoes and would weigh five tons and tower sixty feet into the air.

The clouds and snowshoes were secured on a separate rig. The immense zucchetto, a round skullcap indicating the bishop's ecclesiastical rank, travelled on the back of a pickup truck. The weather was perfect. Crowds lined the road and WMPL Radio broadcast the procession live. According to a local reporter, "cameras clicked happily."

The idea of a sculpture to commemorate the legendary priest of Superior's South Shore originated with Bernard Lambert, author of a 1967 biography, *The Shepherd of the Wilderness.* Other glowing biographies of Baraga have been written in English, and still others have been written in the Slovene language. Besides "the Shepherd of the Wilderness," Baraga is also called "the Apostle of the Lakeland," "the Indian Apostle of the Northwest," and, most famously, "the Snowshoe Priest." As befits a snowshoe priest, the snowshoes that adorn the statue are enormous, twenty-six feet in length, and required their own sculptor to construct them. When first put on display in the Copper Country Arts Studio in Marquette, Michigan, they were said to have evoked emotions of astonishment and awe.

The same has been uniformly said of the bishop, who was born Irenaeus Frederic Baraga in Slovenia in 1797. He was ordained to the priesthood in the diocese of Ljubljana, the capital city, twenty-six years later. As an assistant pastor he performed his duties in the Church of St. Martin, where he fought the so-called heresy of Jansenism. This battle marked the beginning of what Baraga's biographers describe as a love story between the people of Slovenia and Frederic Baraga. People were soon lining up before dawn to attend Baraga's confessionals. Then in 1830, at the age of thirty-three, he arrived in the New World, confident that the Lord had called on him to bring the "true faith" to the Natives.

Fighting depression, sporadic deafness, "frightful rheumatism," and Lake Superior itself, Baraga rendered his service for the next thirty-five years. During that time he was constantly on the move, darting back and forth through an estimated eighty thousand square miles of Michigan, Wisconsin, Minnesota, and even Canadian territory, much of it flanking Superior's shores. The bishop accomplished a great deal of his astonishing travels on snowshoes, including one round-trip journey of seven hundred miles. In 1846, after sixteen years of strapping snowshoes to his feet, Baraga undertook a rare secular observation and made the following notes on the Native snowshoe:

> *As the snow is generally deep and there are no traveled roads, the only way to travel is on snow-shoes. These snow-shoes are from four to five feet long and one foot wide and are tied to one's feet. With them a man can travel even in the deepest snow without sinking in very much. But this style of walking is very tiresome, especially for Europeans [who] cannot travel without extreme fatigue and almost total exhaustion.*

At least once following a typical winter journey, Baraga found the skin on his face had peeled off entirely. The Lake Superior wind, according to the *American Catholic Review,* "was as hurtful to human sight as the burning sand of an African Simoon." Eventually this wind would "suck the very brightness out of Baraga's eyes" and weather his face to the colour of a half-breed's, as one observer noted. Even at age sixty-three, Baraga occasionally found himself waking up in the morning on the forest floor entirely covered in snow, a prospect he dreaded above all. Even so, he concluded that such discomfort was worth it, providing "even one soul can be saved."

In 1835 Frederic Baraga left the Soo and travelled by trading vessel to La Pointe on Madeline Island. The journey, which he estimated as "350 American miles," took eighteen days. He arrived on July 27 with the clothes on his back and three dollars. At this very spot, two hundred years earlier, an unpopular and discouraged Jesuit, Father Claude-Jean Allouez, had taken off his shoes in front of the Chippewa and loudly slapped the dust from them. This way he demonstrated "that I was about to leave them altogether, not wishing to carry anything of theirs with me, not even the dust that sticks to my shoes." These theatrics were so effective that the local people, Allouez wrote, immediately abolished polygamy, put an end to animal sacrifices, and "showed . . . assiduity in all the duties of True Believers."

Here Baraga spent three years founding a new mission, grumbling about the Protestants, who he believed "were deluding the poor Indians . . . into damnable errors," and being unimpressed with the scenery: "Truly this is a dreary country . . ." In 1837 he left La Pointe for a fund-raising excursion to Europe. He brought back with him eighteen oil paintings to hang on the walls of his mission. These paintings were perhaps the first to hang anywhere on the shores of Superior. The altar picture showed Joseph the carpenter working in his shop. "This picture," wrote Baraga, "is very appropriate for an Indian mission church, for Indians are by nature inclined to idleness." All but one were destroyed in a fire.

At La Pointe Baraga demonstrated his renowned piety and generosity. While standing in the pulpit reading from the Bible, he often burst into tears. As he read a passage in Chippewa about the baby Jesus, he once broke down in sobs that resonated throughout the church. Unable to continue, he had to descend from the pulpit and leave the building.

He also demonstrated a willingness to take offence. Here at this Chippewa village—today a teeming tourist destination—he dined with an elderly and impoverished woman, Mrs. Lacomb, who served him mainly corn. She had removed the shell by soaking the cobs in lye. Embarrassed by the paucity of her meals, she shyly suggested to the priest that he might want to consider going to someone else's home in the future. "Do you want to drive me away?" Baraga demanded, and stormed out of the house. The poor woman ran after him, and finally after much pleading mollified him. The priest continued to take meals at her home, and later, in appreciation presented her with a sliver of wood from the True Cross. As of the late nineteenth century this sliver rested in a reliquary at the church in Courtes-Oreilles, in what is now Wisconsin.

In 1841, after eleven years in the North American forest, Baraga underwent a crisis. He overcame it by rededicating and recommitting himself to his work. From that year until his death, the middle-aged man rose without exception at three o'clock in the morning and spent two hours, sometimes three, in meditative prayer. On the one morning the priest slept in, getting up at five o'clock, he was mortified by what he called "a great spiritual misfortune." His diary for that day records "two hours absolutely lost."

Baraga's extraordinary diary is written in seven languages. He wrote primarily in German, freely and competently interspersed with Latin, Italian, English, French, Slovene, and Chippewa. A single brief entry sometimes employed three or more languages. He mastered both the Odawa and Ojibwa dialects in less than twelve months. He once composed an acrostic for his sister in six languages. He also wrote the Chippewa Pastoral Letter, the only Letter in the Catholic Church written in a Native language of North America. He wrote at least eight known books, five of them in Ojibwa, one in Latin, several in Slovene. No one really knows how many books Baraga wrote; some suggest he wrote as many as thirty-three "Indian books."

In the early 1840s he began work on his masterpiece, a dictionary of the Ojibwa language. He spent ten years on this famous lexicon, collecting words, according to Johann Kohl, "as happily as a bee collects honey." On January 4, 1853, he recorded, in German, in his diary, "Now at last I am completely finished with my dictionary. God be thanked." In fact, he was not finished.

By late January he was undertaking a circuitous overland route to Detroit to have his book printed. On Lake Michigan, nine miles from Green Bay, the sleigh in which he was riding broke through the ice and he nearly drowned. In Detroit, after laying out the many hundreds of manuscript pages to dry, he learned he could not get the book printed after all. The dictionary was too large for the equipment in Detroit print shops of 1853, and he was forced on to Cincinnati to have the job done there. His *Dictionary of the Otchipwe Language (Explained In English)*, or "Indian book" as it was called, is still in print and can be purchased in the gift shops of many of the museums that dot the South Shore of Lake Superior.

The dictionary was compiled over ten years while Baraga laboured at the L'Anse mission he had founded in 1843. Nearly twenty years later, in the 1860s, Baraga returned to the L'Anse mission on a visit, and was consoled to find there "a deeply sunken band of Indians . . . changed into a congregation of fervent Christians." He notes that this change had taken place in their own "expressive language" and with heartbreaking humility says of his former study, "In this little room I have laboured much for Indian literature."

The labours and astonishing ability with languages possessed by Baraga and the half-dozen Slovene priests who followed him to Lake Superior is perhaps without precedent in the history of ecclesiastical missions. These men constituted a formidable school of expertise in the Germanic and other Romance and Slavic linguistic traditions. Typically Baraga, following his two or three hours of prayer and meditation, preached five sermons in three different languages, English, French, and "Indian." This was not unusual for him, nor was it particularly successful. In 1857 he noted in his diary, "I will never again preach in all three languages; it is of no use, because it makes the people, including the religious, bored and annoyed."

His associate Father Chebul taught himself both English and "Indian" in *less than ninety days* and at the end of that period preached sermons in both languages. Of the same priest it is said that in winter he could be tracked by the blood oozing through his moccasins. The straps from his snowshoes soon lacerated his feet, and the blood of the too tender priest stained the snow for miles.

Another Slovene, Reverend Edward Jacker, heard confessions in four languages. As the Irish arrived to mine the copper on the Keweenaw Peninsula, Jacker was forced to learn Celtic. With the aid of a grammar that Baraga mailed to him from New York, he was soon preaching in "Indian," French, English, German, and Celtic. It has been said of Jacker that he had "a general knowledge of the grammatical construction . . . of all languages."

The lack of linguistic scholarship proved a handicap to the early days of Protestant evangelicalism in particular. Ministers simply would or could not learn the local language, waiting instead for it to die out and instituting long-term residential programs conducted entirely in English. In establishing his Native schools and giving sermons in "Indian," Baraga flew in the face of the United States government, which refused financial assistance to any school that rendered instruction in a language other than English.

By many accounts, the local language was not an easy one to learn. According to Baraga's first biographer, Chrysostom Verwyst, it contained nine conjunctions, each with a positive and dubitative form, each of them possessing a positive and negative form, making thirty-six conjunctions in all. Each verb possessed eighteen conjugational forms, each with an "affirmative dubitative form," and a negative one, making it necessary to learn by heart nearly four thousand different terminations. According to Verwyst, Chippewa also contained "thousands of words not found in our modern languages."

When Baraga came to write his *Instructions on the Sacraments,* the Native title that he settled on consisted of two words spanning twenty-five letters and included the letter *a* eight times. In Baraga's opinion, the title was best translated as *Nanagatuwendamo-Masinaigon.* As is usual with Baraga's lexicon, the orthography and pronunciation followed the French rather than English, as Canadian French was the dominant non-Native language on Lake Superior.

In October 1856, Baraga left Sault Ste. Marie and, following an immense and "tedious" journey around Superior, arrived in Fort William, Canada, seventeen days later. He immediately began to preach to the Natives. He described his new congregation as "highly delighted to hear a bishop preach in their own language." It was "a thing they had never heard before."

For all of his philological aptitude, and for the great debt the world owes him for his "Indian book," Baraga himself was by no means enamoured of the people who spoke the language, and was sometimes ambivalent about the language itself. He admits that with it an "Indian" could count to a million, but had to do so by terming a million "ten hundred times ten hundred." The Chippewa language he called "strong, expressive, sonorous and beautiful; a perfect oratory language." The Indian as an orator, however, was an utter failure, and of the thousands that Baraga had heard, he could "remember but one who was a tolerable orator."

In all the written accounts of the life and efforts of Bishop Baraga, his love of the Native people is maintained to be so pure and overwhelming that it needs no description. According to one writer, Baraga "stood between his Indians and their own weaknesses." This notion of fatherly protection forms the backbone of the Baraga epic, his selfless dedication to his "poor children," and his unique respect for Ojibwa culture. Exactly how this love and respect manifested itself is never made clear. The "Indian mind," Baraga dismisses it as "poor uninteresting, not capable of much refinement, and generally unfit for the higher branches of education and for literary pursuits." Remarkably, after thirty-five years among the Natives, he observed not one single system by which Native children were instructed in their own traditions. He conceded that older people told them stories, but in his opinion these tales "contain no moral instructions, but mere nonsense and many of them are bad stuff."

In Baraga's estimation, the Indian was "naturally slothful," not capable of becoming a priest or entering the sisterhood, or for that matter even boiling a fish. The bishop had no doubt that his "poor children of nature" were as "lazy as all wild Indians are," or that the holy religion of Jesus would change all this. "It requires much patience and heroic self sacrifice to spend one's life with the poor simple and naughty Indians," observed the priest, forgetting that young Catholic French-Canadian men had been eagerly doing just that for more than two hundred years, and delighting in it so much they refused to return home.

There is little to suggest that the "saintly" bishop despised his flock. Rather, he possessed no interest in the Native whatsoever. When Johann Kohl met up and travelled with him along the South Shore, he was astounded by Baraga's indifference toward nature and his utter lack of knowledge or curiosity in the Natives:

*I was surprised that [he] did not know too much about the history of the region and was completely indifferent to the ethnographic origins of the Indians. All that was not Christian among them or capable of becoming such, did not interest him. All that concerned them, even their remarkable Monotheism, was the devil's work. At first we had some heated discussion over this.*

As people who had lived in an organized and self-sufficient society, who created culture, who rendered the mystery of existence in song and story, who painted symbolic pictorial art on rocks, and even embedded it into leather with their teeth, the Natives held no interest for Baraga. It was all "bad stuff," and the bishop wanted it to disappear. In one of his "Indian books" for children, he wrote, "Pay no attention to Indian religion. It is very foolish, God hates it."

Compared with Kohl, the dedicated Baraga appears wilfully blind. At one point following the winter breakup, the two men shared a canoe journey together as the travelling guests of an Ojibwa family. Kohl's writings on the experience offer a precise and intimate portrait:

*It is impossible to have a quieter and more polite load than a canoe full of Indian children. The eldest boy played the Jew's harp incessantly, and the younger children lay listening to him, with their black heads peering out of the woolen rag and pieces of hide in which their parents had wrapped them . . . The latter ever had an eye on the children and frequently, when they ceased paddling, gazed on them with affectionate sympathy. They would then nudge each other and exchange some whispered remarks.*

This loving attention to even the smallest detail is characteristic of Kohl. Not surprisingly, Baraga had nothing to say about the journey.

Today, the disappearance of "the Indian" beneath the glory of the saintly bishop is perhaps the most noticeable theme in the story of Baraga. In this narrative the Indian's function is to be saved from eternal damnation, or at least the dreadful unbelief in which he languishes, and nothing more. "Here," wrote a breathless Baraga, "souls are saved not by one or two, but by hundreds." Beyond this they hold no interest for him, and no interest at all to Baraga's biographers. His celebrated diary, which spans thirteen years, contains perhaps no more than two Chippewa names, let alone any observation on their ways, beliefs, or activities. For the most part, the diary is a scorecard of apostolic victories:

Aug. 5: *On this mission tour I baptized 56 children.*
Sept. 3: *Confirmation at La Pointe; nearly 100 were confirmed.*
Sept. 10: *Administered confirmation, 20 persons.*
Oct. 1: *Confirmed 43 at L'Anse.*
Aug. 26: *Confirmation at La Pointe, 37 people.*

On Christmas Day, 1855, the author of at least eight known books could only manage one sentence for his diary: "*Dec: 25*–First communion for 18 Indians, and 22 confirmations." On the same day in a news release to a church journal, Baraga, writing in the third person, is much more expansive: "Before communion [the Bishop] made them [the Chippewa] a touching sermon in Indian, from the bottom of his paternal heart." Later in the same letter he exclaims:

*The church was again overcrowded to its utmost capacity, and all were edified and delighted by what they saw and heard. In the afternoon Vespers was in Indian, as usual, [sung] alternately by the Indians and the sisters of the Third Order, who accompanied the singing with their delightful melodeon.*

One scours this passage in vain for any physical trace of the Chippewa. Presumably they are the ones filling the church "to its utmost capacity," being "edified and delighted," singing Vespers "in Indian" along with the Sisters of the Third Order, lost irretrievably behind the delightful melodeon. That the Native even occupied physical space is treated more as an annoyance than anything else. As one of Baraga's biographers approvingly points out, "The soul was all—everything else, nothing."

Today that "nothing" is painfully apparent when one encounters Baraga. *Unum Est Necessarium* reads the motto that he chose for his coat of arms, "One thing is necessary." Everything else was a waste of time, and Baraga would have nothing to do with it. Consequently, it is not just the local Ojibwa who disappear beneath him, but most of nature. Lake Superior seemingly had no effect on him. It was, in his opinion, "a large lake." Admittedly, strange things happened there. At ten o'clock on an October morning in 1856, the day became suddenly so dark that Baraga had to light candles in order to read. In June his church candles entirely melted in the heat. None of these events inspired him to effusiveness. Warm weather he terms "summerlike," cold weather "winterlike." If in thirty-five years he saw a beautiful sunset, he did not think to mention it. In a rare lyrical moment he went so far as to write, "It snowed all day and we had a blizzard." Snow was something the Snowshoe Priest was intimately connected with, yet it did not inspire him into any great descriptive passages: "[Sunday] it began to snow . . . The snow remained on the ground . . . the snow is gone but soon more will be coming."

The bishop's diary abounds in diaconates and subdiaconates, there are consecrations of the holy oils, but there are no animals. There are "plenary indulgences," but no trees. Sinful drunks who have their fingers amputated, "scapular confraternities," and "fresh relics for my pectoral cross" are noted, but no monarch butterflies or fresh wildflowers. He ate whitefish smeared in maple sugar, but he does not say whether he enjoyed it. Camped in the forest in minus 40 degrees Fahrenheit he writes, "I was in danger of freezing my face." He would not hesitate to spell out in full "the Archconfraternity of the Most Holy and Immaculate Heart of the Blessed Virgin Mary," and yet some sentences simply ended mid-phrase, as he did not want to put only a few letters on the next line, thereby wasting space.

It is remarkable that Baraga kept a diary at all. For him it was an act of will and discipline. The trivial, innocuous details that fill a person's life did not pour out of the man's pen with any enthusiasm: "1860, *July 4:* Day of general sinning and misfortune." "*Jan 14:* Nothing special!" "*April 22:* Preached in French on sudden death." "*Feb 19:* . . . Spent the night miserably in a dog sled."

There is something tragic in the priest's silence, as though his zeal for souls had crushed the life out of his own. *"Jan 8–9:* Nothing! It is foolishness to want to enter something every day." A brilliant European scholar stands on the shores of Superior, a consecrated bishop in a powerful new country on the brink of civil war, witnessing the dramatic transformation of the Ojibwa culture from fur to copper and the massive influx of white settlement. In the very heart of such turmoil he opens up his diary and writes, "Sometimes I really find nothing to enter."

In the fall of 1846 Frederic Baraga set out on an unlikely and legendary boat ride across Superior. Rumours had reached him of an epidemic afflicting the Natives near Grand Portage, and he was eager to perform the last rites. To get there he engaged a voyageur, a "half-breed Indian," named "Louis Gaudin," one of the few Natives in the Baraga story to receive a name. This ill-considered dash directly north from La Pointe is often singled out as one of the many miracles supporting Baraga's candidacy for sainthood, and is included in all writings on him.

Although the two men started out under clear skies, the weather soon turned. According to biographer Verwyst, "Louis became frightened." Baraga, on the other hand, was "lying on his back in the boat, reciting his office in an unconcerned manner." That the Indian was frightened and the priest was not is never omitted in the published accounts of this story. A recent flyer from the St. Louis Historical Society confidently states that "the guide was frightened but the priest calmly sang hymns in Ojibwe." As the storm worsened the Native became more frightened, requiring guidance from the implacable priest, who tossed soothing and slightly arrogant reassurances his way: "Don't be afraid . . . the priest will not die in the water. If he died here in the water the people on the other shore, whither we are going, would be unfortunate."

In Verwyst's version, Baraga is steering the canoe. Three paragraphs later, Baraga is inexplicably moved forward, to the bow, with Gaudin now in the stern. The eighteen-foot canoe at one point has a sail, then doesn't.

Somehow Gaudin has either sailed his craft across Superior, or perhaps rowed it. Whether the journey took a day, a month, or three weeks is not explained. Like almost everything concerning Bishop Baraga, physical reality is so neglected that it is difficult to form any firm idea of what really happened.

That this crossing even took place is verified by Kohl nine years later in an interview with Gaudin's cousin. According to Kohl, everybody living on Lake Superior had heard the story. The man also sketched in some of the missing physical details. "The half-breed Indian Louis Gaudin" was named "Dubois." The boat was a birchbark canoe and had no sail, or at least none that he mentions. The journey was what the voyageurs called a "grande traverse" of seventy miles, straight across open water, which, in the opinion of Gaudin's cousin, had never been done before.

If this were true, it would make Gaudin's achievement one of the greatest feats of seamanship performed on Lake Superior. Yet in the telling of this story his skills are never mentioned. His efforts, his nautical training, his lifetime of experience have disappeared. What is left is a familiar tale about a frightened Indian saved by a saintly European priest and his God. In the words of Verwyst, all credit goes to "a special disposition of Divine Providence watching over the precious life of the saintly missionary, allowing them to pass through the breakers unharmed." Louis (or Dubois) Gaudin, who according to Kohl was "a well-known voyageur," is shut out entirely from the story of his own triumph.

When the two men landed safely on the North Shore, they erected a wooden cross to commemorate God's mercy. A granite one has since replaced it at Cross River, a clear, inspiring stream that flows south out of northern Minnesota. The plaque provides a vague description of Baraga's journey with no mention of a well-known voyageur named Gaudin, whose skills saved the life of a stubborn priest. He becomes simply an "Indian guide," and his role in the passage consists of being "spared."

Today it is common to find wild daisies, candles, knapweed, and cobblestones placed against the foot of the cross, tokens of love for a fearless priest and his miraculous journey across Superior.

Despite the removal of the Natives from the Baraga story, there is one thing at which Baraga and his colleagues excelled. Through their teachings and immense travels, they encircled the entire coastline of Superior with the grand narrative of Death. They had arrived in a place already long steeped in it, deaths by drowning, sudden, lonely, bitter, brutal deaths, the deaths of infants, deaths by epidemic, deaths in fire, in war, deaths by alcohol, slow deaths, and deaths in the mineshafts.

Into the middle of all this, they brought the intricate rituals of mortality. They administered the sacraments of the dying and spoke the apostolic benedictions. They sermonized on sudden death, on slow death, and on purgatory. They drew death out through the ancient language of the Romans and mingled it with the ancient language of the Chippewa. They took lonely cold death and illuminated it with the Epiphany.

They also brought with them an eagerness to die themselves, a glorious escape from what Baraga called "miserable, afflicted humanity." When a local seven-year-old girl perished, Baraga wrote in his diary, "Happy angel!" His exclamation mark is a zealous sword through the heart of the miserable flesh-filled marathon that he saw people partaking in all around him.

In James K. Jamison's 1946 book, *By Cross and Anchor: The Story of Frederic Baraga on Lake Superior,* there is this peculiar description of a dying infant's final moments: "A gentle hand rests on the kneeling woman's head. Upon the cot the flame of life flickers. A low sure voice intones the ancient holy words."

In this passage the dying baby boy is rendered invisible. What stands out is Baraga's gentle hand, the low sure voice, the ancient holy words. Death has disappeared behind these comforting rituals. "What things are valuable?" asks the author. "How shall we measure what that kind and gentle countenance [of Baraga's] meant to the young mother?" The author happily points out that despite the impending death of her baby, the ever "swift, untiring figure [of Baraga] approaches on his errand of God."

Dressed in black with a three-cornered hat on his head, a cross around his neck, and a breviary in his right hand, Baraga and his colleagues stumbled across the snowy shores of Superior in search of the dying. Two centuries earlier on this same shore, another Jesuit actually chased Indians across the land in an attempt to convert them.

In one journey Baraga is said to have travelled seven hundred miles on snowshoes. On more than one occasion he dropped to the ground unconscious. "The skin of my face fell off like the fabric of a vestment," he wrote. It seems his skin was forever falling from his face.

A sickly man with burning zeal and an iron will, on March 19, 1861, he refused Communion to a group of people on the suspicion that they had danced. That people danced infuriated Baraga, who preached stead-fastly against it, and he singled out the practice in at least two Church letters. The American bishops of 1866 found dances, especially fashion-able ones, not only "revolting"; they were "fraught with the greatest danger to morals." The frail bishop had no interest in letting people divert themselves from death with a few high-stepping jigs. When the well-known *Lady Elgin* collided with the *Augusta* in Lake Michigan in 1860 and killed three hundred men, women, and children, Baraga could not help noting in his diary that "it was a pleasure trip and . . . people were dancing to the sounds of music when the death blow came."

Although Baraga and his colleagues brought to Superior the ability to translate suffering through the intricate rituals of their religion, they also brought their own suffering with them. Henry Louis Thiele, a classical scholar born in Osnabruck, Hanover, served impressively at Eagle Harbor, but the isolation and loneliness led to mysterious "personal prob-lems." He died at the age of fifty-four. According to the Very Reverend Edward Jacker, Thiele's story "was too long and too sad to tell." Jacker himself, renowned for his mismanagement of mission funds, would die young in broken health, seated at a chair with a pencil in his hand.

All were overshadowed by the zealous antics of the Reverend Laurence Lautischar. Raised by "pious country people . . . in the fear of God," he was enlisted by Baraga in 1853 during a trip to Europe. After a lengthy and dramatic two-month voyage, the new missionary arrived in New York, then spent a short time with Baraga at Sault Ste. Marie. In 1857 he undertook a 160-mile stagecoach ride from St. Paul, Minnesota, to the

Crow Wing reserve. From Crow Wing he set out on foot to Red Lake, an estimated 250 miles away. It is speculated that he *ran* a great deal of this distance, "knocking incessantly right and left with a large handful of leaves" to prevent mosquitoes from clogging up his mouth and nose.

In this place, in what Chrysostom Verwyst calls "the very heart of paganism," Laurence Lautischar died. It took him less than three months to accomplish this. On December 3, 1858, at the age of thirty-seven, he set out on a twelve-mile trek across the ice of Red Lake, to "visit a sick pagan."

The young reverend left with no overcoat and no food. According to his superior, he was attempting "to emulate the great patriarch of the missions" by making the journey there and back in one day. He would make this journey in corporal denial, fasting and praying the entire time. The return trip found him wandering about on the open lake until his legs froze and he was unable to walk. He could crawl, however. According to Jacker, "after crawling around for some time on the ice he finally lay down and died." Before perishing he left a trail of knee marks imbedded in the snow, proof, to his superior, of "how often ascended the pleasant odor of his devout prayers to the heavenly throne, even on the last day of his life."

According to Baraga, his death "grieves us deeply, so, on the other hand, consoles us [with] the assured hope that he now prays to God for our poor Indians." Jacker was confident that Lautischar "made good use of his last moments to prepare for death, offering the sacrifice of his young life to God for the salvation of the poor Indians."

Behind all of the "glory," "poor Indians," "and the pleasant odors of devout prayers" is an ill-prepared young man freezing to death on his hands and knees in the snow. Lautischar's mortal remains were taken out by dog train, eventually removed to Duluth, and buried in the cemetery lot reserved for deceased priests.

As to Baraga's own "Last Sickness and Death," his biographer (and bishop) Chrysostom Verwyst devotes a chapter. The seventy-year-old Right Reverend Bishop had been found unconscious in a corridor of his archiepiscopal residence at Marquette, struck down by apoplexy. In a terrible irony he was wounded in the chest by his own episcopal cross. He had previously suffered a stroke that froze his mouth in a perpetual frown.

Tireless even on his sickbed, the dying bishop's final letter, as with so many previous ones, contained the usual worries about money:

*Last year about this time I received a check from you . . . This year I have as yet received nothing from Vienna. I entreat you most urgently not to abandon me in my need. I was never so much in need of help as just now. My sickness of ten months, of which I still suffer, and my old debts which I cannot pay, make me truly unhappy. If I do not receive help this year from Vienna I do not know how it will go with me.*

At times during the years of Baraga's infirmity, he somehow managed to keep up the renowned pace of his younger days. On one of these journeys, an incident took place that seems to encapsulate the history of Lake Superior. In 1859, a feeble and partially paralyzed Baraga, accompanied by Father Chebul, boarded the *Mineral Rock* eastbound from the Keweenaw Peninsula on its way to Marquette.

At dinner Baraga was unable to feed himself, his hand trembling so much that he could not lift a spoon of soup to his mouth. Seated at the head of the table was Captain John McKay, a competent skipper widely regarded as a very rough-spoken man. The skipper stood up, instructed Father Chebul to take his place at the head of the table, and went and sat next to Baraga. From there he cradled the bishop's head and began to spoonfeed him with his own free hand. The image of this deed, illuminated by candle or coal oil, so struck the other dinner guests that they burst into tears. Men and women alike followed the surly skipper out after dinner and thanked him in the name of humanity and Christianity. This same "very rough-spoken man" had his own relationship to death. During a Superior storm in November 1885, he composed a short note and stuffed it into a bottle: "A terrible storm. I think we are lost. Regards to all in this world. Captain John McKay."

According to Father Jacker, Baraga's gradual decline had begun to manifest itself in the mid-1860s. Finally, after many sleepless nights, on January 19, 1868, the bishop "exhaled his pure soul after an agony of only a few minutes." He was buried in a specially constructed vault in the basement of the cathedral at Marquette. It is said that by common agreement both Protestants and Catholics stopped work on that day. In Father Jacker's opinion, the bishop's dedication to "the most abandoned of God's creatures" ensures that his memory will never fade away.

On May 31, 1972, the slow cavalcade bearing the sculpture of Bishop Baraga reached L'Anse at approximately noon. There was some doubt at first that the overhead clearance of the Houghton-Hancock bridge would prove sufficient, but the statue passed under without incident. At the site the mounting base was waiting, having been completed two years earlier. According to one writer, "The base seemed anxious to hold the exquisite form of the much loved Bishop." The site itself is said to be symbolic, the land being the "actual terrain trod by the missionary and his flock." The view is breathtaking, a vast sweeping command of all of Keweenaw Bay, the shoreline of the peninsula stretching forever to the north. Here too begins the footpath that a grim Jesuit, Father Pierre Ménard, started out upon two centuries earlier, never to be seen again.

Once at the site, the process of assembling the various parts began. The twenty-six-foot snowshoe, webbed with immense brass rods, was welded to the bishop's left hand. The seven-foot cross was welded to his right. Five Catholic priests, one for each ton, conferred their blessings on the assembled structure. A Pettibone Cary-Lift wheeled it within reach of a mobile crane. The massive metal bishop was then lifted into the air, where it "exhibited its iridescent lustre."

As the "swaying mission cross glistened in the sunlight," the people below were said to have prayed and meditated. Finally, within inches of being placed on its base, the bishop's hemline caught on one of the wooden arches. An acetylene torch was called in to cut away the offending bit of material. As soon as the torch touched the metal, the polyurethane lining burst into flames and black smoke swept up the length of the bishop, funnelling to the sky.

As the flaming thirty-six-foot statue of the Snowshoe Priest hung in the air, spectators beneath it "reacted with mob hysteria, praying, crying, exclaiming . . ." Broadcasters for WMPL Radio called live, on air, for emergency help from the L'Anse fire department. The statue was lowered to the ground, and the firemen soon doused it. Two months later, after extensive restoration, the sculpture was proclaimed good as new and mounted permanently.

A year and a half after its mounting the statue was officially dedicated. Forty-five priests and thirty-one Fourth Degree Knights of Columbus attended the ceremony. Also on hand was one of "God's most abandoned creatures," a man of "Indian descent," the Reverend John Hascall, O.F.M. Cap., pastor of Indian Missions West, Marquette diocese. Times had changed since Baraga himself insisted that "Indians" were unfit for the priesthood.

Time has also decidedly caught up to this bizarre sculpture. As it stands, it commemorates an attitude that has been almost entirely excised from the teaching of North American history: the inferiorizing gaze of the white Christian, looking down on the "poor Indian." It stands today as an enormous relic cut off from the body of contemporary thought. In its permanent position it has become a popular and eccentric tourist destination. A sign in the parking lot invites visitors to enter the gift shop where they can experience "state history, famous Pasties, hot chili, and Indian tacos."

On the lawn, suspended some thirty feet in the air, Bishop Baraga stands on clouds made of bronze and wields an immense cross as if he intends to assault someone with it. Unavoidable to passing motorists and even passing ships, the zealous bishop has obviously risen above the rest of us. Intrusive, arrogant, and somewhat frightening, he towers over the trees and the landscape as if compensating for the diminutive stature of Baraga himself, who stood five feet tall and weighed barely one hundred pounds. Like the man, the sculpture also demonstrates an indifference to physical locale, although it does make one major concession to Lake Superior—the statue is designed to withstand winds of 120 miles per hour.

# 10

# *Silver Islet*

*This lake is trying to kill me.*

—WILLIAM B. FRUE

Silver Islet during an abortive start-up in 1921

The story of Silver Islet unfolds on a flat slab of rock that barely breaks the surface of Lake Superior, and lies in Canadian waters close to what Canadians call the Sleeping Giant in honour of the Ojibwa folk hero Nanabozho, who made the world. The Giant is attached to what maps call the Sibley Peninsula in honour of a wealthy American financier, Alexander Sibley, who made a killing.

The story is told in magazines, in tourist and travel brochures, in film, in theatre, in letters, journals, reports, song, and novels (both adolescent and adult), but mostly it is told in the rich language of the amateur historian. It is told straight up, the old-fashioned way, without regard for postmodernist theory, and told proudly, a heroic and inspirational tale about what men can do when pitted against Nature.

Typically the story begins, as it does in dozens of books, with the sentence "Lake Superior is the greatest body of freshwater in the world." In these words from *Silver Under the Sea* by Helen Moore Strickland, Lake Superior is not an average force of nature, but, as she suggests, "a legend born out of the geographical travail of a million years." What exactly a geographical travail is is not clear, but like most things linked with Superior it is presumably powerful and mythic.

The drama of Silver Islet begins with a familiar gesture: the hammering of a spike into the earth. The act was first seen as early as 1671, when Saint-Lusson waved his sword in one hand and a clod of earth in the other. It is echoed later in the driving of the last spike of the railway linking Canada from east to west. Immigrants to western Canada perhaps knew it as the SIB, the Standard Iron Bar, pounded into the earth to mark their new property. It was on display again in June 1868 when an employee of the Montreal Mining Company hammered a surveying stake into the rock of Island No. 4 and first laid eyes on nuggets of metallic silver.

Over the next fourteen years, this tiny slab of rock, rising only six feet above Superior, became one of the most celebrated and discussed mining operations in the world. The fascination had much to do with the mine's location—not on the shore, but in the lake, on an island small enough to fit inside the infield of a baseball diamond. Rumour had it composed entirely of solid silver. From its minuscule surface two shafts eventually reached a depth of nearly a quarter mile beneath the water, and out of these shafts came a quantity of silver such as the world had never seen. The mine would also yield its own history and legends, rapidly becoming one of the most frequently told stories of the Canadian North Shore.

Leading the charge for the wealth of Silver Islet were the engineer William Bell Frue and the capitalist Alexander Sibley. These were not ordinary men but heroes, canonized early on. That they were both Americans has never dampened the pride with which this tale is recited. The major Canadian player was engineer Thomas Macfarlane, who spoke Danish, French, German, and English and, under Canada Patent No. 2889, had invented a "New and Useful Improvement on the Art of Extracting Copper from its Ores by the Humid Process." Macfarlane led the party that discovered the vein, and presumably looked on in quiet disgust as the board of directors of the Montreal Mining Company, unwilling to invest fifty thousand dollars in the region, sold the mine to United States financiers in 1870.

Given Superior's strength and immensity, it was clear that giants were required to do battle with it. Luckily, Irish-born American mining engineer William Frue, according to Silver Islet writers, "possessed a giant frame and a gigantic intellect." We are not surprised to learn that he was "a dogged, persistent, unwavering, dominant type," a "courageous man of great tenacity and strength . . . a man of distinguished talents, of great benevolence of character," who "wrought a wonderful change in the Canadian wilderness." A cynic might wonder if this change consisted of more than cutting down all the trees and transporting $3.5 million worth of Canadian silver into the United States. But the Silver Islet story is not told by cynics. It is a story of heroes, men like Frue, a man of destiny, who in Helen Moore Strickland's opinion, "bested [Superior] through sheer guts and determination."

The only possible black mark against "Billy" was that he was not a handsome man or, at least, as a Wisconsin niece wrote, not "what the artist might classify as handsome." The code is clear. On Superior's North Shore ugliness in men is a virtue. Here, good looks are the stain that colours Morris Longstreth's Long Island dandies, with their chatter and snappy cynicism. The Silver Islet Mine is a story about real men, gigantic men, the way they should be, the way they *used* to be, until the south got the better of them. A fine jawline or a trimmed moustache meant nothing here.

For the women it is a different story entirely, and no female even remotely attached to the Silver Islet saga is allowed to be anything less than charming, attractive, beautiful, or "a magnificent pianeste." At the very least, like Mrs. Frue, she was a "gracious hostess." Along with their accomplishments and good looks, the women did a host of useful things: they fed the men who mined the silver and, writes Mrs. Strickland, "knitted, tatted and laced." Mrs. Sibley, who was in charge of several black servants, including a coachman, seems to have instigated the tradition of having grand pianos shipped across Lake Superior. The "charming and beautiful wife" of later company president John Marvin was not only herself "a magnificent pianeste" and a graduate of the Vienna Conservatory, but her numerous nieces were without exception beautiful. This accomplished woman also had a grand piano shipped across Lake Superior. On summer twilights its notes could be heard against the banging of the stamp mill on shore and the round-the-clock clatter of the pumps that kept Lake Superior from flooding the shafts.

The women of Silver Islet, at least the more accomplished ones, also spent a great deal of time attempting to contact the dead. This remote mining community, with no roads leading into it, did not escape the Victorians' interest in hypnotism and occultism. While heroic husbands oversaw unruly miners on a speck of rock offshore, their wives, according to Helen Strickland, were "tipping tables," conducting séances, and "whil[ing] away many a long hour attempting to contact their loved ones who had been lost at sea or met their death in mine accidents." In this spirit, Sir Arthur Conan Doyle, the creator of Sherlock Holmes, is said to have visited Silver Islet Landing in the 1920s in an apparently successful attempt to telepathically contact the mysterious copper people of prehistory.

In the many tellings of the Silver Islet story, the heroism of Frue, Sibley, and high-ranking mine officials, and the beauty of their wives do not extend to the lowly miners or *their* wives. Of the first batch of these women, which in fairness, included Mrs. Helen Adams Frue and her children, we know that on November 3, 1870, they boarded the paddle-wheel steamer *Algoma* at Houghton, in copper country on the American side. A number of circumstances did not bode well for this crossing. First, Houghton is named after Douglass Houghton, who drowned in Lake Superior at the age of thirty-seven while arrogantly ignoring the pleas of his voyageurs, two of whom (along with a dog) perished with him. Second was the boat itself, the *Algoma*, already forty years old, and four years away from being condemned, dismantled, and buried. Most ominous was the predictable weather of November—Lake Superior's killing month.

The *Algoma*, loaded down with mining equipment, pulled out of Houghton on November 3, with at least twenty-four women and children on board. The morning was cold and ice had formed in the harbour. The *Algoma* steamed without incident until it passed beyond the protection of the Keweenaw Peninsula, at which point the vessel was pounded by a strong northeast wind. Heavy snow reduced visibility to a few feet; the old steamboat slowed almost to a standstill in the wind. Spray froze on the decks and riggings.

As the hours passed the smell of fear and vomit came from the dark quarters below deck. The crying of children, attempts at song, and the intonation of Christian prayer sounded beneath the winds. Mothers hugged their children. Even the crew was sick with fear and showed it. The captain later admitted that he did not expect to survive.

For three days the *Algoma* floundered. Finally, it arrived at Silver Islet, having crossed from the jaw of the wolf on the American side to the ear on the Canadian—roughly 150 miles.

Beyond a faint tribute to their hardiness, history pays scant attention to the actual miners of Silver Islet. They are presented as peripheral players, Native-like in their anonymity, a nameless collective, addicted, like the Natives, to alcohol and bringing with them all the predictable and unfortunate traits of the working class.

To begin with they were foreigners, often Cornishmen who carried across the ocean an already long mining tradition. "Cousin Jacks," they were called on the Canadian side, perhaps a corruption of "Cussin' Jacks." On the South Shore they were known as "Hooies," leading to the expression prevalent there, "drunk as Hooies." A young, indignant, teetotalling schoolteacher, Henry Hobart, who taught for a year on the United States side and faithfully kept a journal, dismisses the whole lot of them as "ditch drunkards." It was plain to the disgusted Hobart that the miners of the South Shore, and even their wives, spent the major portion of their free time "drinking and groveling."

Even when sober, the miners are presented as a problem in need of solving by the real heroes, Frue and Sibley, the upright, teetotalling millionaires who were heroically "besting Superior through sheer guts and determination." At best the miners are "hardy," it sometimes being suggested they would "go to hell and back" for their beloved boss. This is more a tribute to Frue's gigantic personality than it is to any qualities of their own. Frue himself conceded that his men could do "twice the work of ordinary men," but this is a given on Lake Superior, where since the days of Étienne Brûlé and the voyageurs, men have been expected to do the work of two men while receiving the salary of one.

That these drunken agitators also worked like pack animals cannot be denied. At Silver Islet, Frue soon realized that the rock was not a tenable base from which to operate a deep underwater mine, so he set about to enlarge it. Enormous breakwaters were achingly constructed from thousands of tons of piled stones barged from the mainland a mile away, all of it enclosed within a complex timber cribwork that served as the foundation for the hoisting machinery, the headframe, and the community of men that grew there.

The men who piled the stones and helped with the cribwork were the Hooies of Hobart's journal, the carousers and notorious consumers of "Paddy's eyewater." Their immense breakwaters served as monuments to the intensity of Superior's storms, some of which halted work for as long as three weeks. The Islet grew quickly, against enormous odds, in the teeth of gigantic winter blows. In 1870 a gale tore out the cribbing,

which, for the first of many times, was rebuilt. By that year the surrounding land was so denuded that Frue offered a reward to any man who
could locate a stand of trees. Some Norway pine was discovered, cut, and
assembled for the replacement cribbing. All of it was obliterated in a
March blow that snapped the two-inch metal bolts joining the cribwork
together. "They might as well have been my wife's hairpins," said Frue.
Men caught out on the cribwork during a storm were, in his words,
"tossed about like nutshells . . . The sea rolled up and picked five of them
up at ease, throwing them up in the top of the lumber pile."

Despite such setbacks, Silver Islet stretched for five acres, then ten,
ringed by massive piles of rocks and cofferdams to keep out Superior.
Eventually the island swelled to thirty times its natural size. Rock against
water, man against nature: the northern story illuminated by the bril-
liance of metallic silver. On to this now artificial island a community was
constructed. This included the erection of at least three boarding houses
for the single men. Each boarding house was built to house specific ethnic
groups, to avoid what Strickland calls the "flare ups" and "fatal brawls"
that dog the working man. She means the *single* working man of course,
and is careful to distinguish these brutes—"by nature drifter[s] inclined
to prolonged drinking bouts"—from their dependable and safely married
counterparts. These wonderful fellows, instead of getting pie-eyed, were
apparently making pull toffee, "a delicious treat that afforded hours of fun
and pleasure." As to the Islet rooming houses, Frue divides them into
"one for the Cornishmen, one for the Swedes and one for the others."
These others, writes Strickland, are "Finns, Bulgarians, Italians, Irishmen
and what have you."

In the writing of Silver Islet, these men are typically presented as tough
characters who drank hard and fought even harder. At one point, Strickland
is caught red-handed, declaring that one of them could "outfight and
outdrink any man." His toughness is predetermined by prevailing concep-
tions of the North; all he needed to do was step into it. He would be a hard
man, of course, strong enough to break the frontier. His wife would be
quiet and uncomplaining, and she would possess the determination necessary to bring her husband into the fold of a Christian family.

One of many photographs taken on the Islet show the miners, craggy, arms folded insolently over their chests. They stand on a wash of rubble and plank gangways; eleven wooden sidewalks totter off in all directions. Their bearded faces show the indignant looks of busy men. Their postures are awkward, the uncertain formal poses that mark the first days of photography when people were unsure what it meant to be photographed, and in what way it differed from having a portrait painted.

They stand solemnly, faces forward. Something feels staged about the whole thing, as though they sense already that they are mere actors in a northern drama. All of them have their meanest faces screwed on tight. Over their heads can be seen the many water barrels, perched like bowling pins on the roofs, ready at any moment for the next fire and explosion.

Peeking between the legs of the men, in the foreground amid the rocks, is a little girl. Like them, she stares in the direction of the camera with the same impatient gaze. At first a viewer does not notice her; she sits unobserved, coming into focus only later, a child in a frock whose presence seems to undermine the whole scene. The little girl's name was Maggie Cross, the daughter of J. W. and Helen Cross, who ran one of the Islet boarding houses. Her mother gave birth to a son on this rock. Other children would be born here, to grow up on a fairy-tale landscape, nearly a mile into Lake Superior, surrounded by more than one hundred men.

Company bylaws permitted these men three drinks a night and a quart on Saturday. The company bar on the Islet resembled a fortified bunker, sealed at both ends and standing five feet high, with no way in except over the top. There was also a library, which Strickland assures us the miners had little use for. In a wonderful convergence of roles, it turns out the librarian and the bartender were the same man.

A jail was built on the mainland to house the miners, although there were no convictions and very few incarcerations. This opens the possibility that Silver Islet was, in fact, a rock full of law-abiding foreigners entrusted with the care of little girls and boys, reading books after work, and staying out of jail. The description hardly accords with the way the story is told, and, in fairness, it is not perfectly true either. The Constitution and bylaws of the Silver Islet Employees Benefit Society stated that a five-dollar injury compensation would *not* be provided to men injured in a fight. However, a claim could be made if those injuries were suffered in "self-defence." This is the kind of legal hair-splitting one expects to find on the frontier, but it does not prove beyond a doubt the violent nature of the men that William Frue had to tame.

For her part, Helen Moore Strickland runs into trouble when she tries to negotiate her way through the path of these brutes, particularly when it comes to celebrating Canadian decency in the face of American Wild West–style lawlessness:

*Silver Islet never had nor needed a Boot Hill, thanks to the wisdom and kindly but firm hand of Captain Frue. People did not go around gunning down others. They were never allowed to get that drunk, nor were they permitted to flash shooting irons . . . Silver Islet has a scenic, tree-studded cemetery but no Boot Hill, even though it was a romantic mining town.*

Many of the texts that carry the Silver Islet story forward are reduced to such hapless characterizations. We are informed that the Cornishmen turned out to be "as troublesome as the Norwegians," although no evidence is provided of this trouble. It seems these chronic bellyachers had the gall to complain about unbreathable air in the shafts and poor lodgings. Perhaps they objected to being blown up, which happened with some frequency on Silver Islet. Supplies and machinery to be stored there were routinely ordered in double quantities, a hedge against their being destroyed in explosions, fires, or both.

There were other problems as well, as indicated by the company assayer's report, 1877:

*At a depth of about 360 feet, it was found that many of the vugs [small pockets in the rock] were filled with flammable gas . . . In some cases,*

*the volume of gas under pressure was really startling . . . In one case, a*
*flame was thrown 40 feet . . . some men were seriously burnt in this*
*instance, and after the flame had somewhat subsided it became possible*
*to creep along the floor of the level and plug up the drill hole . . . This*
*regulated jet burned steadily for about six weeks.*

As the shafts descended level after level beneath Superior, other difficulties arose. Pockets of water and gas were found mingled together, a
phenomenon rare in mining. Below the eighth level, seeping water was so
caustic that blisters broke out on the miners' skin on contact. According
to analyses undertaken at the time, every two gallons of water at that level
contained a pint of "very acrid and deliquescent" calcium chloride.

Of the men who worked in these conditions, an unimpressed Frue said
they were "as opposed to compromise as the quills on a porcupine." One
of the compromises they opposed in particular was being strip-searched
twice a day. On their way into and off a shift the miners were required to
pass through Watchman's Tower, where they removed their clothes and
boots and were searched. Anyone refusing to undergo the procedure was
fined ten dollars.

Writers of the Silver Islet saga tend to assume that these crude
Cornishmen "and what have you" were stealing the heroic Frue blind.
According to Helen Moore Strickland, they would toss choice pieces of ore
out onto the ice and retrieve them after they had been searched. In summer
they fastened the ore to the underside of a log or plank, sent it toward Burnt
Island, and collected it later. Others relegate most of this to a tall tale. With
silver prices running high at the time, at about a dollar an ounce pure, it
would seemingly require a great deal of ore tied to a great many boards for
a man to profit by his thievery. The author of *Silver Under the Sea* is
adamant that seven barrels of stolen silver are still hidden on the island.

Noticeably missing from all the breathless accounts of Silver Islet, with
its heroism and hints of buried treasure, are the "Indians." By 1868 the

landscape is void of them. We are told by Strickland that their "picturesque" and "dimly lit wigwams" showed beneath the windows of Alexander Sibley's summer residence on shore—almost the lone mention of Native people at all. By the early 1870s they were cast exclusively within the framework of the picturesque, and in that capacity helped to sell steamship excursion tickets for sightseers out of Toronto. These popular return trips from Toronto to Port Arthur featured a picnic-lunch stop at Silver Islet Landing.

In the extensive literature on Silver Islet, the Native inhabitants are described in passing in opening pages, an indistinct collective with a conspicuous absence of individual names. The one name that surfaces at all is that of Hiawatha, not the flesh-and-blood Hiawatha, but the famous and now often vilified poem by Henry Wadsworth Longfellow.

It is the Natives who supply the exotic and colourful legends that are freely interpreted by others and then, once the real story gets going, are not heard from again. The omission is unfortunate; in the 1950s archeologists on the Sibley Peninsula uncovered a site used as a camp and workshop by the Aqua Plano Indians about nine thousand years ago. These people, the earliest known inhabitants of the Great Lakes basin, had developed a tradition of hunting mastodons using taconite tools.

By the time silver was discovered here, the Natives had been pushed from the main stage and transformed from hunters into "the party of the second part." This was accomplished on the Canadian side by the Robinson Superior Treaty of 1850. Under its terms a region extending roughly from the base of the wolf's neck northwest to the eye—a land mass about the size of Spain—was ceded by the Ojibwa to the government of the Province of Canada for "two thousand pounds of good and lawful money."

In a meeting on the Canadian side of Sault Ste. Marie, George Johnston, son-in-law of Henry Rowe Schoolcraft, was on hand to translate the document. Leaving their *X* marks were a number of "prominent men of the Ojibewa Indians," men such as Manitou Shainse, Chiginans, Mishe-Muckqua, Totominal, and Ah-Mutchinagalon, names that are seemingly extinguished from history by the time of Silver Islet. Although these tantalizing and difficult names do not find their way into the *Canadian Biographical Dictionary*, they are the sound of Lake Superior itself. In their cadences can be heard the soughing of wind, and the lapping of waves on cobble beaches.

The *X*s were witnessed by six men who bore very different names. George Ironside, Astley P. Cooper—names that signify metal and the working of metal. Swanston, Balfour, and Keating sounded a very different history, lapping on an entirely different shore. Their names do not reflect thousands of years of woodland habitation, do not so much reflect Lake Superior as contain it, taking away the connotation of the word, and reducing it to "the said lake."

With the Robinson Superior Treaty it was established that the party of the second part would go willingly away from the said lake and onto reserves set up "for the purpose of residence and cultivation." What exactly was to be cultivated here, at nearly Latitude 50 degrees north, was not specified. It was also understood that the party of the second part would not "at any time hinder or prevent persons from exploring or searching for minerals or other valuable production in any part of the territory hereby ceded to her Majesty." In the language of the treaty, hunting and fishing was hereafter "a privilege," granted by the Crown.

The treaty was hurriedly concluded following the dramatic events of the previous year. Since the early 1840s the Canadian government had issued mining permits to mining companies without treaty arrangements with the Superior tribes. In 1848 this resulted in what the press called the Mica Bay War, in which a respected Ojibwa chief, Shingwauk, and a group of armed followers entered the mining site of Mica Bay on the eastern shore, knocked on the door of the superintendent of the Quebec Mining Company, and explained that his mine had been taken over. The government dispatched the army from Montreal; Shingwauk and another leader spent two weeks in Toronto's Don Jail and were released. In the face of this embarrassment, the government sent Benjamin Robinson north to negotiate.

Benjamin William Robinson was born in 1797, the youngest and least distinguished of the Robinson boys, although it is said he shared equally in the "Robinson charm." When Benjamin was one, his father died, and he was raised in York—renamed Toronto in 1834—in some poverty by his mother, Esther Sayre. At twenty-two he married well and moved into the fur trade in the Muskoka area. He was soon widely known and supposedly well respected by the Natives for his fair dealing. In the early thirties he went into politics, running on a strong anti-reform platform. By lavishly giving away Crown land to supporters, he defeated his reformer counterpart and rebellion sympathizer, Samuel Lount, who in 1837 took part in the rebellion and was later hanged. As a politician, Robinson was successful in macadamizing the roads of Toronto. In 1841 during a bitter election that Robinson lost, the local militia was called out. By 1845 the *Globe* newspaper was calling him "the only honest politician." In 1850 he was commissioned to clear up the legal mess on the shores of the upper lakes.

Robinson arrived in a compromised position. To begin with, he actually sat on the board of directors of the mining company that had been driven out of Mica Bay. In his words, the Superior region was "notoriously barren and sterile." In the words of an annual report of the Quebec Mining Company, the region was "abounding in mineral treasures."

On September 7, 1850, the Native people of Lake Superior were persuaded to surrender the entire northern coast, from Batchawana Bay to Pigeon River, to the government of the Province of Canada. Robinson's treaty, said to have "ended the difficulties on the upper lakes," was later used as a treaty model. Besides the usual concessions of annuities—one pound per Native per year—it entitled the inhabitants to royalty payments for any minerals discovered on their reserves. A unique feature of the treaty was an "escalator clause" to ensure that annuities increased correspondingly with any increase in the value of reserve land. Robinson's work was so successful that a local newspaper attempting to attract settlers soon confidently claimed there were "no troublesome Indians" in the Algoma district.

How many of *anyone* inhabited the North Shore of Superior in the nineteenth century does not seem to be known. During the 1870s the employees and families of the Silver Islet Mine were said to represent the largest concentration of people on the Canadian side. Whether this number included Natives is not stated. Similarly, by the time the first white settlers homesteaded on the banks of the Kaministiquia near Fort William in the 1860s, twenty thousand Americans were thought to be firmly settled on the opposite shore of Superior. Whether Natives are accounted for in this number is not clear either. By the 1860s, forced marches, deportations, disease, and reserves had all worked to render the local people almost invisible. Their rapid disappearance from the pages of history—the journals, diaries, and books that spring from the southern region of Superior—is a startling phenomenon of Superior history. Barely thirty years earlier the Ojibwa had been the one subject that every visitor wanted to write about.

As the Natives evaporated from the physical stage, they appeared more manageably in books, *many* books, with readers searching them out in the swooning pages of Anna Jameson, the emphatic Finnish rhythms of Longfellow's *Song of Hiawatha,* and the heavily sanitized folk tales of Henry Rowe Schoolcraft.

In a letter to the Canadian government, Alexander Sibley insisted that by operating his Silver Islet Mine he had opened up a region of the earth that had been "a sealed country." Presumably sealed in it were a small number of Native people. "We have given great encouragement to the Indians," Sibley insisted. "We employ them in large numbers and give them the same pay as we give to others."

That Sibley and Frue were scrupulous toward Natives and hired them in numbers is a staple of the Silver Islet tale, although somehow the faces of these Native men never appear in the many photographs taken during the mine's lifetime. In the major texts on Silver Islet, only one Native (besides Hiawatha) is ever named, an Ojibwa, John Messiah, a cook. He is passed down in the reminiscences of a woman named Jane Livingstone, wife of the local postmaster. "The culinary operations were performed by our trusted servant, John Messiah, generally known as Omishomiss." Strickland later adopts the sentence as her own when she writes: "The culinary operations were performed by a trusted servant, John Messiah, known as Omishomis." Although she gives his Ojibwa name with one *s* instead of two, she makes a careful point of repeating the "trusted servant" part. With these references, the Canadian "redskin" of the

Silver Islet story is transformed into the more familiar "step 'n' fetchit" of American plantation servitude—reliable, obedient, and trustworthy with the uniquely northern gift of being a culinary genius with a trout or a whitefish.

For all of its complexities, the story of Silver Islet can be reduced to the size of a plaque erected by the Department of Highways. It tells the story of great men (Americans) working under harsh conditions (Canadian) to produce "a miniature Eldorado."

The story is archetypal and leaves out a great deal of local colour. This includes the Jesuit Father Richard Baxter, known as "the pioneer priest" of Thunder Bay, whose diocese included Silver Islet Landing. Strickland writes of the man that "he carried crisscross on his shoulders numerous canvas bags and bundles which contained his vestments, candles, his portable altar, and the famous horn on which he was wont to blow a strident blast to summon the Catholics together." Whether the famous horn was a moose horn or a trumpet is not clear. Father Baxter's church at Silver Islet, the St. Rose of Lima Church, was named after the first Catholic to be canonized in the Americas. Apparently this tropical saint never swatted a mosquito and in gratitude they refused to bite her.

A separate and intriguing story is the grand pianos of the presidents' wives, coming fast and furious across Superior, being played by white fingers in a burnt and heavily cut boreal forest, on a foundation of three-billion-year-old rock. Worth noting is a man named Biggar, an overlooked Canadian cook and the only man on the island who could construct a cartridge that successfully exploded underwater. Exactly what this says about his cooking is unclear. There was the fervour and madness of a mineral strike: the stocks bought for fifty dollars and sold for twenty-five thousand dollars; burly, knowledgeable men seated on barstools at Fort William and Port Arthur, removing hunks of glittering galena from their pockets and holding forth like mineralogists to anyone who might listen.

Pushed to the sidelines, disgusted veterans of the fur trade, a commerce long since in its twilight years, could barely contain their contempt. The Hudson's Bay Company manager at Nipigon noted, "I'm thinking of sending down a few iron spoons we have here to see if the eternal chattering won't turn them into silver." He groused further that "what with mineralogy, geology, etymology, syntax and prosody veins, shafts, nuggets, lump mass & veins, lead indications, mica specimens, fire and earth and water I did not know where in the world I had got to."

Like many mines, Silver Islet boomed and then busted. In the solemn words of a Department of Highways plaque, "Nature again claimed The Silver Island for her own." In fact it was not Nature so much as greed and alcoholism that shut down Silver Islet. By 1882, having already delivered up nearly $3.5 million worth of silver, the veins were exhausted and yielded a meagre thirty thousand dollars, which fell to two thousand dollars the next year.

In a last ignominious gesture the storied mine closed for good because a group of sailors got drunk in port at Keweenaw Peninsula and failed to deliver a crucial boatload of coal. With winter closing in, Silver Islet employees threw everything that burned, including several buildings, into the boiler in a losing effort to keep the pumps running until spring breakup. Eventually the mine manager ordered the pumps shut down, and the shafts, by this time extending 1,230 feet beneath Superior, quickly flooded with water.

William Frue, inventor of the Frue Vanner for separating ore, and the personality that still animates the Silver Islet story, resigned his position for unstated reasons in 1875. A mere six years later he died in Detroit— in poor health since his years on the Islet. Alexander Sibley had died from a stroke in New York a short time earlier. Thomas Macfarlane, the Canadian engineer who surveyed and named the Islet, would later state reservedly that the Silver Islet story should teach Canadians to have more confidence in their country's mineral resources.

Today the shoreline village of Silver Islet remains as picturesque and ghostly as ever. A silent cemetery, with its rare wood-slab markers, flanks the settlement. The miners' cabins, quaint, sturdy pine buildings spaced distinctly apart in case of fire, resolutely line the coast of the mainland and will for a long time yet. Their current owners occupy them with a sort of reverent humility, a few handmade plaques indicating the name or position of the miner who lived there 135 years ago. There is no electricity, and gas-powered pumps suck water from the lake into enormous drums mounted on wood scaffolds.

The company store still stands, and occasionally famished and wind-blasted kayakers stagger into it, desperate to resupply themselves with dried foods and essentials. They find instead Silver Islet T-shirts, a display case of mood rocks, and lovely ceramic cups that read Silver Islet Mine. For their trouble, a slice of extraordinary blueberry pie can be had, in season, in the adjoining Tea Room.

Out the window of that room can be seen Burnt Island. Behind it, off in the distance, two flooded shafts loom jet black beneath the surface of Lake Superior.

# 11

# *Superior Piscine*

*Is he fishing for me? The Lord of Lake Superior?*
—FROM AN OJIBWA TALE RECOUNTED BY JOHANN KOHL

Whitefish: "caribou of the water"

ike many North American towns that border on water, Bayfield, Wisconsin, is named after a British naval surveyor, Henry Bayfield, who, at the age of twenty-two, undertook an exhaustive hydrographic survey of North America's inland waters. Over the next forty years, using a chunk of lead attached to a rope, he measured the depth of water from Canada's Thunder Bay to Newfoundland. In 1823 in the schooner *Recovery,* rented from the Hudson's Bay Company, Bayfield reached Lake Superior. For the next three years, sleeping on a buffalo robe and covered in blood from a plague of mosquitoes so thick that he and his men could not open their mouths, he conducted the first hydrographic survey of Superior. He also wrote an obscure paper on a subject that by now he knew something about: the "Transportation of Rocks by Ice." Bayfield's soundings, improved upon slightly in the first two decades of the twentieth century, were what the officers of the S.S. *Edmund Fitzgerald* relied on as the great carrier blew closer to the Six Fathom Shoal off Caribou Island on a November night in 1975.

Today in Bayfield, Wisconsin, as in many towns on Lake Superior, it is possible to buy fresh fish. In this case, they are being sold by a man named Oly, the driving force behind Wisconsin's northernmost barbershop/salon-and-fresh-fish stall. As a cutter of hair, Oly caters to men, women, and children, but draws the line at pets or farm animals. He will cut your hair and also serve you a drink, although it is not clear whether it's the customer who gets the drink or him. "I have been known to have a few," he admits in reference to nothing in particular.

Oly is wrapping up a story about a police officer who once visited the area. Lately the officer had become involved in what Oly calls "a nasty shoot-out with some bad guys," who ran over the officer's legs. They had to be amputated, and the man died as a result. Oly seems to have no shortage of stories like this, all of them ending badly, and when he finishes with his customer and says, "What can I do for you?" it is tempting to say, "Please keep talking."

Instead people usually answer, "Whitefish." A flyer on the counter announces: *Oly's: The trout, the whole trout, and nothing but the trout, so help me cod.* But it is still whitefish that people want.

"Smoked or fresh?" he says.

"Fresh."

Oly disappears, comes back moments later with two fillets. "You're in luck. Still has a pulse. Just came in."

Only minutes ago these fillets were the legendary whitefish of Lake Superior. At one time they were known locally as *aattikumaig,* "caribou of the water," a term that notes their importance to the local diet, and the sheer amount of meat to be culled from them. The Ojibwa name, sometimes spelled *atikameg,* also indicates a predominant feature of whitefish: that, like the caribou, they assemble in great numbers.

Until recently these enormous herds of fish congregated in the rapids at Sault Ste. Marie, the vast majority of which were blasted away by the building of the Soo Locks in 1845. In her *Winter Studies and Summer Rambles in Canada* in 1838, Anna Jameson was wont to call them "*my* rapids" and likened them to "an exquisitely beautiful woman in a fit of rage." The waters at Sault Ste. Marie, she insisted, "are to be treated as a man treats a passionate beauty—he does not oppose her, for that were madness—but he gets *round* her." The Ojibwa were less fervid in their description and called the place simply Bawatang, meaning "shallow waters rushing over stones," or perhaps "the place where the fish gather."

When spring ended and the sugaring season came to a close, families converged at the Soo for the summer to net and spear the whitefish that milled together here in such numbers that canoes could be poled over top of them. As early as 1705, it was observed that Indians at the Soo rapids caught as many whitefish as they wanted, whenever they wanted. Few travellers passed near these rapids without describing the Native fishing done here.

While staying at the Johnston home in the 1820s, Colonel Thomas McKenney managed to procure himself what he called "a perfect drawing of a whitefish." From it he observed that "the head is smaller and more pointed than the shad." More than a century later he was outdone by officials at Ontario's fish and wildlife branch who infused substantially more poetry into their own observations. According to the bureaucrats, the spawning whitefish is adorned with "a breeding dress of nuptial tubercles on the head and rows of elliptical pearl organs on the sides."

Elliptical pearl organs or not, McKenney was adamant that the whitefish was "in universal estimation, the finest that swims." The first serving of this fish was considered such an event that the hard-eating Governor Lewis Cass awakened from a deep sleep. After the meal, McKenney crooned, "I have never tasted anything of the fish kind, not even my Oneida trout, to equal it."

Charles Penny had not spent long at the Soo in 1835 before he noted in his journal, "I have already eaten so many whitefish that my tail wiggles as I go along." Like McKenney, he thought the Lake Superior whitefish was the finest fish on earth: "One can never get tired of them at this latitude. The meat is so fine, hard, and white, and so sweet, that other fish seem flat stale and unprofitable when compared to them."

At times both the white and Native communities were feeding themselves entirely on whitefish. The Reverend McMurray was said to have eaten them every day of his life for seven years with undiminished relish.

As she was wont to do, Anna Jameson also waxed poetic about this remarkable creature. A veritable connoisseur of fish herself, she had eaten tunny from the Gulf of Genoa, anchovies fresh out of the Bay of Naples, trout out of the Salz-kammergut, and "divers other fishy dainties rich and rare." The Lake Superior whitefish exceeded them all. "The most luxurious delicacy that swims the waters," she called it. She also invoked the familiar North/South dichotomy when she insisted on the quality of the Lake Superior whitefish compared with those found in the lower lakes. Like comparing a Sandwich oyster to a clam, she wrote. In 1887 C. S. Osborn, author, prospector, Michigan politician, and staunch critic of "heated cities and [the] malarial atmospheres of . . . Cincinnati, St. Louis and Chicago," carefully distinguished the local fish from the "stale article of the southern markets that has been packed and repacked and shipped for hundreds of miles until it is fresh only in name. The Soo whitefish goes into the frying pan, as the Indian says, 'a-kicking'" The Ojibwa origin of the term "a-kicking" he does not specify. Perhaps the word he heard was *aattikumaig*.

In English the study of fish is known as ichthyology. Johann Kohl, in 1855, noted a rough equivalence to the Ojibwa term *"Nin gigoike."* Kohl translates the word literally as "I make fish." Similarly, *"Nin pgibadi"* means "I catch fish with a line on which there are many hooks." The Natives displayed considerable skills in catching fish. Using *watab,* the twisted roots of the cedar tree (also used to sew together the birchbark canoe), Native women very capably produced fishing nets 150 feet in length. These cords resisted water and could be laid up for two years without deteriorating. Upon touching the lake water, they became supple as leather. The nets were dipped in a concoction made of boiled sumac leaves to wipe off any lingering odour that might scare away the fish. Spear technology in particular was highly developed. "They have transformed Diana's spear," wrote Kohl, "and turned it into Neptune's trident." Kohl was one of the last white men to see the Chippewa's full array of fishing-spears. These spears generically were called *anit.* Kohl wrote that the Natives had specialized names for different types of spears. "They also have a species of spear-head which, on striking, comes loose from the pole and is merely attached to it by a cord. The fish so caught drags a wooden bob until it exhausts itself and is captured without difficulty."

Some of the local fishing lines were woven from the white fibres of the bulrush. Presumably women did this work, also making menstrual pads and diapers of the same material. Fishing lines are reported to have achieved lengths of three hundred feet, long enough to troll for the lake trout in summer. Raudot attributes the invention of fishing nets to a Native named Sirakitehak, who spent his life watching spiders weave their webs. According to Raudot, the Natives of Superior claimed that their ability to fish had been taught to them by Mishipizheu.

At the Soo rapids, a skilled Native fisher standing upright in his canoe could take out five hundred whitefish in two hours. Even children were skillful fishers. When McKenney, like most white observers, stood watching the activity in the rapids, he found "it is not possible to look at these fisherman Indians, and Canada French, and even boys and girls, flying about over these rapids, and reaching out this pole with a net to it, without a sensation of horror." These fishers rarely drown, he added, "unless they are drunk."

Non-Native fishers also proved adaptable in learning the ways of fish. In 1984 when the Canadian government banned logging companies from driving cut logs down Superior's rivers, more than a few sport fishermen were disappointed. They had discovered through a century of trial and error that fish congregated at the perimeters of these massive log booms. The trees, cut with the bark still on, were infested with bugs that soon dropped off in the cold waters of Superior, bringing the fish to feast on them.

In his cavorting about Superior, Charles Penny camped at what he incorrectly believed was the mouth of La Rivière des Morts, and noted in his journal, "We had great sport catching trout. We took fifty in little over an hour. Our men clean and cook them before they are fairly dead." Members of John Johnston's family, using nets, were taking 1,500 fish a night out of the Soo rapids. J. Elliot Cabot, in Louis Agassiz's 1850 *Lake Superior,* discovered that their voyageurs could catch lake trout by simply attaching a line to their paddles.

With white men catching trout on a hook and line at the rate of nearly one fish per minute, and single families hauling out a thousand whitefish a night, it was only a matter of time before the fish, as a resource, followed the furs into practical extinction. In 1835 Anna Jameson stated that eight thousand barrels of whitefish were shipped off the lake. By 1839 fishing in the Lake Superior district of the Hudson's Bay Company was considered extremely productive. In the same year one million pounds of Lake Superior fish were shipped to Detroit. An 1857 description of La Pointe on Madeline Island describes inhabitants packing fish in "barrels, half-barrels and quarter barrels."

Merchants did not turn to the fish stocks by choice. By 1840 so many pelts had been taken out of North America that professional trappers began to concentrate on raccoons for income. The raccoon was soon hunted into near extinction. In these straits the American Fur Company attempted to keep itself alive by commercially fishing Lake Superior. From that point on, the history of Superior fishing becomes largely a story of greed and depredation. At its Michipicoten River post, the Hudson's Bay Company, in an effort to pinch pennies, attempted to feed fish to cattle.

With the game gone and huge incursions taking place in the fish stocks, the Native populations of Superior faced the destruction of another traditional source of food. In Johann Kohl's opinion, whitefish were "the daily bread of the fishermen on this lake." The quick disappearance of this daily bread furthered the dependency of local tribes on white officials and may explain their willingness to put *X*s on the Robinson Superior Treaty and on agreements south of the border, including the July 1838 treaty, by which they gave up the perpetual right to fish the Soo rapids.

By 1836 it was clear to Charles Penny, at least, that the fish stocks of southern Superior were in decline. In an effort to save the fishery there, the U.S. government closed Chequamegon Bay to fishing in the late 1880s. Under pressure, it opened it again in 1891. During the same period a desperate Ontario government tried to supplant fish stocks by planting the eggs of the rainbow trout at Sault Ste. Marie, Ontario. The rainbow was not native to Superior or any of the Great Lakes, but it flourished and soon became part of the commercial catch. In 1903, 7 million pounds of fish were taken out of the lake commercially. In the rapacious year of 1941 more than 25 million pounds of fish were removed from Superior. Its generous back was broken. By 1960 the total catch fell to some 600,000 pounds.

Today government and local publications blame this astonishing collapse on a foreign invader, *Petromyzon marinus,* the sea lamprey. These nasty-looking creatures made their way up through the canals linking the lower lakes, devastating the fisheries as they passed through, and finally reaching Superior in 1946, following the construction of the various canal systems.

At Neys Provincial Park, just west of the old fishing village of Port Coldwell, Ontario, there is a young biologist who will have nothing to do with the lamprey theory. The stocks, she says, "were fished out, plain and simple."

The woman running the Rossport gift shop also refuses to hold the lamprey responsible. "Hah," she snorts. "Hah." She is old enough to remember the slaughter that was the Rossport Fishing Derby—ten thousand people, banjo reels in hand, surging forward at the sound of a gun. Books were written: *How to Win the Rossport Fishing Derby*.

On the American shore these troublesome opinions are rarely voiced. Tour guides confidently insist that commercial fishing on Lake Superior was brought to an end by the lamprey. They give little hint that the fishing here was as predatory, unregulated, and short-sighted as the mining, the timbering, and the fur harvesting. According to some estimates, the commercial stocks were depleted in less than two decades.

Even a lone sport fisherman could exact a deadly toll. One black day in July 1926, William "Uncle Billy" Brown showed up on the South Shore near Munising, Michigan, and began trolling for lake trout. Employing the deep-sea techniques he had perfected on the salmon of the West Coast, Uncle Billy pulled 1,430 pounds of lake trout out of the water in half a day.

At Rossport, Ontario, there are accounts of local fishermen chopping off the heads of all trout in their nets weighing less than six pounds—to diminish stock and increase prices for the fish that were left. During the first half of the twentieth century, an estimated 375 tons of fish were being shipped out of Rossport alone, packed in 375 tons of ice and transported in wooden crates. Some twenty coal-fired tugs caught the fish, each tug able to lay as much as seven miles of net.

The fact that these nets were hauled by hand may at first seem an innocuous detail. Only when you realize that many of these nets hung six hundred feet into the water do you understand why an ageing fisherman would cite this detail with pride, on those few occasions he was interviewed. After hauling a net up the length of two American football fields, his hands were raw and frozen; blood seeped from beneath the nails.

A story is told of a Native fisherman of the Ottawa tribe who worked the nets on Superior for the first time. In the endless procedure of lifting one hand over the other, his fingers turned black. Having hauled his nets up two hundred yards, with fish bursting on the surface from the pressure change, the silent Ottawa was heard to say, "Pretty tall water here."

The situation was magnified if you had only one arm, as did a man named Winterton who worked his nets out of Port Coldwell. According to researcher James Mountain, the fisherman, of necessity, developed a sensible method of working the heavy Superior seas: "You get a sea on there so you're going way up high and then coming down . . . I'd wait til I got down, and then I pulled all the slack in. Then I'd bind it on the side of the boat . . . and when she'd go up, she'd pull my net up high, and then I'd wait until she'd start to drop and I'd start pulling to beat hell."

Superior's depths demanded such innovations. Sometimes the strategies were basic; winter fishing in the Ashland, Wisconsin, area involved cutting holes through ten-inch ice and dropping weighted hooks at the end of 125-foot lines. Whenever a man felt a tug, he ran with the line, and that brought the fish onto the ice. The same author describes a single fisherman dropping at least sixty nets into the waters. On the Canadian side during the final, dying days of the fishery, a man could pull up seven miles of nets—and not find a single fish.

When Canadian journalists made it up to the North Shore in the 1940s and 1950s and discovered that a commercial freshwater fishery was still operating in their own country, what astonished them was that the fishermen could not swim. Unrepentant locals would point at the waters of Superior and say, "Where you going to swim to? You're a dead man, even if you could swim."

Trout and whitefish taken from the coastal towns of Jackfish, Rossport, and Port Coldwell, ended up in the dinner plates of the CPR, sometimes within minutes of being caught. These ultra-fresh dinners were an esteemed luxury on the Canadian passenger trains, and contributed to the golden age of rail travel. From these towns fish were shipped south to the restaurants of Chicago, New York, and the eastern seaboard. Before the stocks collapsed, a fisherman in the Rossport area recalls looking into a wooden box and counting eight trout—their total weight 310 pounds.

This sort of plenitude is gone, and the sea lamprey has been fingered as the cause. Ugly and foreign, the lamprey makes a handy target. Lacking bones, scales, paired fins, a lateral line, and a swim bladder, it is a poor swimmer and ensures its movement over vast ranges by attaching itself to a host and victim. The lamprey has exterminated three types of Great Lakes cisco. Eighty-five percent of the fish that survive a lamprey attachment show as many as eight previous wounds.

In the spring, rivers that flow into Superior and provide breeding waters for the lamprey are laced with a lampracide to kill the larvae that reside there for as long as six years. The chemical TFM successfully reduces lamprey populations, but it also harms other fish, including the walleye, which is the backbone of Canadian sport fishing. In the 1950s, in an attempt to electrocute the culprits, officials constructed electro-mechanical dams on more than one hundred spawning rivers that flow into Superior.

The Great Lakes Aquarium in Duluth, a fifty-thousand-gallon fresh-water tank, contains almost every species of fish to be found in Superior, including perhaps the slimy sculpin (which migrates vertically), the large-scale stoneroller, and the three-spine stickleback. Noticeably absent is the *Petromyzon marinus*. Even though the lamprey has been found in Superior for more than half a century, this common and abundant resident is not welcome at the aquarium. Instead a dead eel lies twisted in a jar of formaldehyde, a freakish thing put on display to frighten people.

The Old World attitude to the sea lamprey contrasts sharply with the North American one. Lucullus, the Roman general and consul noted for his self-indulgence, was said to have personally fed the lamprey that he kept in a private pond. Villagers in Portugal evidently help lamprey around dams so they can continue their spawning migration. Secret societies are rumoured to exist in Portugal; their only purpose is to eat lamprey.

Given this, the most promising solution to the Lake Superior lamprey problem might seem to be to net and sell them to Portugal and Spain. It's unlikely this will happen. To almost everyone's surprise, the lamprey of Superior and the other Great Lakes have been found to contain high levels of mercury, exceeding in some cases 1.3 parts per million—more than four times the allowable European standard. As of the 1990s, the United States and Canadian governments were spending $10 million a year attempting to control lamprey populations, with another $12 million being put toward boosting the Lake trout stock.

In the mid-twentieth century, with the stock in ruins, fishermen set their sights on a mysterious creature called the siskowet. To reach it they dropped their nets more than six hundred feet deep into Superior. Today residents sometimes call this fish "fat trout." Johann Kohl called it "a rather large and very fat fish found in the Canadian lakes." As late as 1963 Canada's fish and game scientists were still unsure about the range of this fish, stating it was found conclusively in the deep water of Lake Superior, and probably in the other Great Lakes as well. Today officials at the Duluth aquarium are adamant that the siskowet is found nowhere in the world but Lake Superior.

In an Ojibwa tale recorded by Kohl, the siskowet preceded the sturgeon to the semi-divine Nanabozho, who sat in his canoe luring the fish to his hook by singing to them: "Brightly speckled fat siskawat, you are not the animal I fish for either." These mentions of the siskowet are among the first, if not *the* first, appearances of the word in writing. Anna Jameson called the fish "skevat," although she was admittedly "spell[ing] the word as pronounced, having never seen it written." A small schooner, the *Siskiwit,* had been sailing on Superior since the early 1830s. In Jameson's opinion the fish made a luxurious pickle, but was far too oily to be eaten fresh. Anyone who has attempted to fry a "fat trout" has watched its flesh dissolve entirely into globules. Scientists today believe the siskowet trout is composed of 88 percent fat. They also believe that some of this fat is good for the human heart. More than one hundred million siskowets one year and older are currently swimming around in the depths of Lake Superior.

On June 29, 1922, a commercial fisherman working the Batchawana Bay grounds brought up his nets to discover a very large sturgeon. This fish, the largest ever caught in the Great Lakes, was nearly four feet in girth, weighed 310 pounds, measured seven and a half feet in length, and was estimated to be a hundred years old. Swimming the waters since before Henry Rowe Schoolcraft pondered "the dark cave of the Indian mind," its birth predated the removal of the Ontonagon Boulder, the Civil War, and *The Song of Hiawatha*. A New Yorker bought it for $150.

Unfortunately this remarkable species, *Acipenser fulvescens* Rafinesque, the lake sturgeon, swims the waters in significantly fewer numbers than it did a century and a half ago. At one time, in order to spawn, sturgeon ascended almost all the estimated two hundred rivers that drain into Superior, and all the large rivers of all the Great Lakes. The lake sturgeon has no scales and is the largest and longest-living fish in the fresh waters of North America. It is a fish that draws the dividing line between immigrant and Native cultures. The Ojibwa once called it *Mishe-Nahna*, "the king of fishes," the fish that swallowed Nanabozho and his canoe whole and plays a crucial role in the Ojibwa creation myths. In the tale rendered by Kohl in which Nanabozho is swallowed, he dances for three days in the sturgeon's stomach, finally set free by gulls who pluck a hole in its side. After feasting on the oil of this dead sturgeon, the black bear became so fat that he had to sleep for six months of the year to grow thinner. The animal kingdom filters through the body of the sturgeon. Modern historians believe the sturgeon was as important to eastern forest Indians as the bison was to the peoples of the western plains. As early as 1669, the *Jesuit Relations* tells of a single fisherman taking out twenty large sturgeon a night.

For better or worse the lake sturgeon played no such role in the theology of the newcomers. By the mid-1800s, fishermen were dragging tons of sturgeon out of the Great Lakes as a nuisance fish, dumping them on the shore to die or feeding them to their hogs. By that time logging operations had substantially poisoned the rivers of Superior. Harbour construction and increased shipping at river mouths also put massive pressure on the sturgeon. Their plight worsened in the 1870s when someone discovered that lake sturgeon roe could be sold as caviar and the skin worked into leather for clothing. Isinglass, produced from the sturgeon's swim bladder, was marketed in Europe as a glue and lamp fuel. North Americans living in remote regions sometimes stored eggs in barrels of isinglass to prevent their spoilage through winter. Some people today can still remember being sent into the basement as children and reaching into a slimy barrel of isinglass to come up with cold eggs for their mothers' baking.

Like isinglass, the lake sturgeon points back to a time that is gone. The fish is a dinosaur. In the language of Ontario's Ministry of Natural Resources, the sturgeon "has retained a cartilaginous skeleton, in keeping with its ancient and primitive relationship." It has been swimming on the planet for 136 million years. In less than two decades after the mid-1800s, it was nearly wiped out. Now only ten rivers in Lake Superior support any sort of self-sustaining sturgeon populations, and these populations are substantially reduced.

Today throughout their entire range from Duluth to the Atlantic Ocean, the sturgeon is listed as threatened or endangered. A sturgeon requires twenty years to reach sexual maturity, a pace that the modern world finds intolerable. Even once sexually mature, the sturgeon may wait seven years between broods.

In 2001 a Lake Superior technical committee came up with a comprehensive plan for the "rehabilitation" of Lake Superior sturgeon. This was no easy task, given the daunting obstacles that face the stock. For a creature nearly wiped out in the 1880s, things have only got worse. The 1930s saw a further deterioration of Superior's water quality, combined with the construction of hydroelectric dams and other barriers. Sturgeon are difficult fish to coax around these barriers—after 136 million years they tend to do things the way they did them before. Spawning beds have been buried by infilling. Young sturgeon are susceptible to the same chemicals dumped into the lake to kill the lamprey. Despite improved water quality and regulations against commercial harvesting, the lake sturgeon has not recovered from its decline of the 1930s.

Just how difficult it will be to achieve this recovery is indicated by the Sturgeon Rehabilitation Plan itself. Awareness of the sturgeon, the paper notes, "is usually only on a local level." Most people in North America have never seen a sturgeon and never will. For the time being, a marvellous four-foot-long specimen swims in the giant freshwater tank at the Duluth aquarium. For ten American dollars, its grey sides and snow-white belly can be seen flashing magnificently behind the glass.

For the future it seems that the survival of this dinosaur will depend on public relations. Those relations will consist of educational brochures and posters that "help increase public respect" for the sturgeon. Promotional materials are to be distributed at fishing derbies, schools, and tribal meetings, and they represent the easy part of the plan. More difficult than learning to respect the sturgeon will be removing the sediment from riverbeds so the sturgeon can spawn there again. It will not be easy to dismantle hydroelectric dams and barriers, nor to convince road crews not to begin their bridge repairs until larval sturgeon have drifted past the construction sites. Once these strategies are in place, scientists can get down to the daunting task of assessing the genetics of sturgeon stock stream by stream. An estimated 1,525 tributaries of all sizes drain into Lake Superior.

Legally protected in U.S. waters since 1921, sturgeon—like timber, the mineral resources, and the fur stocks—are not expected to recover from the ferocious depredations inflicted on them during those brief later years of settlement.

Today, miraculously, there are still fish in Lake Superior; there are still lamprey too. But it seems there are fewer of them, and it seems that the fishing industry is far from extinct. Shoreline restaurants can be found where for ten dollars a fresh trout, lightly breaded, will hang over both sides of your plate. Ask the waitress where the fish comes from, and she points to the window fronting Lake Superior and says, "Out there." Fishing boats are still setting nets, stout, snub-nosed affairs, open at the sides, many of them run by Ojibwa fishers. They still bring the fresh fish to the docks at Bayfield, Wisconsin, to a fish-and-chip stall at a wharf in Rossport, Ontario, to other spots along the highway, and to places like Ferroclad Fishery Ltd., of Batchawana Bay, Ontario, although the sign that advertises it has toppled over and lies face down in a mantle of blueberry bushes. Here amid the rubble of derelict fishing boats, acres of abandoned nets, and ancient prototypes of the personal watercraft, you can still find a professional freshwater fishery, men and women dressed in white, wearing hairnets.

For little more than pennies per meal, a fillet of legendary whitefish, the length of an arm, is folded into a plastic bag and wrapped in ice. A lot of ice. The ratio from a century ago is still preserved, about a pound of ice per pound of fish. Five minutes later that fish, cooked at a roadside picnic table, spatters in oil, releasing a fragrance that turns your head. The meat is white, "white as a partridge's breast," wrote Thomas McKenney, with the slightest touch of pink to it. Caramelized to a darker shade, it parts with a fork or the fingers. The first mouthful is a taste of the world in a previous century, a taste of freshness and plenitude. Not long ago people poled their boats across immense schools of these fish. Factors at Michipicoten tried to feed them to cows. Some of the nineteenth century's more sophisticated travellers called this fish, taken from right here, the finest tasting food on the planet.

The first mouthful sucks the air from around you. The rest is the physical taste of indulgence, like something beyond what we deserve in this life. The experience conjures up pictures painted by Eastman Johnson of grinning Native children, whitefish seasoned with maple sugar sticking to their fingers and faces—boys and girls with life shining from them. The first governor of Michigan was wakened in the middle of the night, led by candle to the dining-room table, like an initiate, to eat the whitefish. The ubiquitous Lake Superior potato was served on the side, and after that perhaps a bowl of blueberries. When the plate is cleared, there is nothing but sustenance and satisfaction. The meal leaves no heaviness because the whitefish possesses little or no fat. Only a type of idyllic aftermath of fullness that lasts all day, a gratitude to the Great Creator, to Nanabozho, to Christ himself, who is symbolized by a fish.

According to a man who drives a train along the North Shore, sport fishing on Superior is making a bit of a comeback. The lamprey are still out there, he says, the scars still visible on the sides of the caught fish. But at least to him, the fish seem to be coming back.

Today the sportsmen who go after these fish are serious and possess the technology and the determination of astronauts. On the Bayfield dock beneath Oly's fish stall and hair-cutting salon, the word is out: the fish are "moving." As they have done for thousands of years, the great trout are shifting down the passageways of the Apostle Islands, and this has created a thrum of excitement on the public docks. Men who own yachts and wear billed caps are uttering the code words of their secret freemasonry.

"What you using?" shouts one millionaire to another.

"We're using flashers and flies."

"You stacking 'em?"

"Sure, we're stacking 'em."

"How deep?"

"Thirty, fifty, and seventy feet."

The first millionaire nods solemnly, and both men disappear into the cabins of their respective yachts. Soon they're directing beams off satellites in outer space, collating data, fine-tuning their Global Positioning System equipment, snapping on radar and sonar units to locate the position, depth, number, and even the size of the ancient trout.

They are ready once again to be fishers among men.

# 12

# *South of Superior*

*Mrs. W. R. Durfee, in one of her inimitable stories . . . advis[ed]*
*Mrs. [Abraham] Lincoln not to stop at the Cramer Hotel*
*at LaPointe, as it was "full of knot holes, and the*
*men snore something awful."*

—GUY M. BURNHAM, 1929

Cemetery at L'Anse: "as far as anyone can remember"

*T*here is something robustly well used about the American shore of Lake Superior. It has the feel of a place that has been cashed in a long time ago, the furs, the copper, fish, timber, the iron ore, all of it exhausted in a hurry, like liquor during a determined binge. Even the "Wild Upper Peninsula of Michigan" is not so wild anymore. The estimated twelve thousand bears here do not roam as freely as they once did. A few reside on "bear ranches" like Oswald's, where you can visit Tyson, billed as "the Largest Black Bear in the U.S. and possibly the World" at 880 pounds, "certified." The truth is you can't see Tyson anymore because, as the fine print explains, Tyson died some years ago. For eight dollars, though, you can still visit "the home of Tyson," and while you're at it "see wild roaming bears."

Most of what is left here now is the shoreline of Superior, the highways and the golden dunes, the water of the great lake, and history, which is being harvested and sold as fast as any other resource. No one seems bothered by this, and it's not clear they should be. Why shouldn't the Keweenaw County Road Commission erect a sign stating that the Knights of Pythias ritual was written here, at this spot in Eagle Harbor, by Justus H. Rathbone during the winter of 1859–60?

In the midst of this history, trailer parks press the shore. Children run about as barefoot and gleeful as Huck Finn ever did. Happy, overweight men crush beer cans in one hand and order their wives about with the same easy confidence with which their wives totally ignore them. Even the dogs are friendly and optimistic and want to lick your face.

The Munising Tourist Park is such a place, a simple strip of delicate freshwater sand dunes with Lake Superior on one side and the M28 Interstate on the other. The people here are in a mood to be friendly. They tell stories of travels, of places not so good, of places better. One young man tinkers with his massive outboard anchored a few feet offshore, then gamely leaps knee-deep into the water and tries wading out. He comes back in quickly, wincing. "It'll be better tomorrow," he says, meaning the water. It won't, but with this statement a mantle of American optimism has been thrown across Lake Superior.

The man's wife, like him, speaks in the broad and open accent of the northern states. The two of them have been coming here, to this park outside Munising, Michigan, for the last nine years. "So have they," she indicates a family of sparrow hawks that have been returning for many years as well. The sparrow hawks, or American kestrels, are the smallest of the falcons and make a furious *klee klee klee* as they dive through the pines screaming at each other. During mating season they copulate fifty times a day. Now they perch in the trees jabbing at a snake or songbird, letting bloody scraps of flesh and feathers drop to the ground.

The woman is a self-confessed collector of *Edmund Fitzgerald* memorabilia. "Just paintings," she says, to distinguish herself from the *Edmund Fitzgerald* paperweight, key-chain, and billfold collectors who swarm the southern shore. While she talks, the traffic on the M28 Interstate rumbles close behind us. But we are camped on the banks of Superior, and the sound might as well be the rustle of the northern lights on the tundra.

Like the voyageurs before us, we have pitched our tents on the sand. In 1848, perhaps at this very spot, J. Elliot Cabot, who squired the learned Louis Agassiz around Superior, reported "no vestige of human habitation in sight, and no living thing, except the little squads of pigeons scudding before the wind." The squads of pigeons are gone for good now, but the feeling Cabot experienced as he stood before the campfire, that "unusual and unaccountable exhilaration," is still to be had. Cabot speculated almost hopefully that this exhilaration was "an outburst of that Indian nature that delights in novel modes of life, and in going where nobody else goes."

Unlike the voyageurs, not all the men smoke now, there are decidedly more women, and no one is throwing soup onto a rock and lapping it up like a dog because he doesn't own a spoon. The eating habits are relatively civilized, although a certain species of South Shore frog is known to use the back of its eyeballs to push food down its throat. Otherwise nobody here seems to lack spoons or anything else. The unmistakable shadows of a television flick from a pup tent. A few satellite dishes have been stabbed in the ground and are sucking in television shows from outer space and bringing them here. The sunset is stunning and being archived on digital cameras, and people fifty feet apart are communicating on hand-held family radios: "I'm almost at the bathroom now . . . I'm *at* the bathroom . . . I'm going *into* the bathroom."

Two girls are attempting to bring their brother to the shore of Superior. In doing this they are obeying Herman Melville's belief that humans will march instinctively to the brink of water, the inexplicable spot where the aqueous meets terra firma. The boy is in a wheelchair, and no matter how hard they pull the sisters can't haul the wheels over the loose sand. The boy, sensing that he will not reach the lake, begins to wail, and one of the girls bends to embrace him. In a moment she lifts him from his chair. She proceeds to carry him the way a small child carries an extremely large cat. It is twenty steps to Lake Superior, and with much effort she soon gets him there.

The collecting of jasper and agates is an old pastime on these shores. In the nineteenth century a man is supposed to have become so absorbed in picking Lake Superior agates that he failed to hear the whistle of his steamer, and was left behind to die.

Unfortunately for the children, the stones start twenty-five yards down the way, and the girl does not have the strength left to carry her brother any closer. He doesn't seem to mind. He has reached the brink of Superior, and is content. They sit in the sand for several minutes, and then she lifts him back into the wheelchair.

By this time the sun is going down, a mass of purple on the horizon where Canada should be, sixty miles due north across the water. One by one fires are lit; rings of flame space evenly down the beach. Laughter is heard, the sizzle of a pine branch thrown in the fire, spattering like bacon. A few fireworks whistle through the dark. Suddenly there is a community on this beach; a group of people has gathered to do what has always been done here, to light fires, to camp, to tell stories. Obligingly, and right on schedule, the space station glides across the sky. "There go our taxes," someone shouts.

The stories here are not spoken in Ojibwa, although Native words slip in and out of the conversation. The geography is a different matter. No one camping at this spot can explain where they're from, or where they're going, without speaking the language of the Ojibwa, or some Native North American group. A man is driving his Pontiac from Wisconsin to Ontario, and plans to visit relatives in Chicago, Illinois. He was a fighter pilot once, and flew the first jets in a brilliant arc through the Korean sky. His wife is delicate, fair-skinned, and easily burned in the sun. They have come to the shores of Superior to escape the inland heat. Recently someone they loved very much was found in the Wisconsin River, stabbed to death.

This is who we are, clustered together in tribal gatherings, sharing camp fuel, exchanging stories, grieving the death of loved ones, and attempting somehow to crawl back up next to nature. On a few occasions the fog comes dancing off the lake, almost ten feet in the air, silver wisps that shift their shape and are as evasive as superstition. No one here is Ojibwa. We are not of the Anishnabe Nation, "the first ones." We are hardly even the second ones. We can only be described as "non-Natives," camped on a municipal campground outside a place that was once celebrated for the manufacture of large salad bowls.

*Munising* translated from Ojibwa means approximately "the place of the big island." That island, Grand Island, lies a few hundred yards off the beach, the largest island on the southern shore of Superior. Along with Munising Bay, it forms the largest natural harbour between Marquette and Sault Ste. Marie. Forty miles out from shore, Superior plummets to 1,332 feet, its greatest depth.

In the 1836 treaties the Ojibwa turned over Grand Island to the United States government for a promise of tools, cash, and medical care. Sixty-five years later the island was sold to an iron magnate, William Mather. He then imported Newfoundland caribou, Ontario moose, Swedish game birds, and Belgian hares. "My little Yellowstone," he called it. As soon as he died in 1951 his iron company came ashore, cut down all the trees, and eventually sold the denuded island to the taxpayers. Today it is a National Recreation Area, located within the Hiawatha National Forest.

Two very old lighthouses exist on Grand Island. The North Light stands higher above sea level than any lighthouse in the world. It was the last light the crew of the schooner *Oriole* saw when it was rammed in the night by the steamer *Illinois* in 1862. The sole survivor is said to have clung forty hours to a piece of flotsam—an extraordinary display of endurance. Coast Guard estimates suggest that with Superior at its warmest, a man has four and a half hours to live. The survivor watched in horror as the *Oriole,* in full sail, disappeared into the fog with her stern sliced off. The cries of the drowning men and women were clearly heard by the passengers of the *Illinois,* and they were outraged when the captain refused to stop for them.

The East Channel lighthouse was made of wood in 1867 and left derelict in 1913. It still stands, crooked, bare, church-like, except that it is made of barnboard, and looks itself like a dying barn with a steeple mounted on it. As it is one of the most photographed structures on the South Shore of Superior, if not the entire Great Lakes, no boat tour out of Munising is complete without pulling up close to what is left of it. "In that lighthouse," announces the tour captain, "the keeper's wife gave birth to two children." This comment brings dismayed groans from the women on board. They can imagine themselves, legs splayed and yelling beneath a coal oil lamp, the wind sluicing in between the cedar shakes of a clapboard lighthouse. "I guess *she* didn't have an epidural," quips a young woman and makes a face. Attempts are being made to save the lighthouse—an admission that when we let the past die we become ghosts ourselves, less than ghosts, for we lose the ability even to haunt.

The Munising Tourist Park is on a beach next door to Schoolcraft County in a national forest called Hiawatha, after a poem inspired by the ethnographic writings of Henry Schoolcraft. The historical, or at least "half historical," Hiawatha (also spelled Hayenwatha, Ayonhwahtha, and Taoungwatha) was an Onondaga nation-builder, not Ojibwa, and is sometimes presented as a notorious flesh-eater until shown the light by the Heavenly Messenger, Dekanahwideh. Dekanahwideh was the son of a virgin mother and suffered from a double row of teeth, necessitating his use of Hiawatha as his messenger. Hiawatha's early great achievement was to comb out the live snakes that formed the hair of Atotarho, head chief of the Onondagas and a cruel murderer: thus "Hiawatha"—"he who combs," although Horatio Hale in his 1883 book *Iroquois Book of Rites* interpreted the name as "he who seeks the wampum belt."

In *The Song of Hiawatha*, Longfellow consciously attempted to construct an American folk epic out of what he presumed was a romantic and disappearing race. In his own mind he believed he was "weav[ing] together their beautiful oral traditions into a whole." As a poet he planted language that has imbedded itself into English speech. He wrote "ships passing in the night." He wrote "footsteps on the sands of time" and "the forest primeval."

His first wife died of a miscarriage. He courted his second wife for seven years before she agreed to marry him. In 1861 her dress caught fire. Longfellow tried and failed to put out the flames that burned her to death.

Hugely popular in its time, *The Song of Hiawatha* has been largely relegated to the status of a children's story today. Among adults the poem is widely singled out as a cultural fraud, a shameless appropriation that solidifies two centuries of racial stereotypes. Its pounding "Indian" rhythms were borrowed entirely from the *Kalevala*, the national epic poem of Finland. In the nineteenth century, Oliver Wendell Holmes said of *Hiawatha* that it was "full of melodious cadences." In the twenty-first century the *Times Literary Supplement* called it "a headache set to poetry":

> *By the shores of Gitche Gumee,*
> *By the shining Big-Sea-Water,*
> *Stood the Wigwam of Nokomis,*
> *Daughter of the Moon, Nokomis.*

We are camped by the shores of Gitchee Gumee by the shining Big-Sea-Water. On the picnic table sits a pound of Land O Lakes butter, useful for frying the whitefish that can be found, relatively fresh, in the local supermarket. On the package is an image of a kneeling "Indian maiden," erotic and submissive in a way that pictorial Indian maidens tend to be. Her lips are parted and painted red.

She too is a part of Longfellow's legacy, the lithesome Indian maiden, and she is offered here as an example of better sex, and presumably better butter, the exotic "other." "Satisfaction Guaranteed," the package says. But what exactly is she? And why is she on her knees in a short, beaded miniskirt, on a package of butter? Who did her nails?

Indiantown is down the road. So is Ispheming. So is Indian Lake, and Zeba, and Pequaming, meaning "a narrow neck of land almost surrounded by water" (*Pequa quaming*). So many Native names, a language, a continent full of Native words. Henry Schoolcraft, who never managed to master the language, condemned it as "having a tendency to clutter up general ideas with particular meaning." It was these particular meanings that contained the information that kept people alive in winter. But to Schoolcraft such terms got in the way of the word of God. Schoolcraft would be immortalized by having several places, as well as a blast furnace, named after him, very close to here.

When Colonel Thomas McKenney came through in 1825, he wrote, "The Indian has a most appropriate name for anything in nature. Nature is their book and they read no other." The Ojibwa had a word he could not remember that described the Milky Way. He thought it meant "The Path of the Ghosts." Longfellow, who had done his research, would later write in his *Hiawatha*:

> *In the frosty nights of winter;*
> *Showed the broad, white road in heaven,*
> *Pathway of the ghosts, the shadows,*
> *Running straight across the heavens,*
> *Crowded with the ghosts, the shadows.*

The Big Dipper hangs directly overhead of us, pouring down the final drops of the Big-Sea-Water from heaven. East of here, running into Superior, is the Big Two-Hearted River. A very young Ernest Hemingway wrote of the "burned-over land" along the banks, describing the grasshoppers that had turned black in the aftermath of a fire, and the instinctual pleasure of making camp:

> *Nick was happy as he crawled inside the tent. He had not been unhappy all day. This was different though. Now things were done. There had been this to do. Now it was done. It had been a hard trip. He was very tired. That was done. He had made his camp. It was settled. Nothing*

*could touch him. It was a good place to camp. He was there in the good place. He was in his home where he had made it.*

A very young man, already purging from language all the learning, adornments, and punctuation that Longfellow had spent his life putting into it.

West of here is a place called Laughing Whitefish. Iron ore was discovered in this region in 1844. Philo M. Everett was guided to the site by a Chippewa, Marji Gesick. For his service the man was promised a share of the fractional interest in what soon became the fabulously successful Jackson Mine. This interest was never paid, and years later his daughter, Charlotte Kawbawgam, with the help of a good lawyer, successfully collected her father's share. This affirming incident was written up as *Laughing Whitefish,* a long-out-of-print novel by John D. Voelker.

Farther on is L'Anse, "the handle" or hub. In the early nineteenth century an opera house was built in L'Anse. Whether any operas were actually performed in this structure is not clear, although it is known that some vigorous basketball games were played in it. In 1896 the town was entirely obliterated by fire.

In the mid-eighteenth century a Houghton hotel owner, in anticipation of the railway passing through there, moved to L'Anse. Since L'Anse did not have a hotel, he brought his own. Straddling two large scows lashed together and extending well over the sides, the intriguing contraption was towed thirty miles by tug in the dead of night by a Captain Bendry, on the assumption the lake would be at its calmest.

Captain Bendry was born in Wiltshire, England. At the age of twelve he began sailing the Mediterranean and the West Indies. As a nineteen-year-old he came to the Great Lakes. In 1845 he was deckhanding on Superior's first steamer, the *Independence.* A year later at the Soo he married an Indian-French-Canadian woman, Charlotte Contoui, and had eleven children with her. Two of these children, his wife, and he were stranded in Keweenaw Bay during a nasty winter blizzard. As a result, they became the area's first non-Native settlers. Married for forty-six years, Bendry and his wife are buried together in the Catholic Indian Cemetery at Assinins.

The hotel that Captain Bendry transported on that remarkable night was in complete working order, everything still in place: the cutlery, the plates, the cups, even the guests. All of them had placed lamps in their windows to help avoid collision.

This is what the frontier was, a place where men, without filling out forms or asking permission, towed hotels across inland oceans. In the absence of docks, they, like Horace Greeley at Eagle River when he arrived on the *Independence* in June 1847, tossed protesting cows overboard to make their own way to shore. It was places like Zeba, where the trapper Benjamin George, savagely burned in a fire, crawled on his hands and knees seven miles to the nearest neighbours, and died there. Near Fish Creek in the 1870s a duck hunter named Holton accidentally discharged his rifle into his own knee. When two surgeons attempted to administer a painkiller he told them, "Never mind the dope, cut it off." He endured the amputation without a sound, complimented the doctors on their work, and, according to written testimony, soon became "an expert one-legged ice skater."

The frontier was also the commonplace bravery of small children. Little Ida Hatch was visiting a sawmill at Houghton Point in the 1850s when she stumbled on the blade, cutting her chest four times before the owner could stop the machine. Her aunt stitched her back together using a buckskin needle, some white silk, and a piece of beeswax. The sawmill owner held the girl's legs "so she couldn't kick," and his wife held her arms straight out from her body. Pressing the edges of the flesh together, the aunt sewed them tight and bandaged them. Later the little girl exclaimed, "I wouldn't do that again for a farm."

In 1919 the ambitiously named Silver City contained exactly three permanent residents. One of them was Charles Wells, who kept a well-manicured garden and a spotless cabin. Another was Jim Cusick, a trapper who got drunk one night and shot up Robinson's saloon in Ontonagon. The third was Charlie Miller, a miser who counted the number of matches in a matchbox to prove that match companies were not putting as many in as they did before. He was known to make a single box last a year.

In 1902 two tugboats towed a long boom out of Silver City toward Bayfield, Wisconsin. A swift Superior storm obliterated the boom; *seven million board feet* of logs were lost. The logger, J. C. Brown, declared bankruptcy and abandoned half a dozen logging camps in the interior. The knives and forks were still on the tables.

By 1910 a type of road ran east out of Silver City to Ontonagon. At least one stage horse had dropped dead on it. Passengers discovered that if they tied themselves into their wagons with rope when they travelled this road, there was less chance of being pitched out of their seats.

It would not be fair in this catalogue to leave out Jemmis Tresize, "a miner of Herculean strength," and a notorious drunkard and brawler, who worked the copper fields of the Keweenaw Peninsula. The Eagle River town council resorted to some ingenious lawmaking to pacify him: they ordered a two-hundred-pound iron ball from Detroit. Every night after work they attached it to the man's ankle by a chain before he started drinking. Despite these precautions he was routinely observed in local saloons, with a drink in one hand and the iron ball attached to his leg.

Eagle River quickly gained an unsavoury reputation. Henry Hobart, a schoolteacher writing from the nearby Cliff Mine area, wrote of it on Christmas 1862, "I have taken a tramp to Eagle River where drunkenness & carousing seems to be the main thing . . . It is a drunken dirty place. I know of no place so deserving the vengeance of a drunken dirty place." In the teacher's opinion, it was a "God-forsaken hole."

As early as 1849, the *Lake Superior News and Miner's Journal* bragged of Eagle River that it had "the appearance of a thriving village." By 1862 the Eagle River Fuse Company, one of the first in the United States, was turning out twenty-five thousand feet of fuse per day for use in the mines. By that time the village claimed two breweries, at least thirty-two saloons, and three hotels. The town jail was located in the third storey of one of these hotels. The Phoenix boasted twenty-four rooms and was considered Michigan's leading hotel north of Detroit.

The Keweenaw Peninsula is a world unto itself, like an island that is not an island but shut off just as effectively. It constitutes the open jaw of the wolf that juts sixty miles into Superior on Michigan's Upper Peninsula. From the vast reaches of these forests comes the inner layer of corrugated cardboard. A full 10 percent of the copper the earth has ever yielded came from this little strip of land. This is "native copper," "virgin copper," found almost nowhere else on earth. It can be bashed out of the rocks by slamming rocks against it. The copper from this peninsula produced the sheathing on wooden warships, naval equipment, bronze cannons, pots and pans, brass buttons, cans, and coins.

In the 1840s a mining rush flooded the Keweenaw Peninsula. To guide this steady influx of miners and supplies around the rock shores of the Keweenaw, ten lighthouses were built on the peninsula alone. They were not enough. An estimated 170 ships have wrecked against this rugged point.

Today, like all vital history, the story of Superior's lighthouses is being kept alive by amateurs and volunteers. Kerry is one of them. An astrophysicist in real life, he occupies his summers guiding tourists around the Eagle Harbor light. A large number of these people are avid followers of the lighthouse, and they are fiercely knowledgeable. They know how to pronounce *Fresnel* correctly (the *s* is silent), and they know why the remarkable lens he invented in the early nineteenth century had to wait nearly half a century before being installed in American lighthouses. Winslow Lewis, who held the patent on the previous and much inferior lamp, was a close personal friend of the U.S. harbor master. This friendship caused Jean Augustin Fresnel's invention of 1822 to be shut out for another thirty years. There are no estimates of how many ships and lives were lost because of this exclusive and profitable intimacy.

Kerry is a bit tired today but as polite as ever. Among the visitors are those eager to trip up an unwary lighthouse guide with their inexhaustible knowledge. "Is that a fourth-order Fresnel?" demands one querulous devotee, "or a third?" Kerry has developed an ingenious and diplomatic way to deal with such people. He modestly prefaces his answers with the words, "Please correct me if I'm wrong, but my understanding is that . . ."

The standard means of lighting lighthouses on Lake Superior and all the Great Lakes was the oil of the sperm whale. When the species was hunted to extinction in 1852, lard was used, then, by 1885, kerosene. At Eagle Harbor in 1980, following a succession of twenty-one lighthouse keepers, the light was automated. Today a bell buoy clangs offshore. The Fog Signal Building is now decommissioned, but not before the local council found it necessary to spend ten thousand dollars on a new foghorn and building. A councillor complained at the time, "Ten thousand dollars for a foghorn and we've *still* got fog!"

The copper rush of the Keweenaw Peninsula was led largely by Cornishmen, the originators of the "Cornish pasties" found in the restaurants and supermarkets of the Michigan section of the South Shore. The schoolteacher Henry Hobart had some difficulty accepting these folk, and the region itself. In the course of a single day he discovered the thermometer could change by sixty degrees Fahrenheit. "This is a fine country," he noted, "for bed bugs, mosquitoes, black flies and Cornishmen." As to those bedbugs, he routinely squashed "nearly a pint before retiring." He also found them in the head of his scholars in large enough quantities "to make a Cornish pastry." When he was not recording insults about Cornishmen, the young Hobart jotted down some details about the lives of the local people as well. Among women, it turns out, tobogganing was an extremely popular activity, even among women of advanced age. He had a fondness for recording jokes: "The experience of many a man's life—'what a fool I've been.' The experience of many a wife—'what a fool I've got.'"

Writing from the Cliff Mine area in 1863, Hobart indicated some of the toughness of the locals when he observed that a brick had fallen fifty feet onto the bare head of a local miner. "The skull was all right," he wrote, "but the brick broke in two." Not all were this lucky. His journal is also filled with the mundane, daily deaths of the miners: "The engine driver . . . was caught in the fly wheel . . . and smashed to a jelly." The nearest hospital for these men was in Detroit and could not be reached during the freeze-up.

Superior presses in tight on two sides here, cramming the ghost towns against the ghosts, the rock against the grave. People came here to mine copper and they died young, very young, in falls, in childbirth, after three months, at sixteen years. The 1843 Evergreen Cemetery is one of many testaments to them. The day is extremely hot, and cicadas make a noise overhead like chainsaws; grass crunches, and the yarrow is in white, hard flower. On the stones the inscriptions are stark and accusing:

> *Tom Harper who was killed by the falling of a rock.*
> *Aged 19 years.*

> *Henry Hunt killed at Copper Falls Mine.*

> *Joseph B. Stephen Born In Cornwall England,*
> *killed at Cliff Mine*
> *"That lip and voice are mute forever."*

Four-year-old girls and teenage boys parting from this life as if in a hurry. Baby Willie B. died at three months. His mother died at the age of twenty-four. Their two stones lie next to each other; a bird's nest links them physically. It's not clear whether someone has deliberately set this nest here to straddle the two graves, or whether a bird did this. What's clear is that the nest is empty, that the boy and his mother are dead, and that the young husband has taken his grief into the hard rocks and the cliff face of Copper Country.

Today in L'Anse there is a tourist office. A young woman working in it occasionally advises people to visit what she and just about everybody else calls "the old Indian cemetery."

"It's very cool," she says.

The Pinery Indian Cemetery is located several miles down a dirt road. A large steel plaque states, "As far as anyone can remember, this burial ground has been here." Low pine spirit houses, covered in moss, are sinking to the earth, becoming earth itself. A small gash has been cut in the western sides of them, presumably so the spirits of the dead, the higher soul in particular, might move out through the western door on an endless journey into the other world. Roofed with shingles, the structures are designed to protect the departed from wolves and other animals. Clustered together they form a low-lying village of the dead, merging with the earth, growing out of the red loam of the tall red pines.

Esther Mitchell lies here. She passed over on November 6, 1925, at the age of 107 years. When she was a young woman of twenty-four she grieved for the death of a local child also buried here, daughter of Benjamin and Clara King, Lucy Jane, who died on a winter night in 1842 at the age of twenty-five days. This fact is carved on a fallen tombstone, followed by the grief of a common epitaph: "Our babe sleeps." Robert James Miller, PVT, HQS Infantry Div., died on a very hot day in August 1971, far away from these shores in a country called Vietnam. Another Ojibwa man, twenty-two years old, died fighting in Cuba; his tombstone is all but illegible.

At one time the Ojibwa placed their dead on high scaffolds. White observers assumed this was because they lacked the tools to inter the bodies in the frozen ground. A local chief gave a better reason: he told a white visitor in 1826 that the dead were put there because it was better not to lose sight of them right away.

At the Munising campground cigarette butts glitter from the sand of a fragile dune ecology. These are freshwater sand dunes; Lake Superior provides Michigan with more freshwater sand dunes than are found anywhere else in the world. Evening is coming on and the wind roars out of nowhere, like a truck crashing through the tops of the pines. Healthy shirtless boys are still playing tackle football amid the rare and stubborn grasses. Hordes of monarch butterflies, like fluttering orange cloths, cling to the purple knapweed as they move erratically south.

More than 350 years ago, Radisson and Groseilliers tried to winter on this shore. They built a small hut for themselves. Radisson was not old enough to shave, and Groseilliers was epileptic. Both were young, brave, and armed to the teeth, none of which prevented them from starving. When the Ojibwa returned they found the two men nearly dead, having roasted and eaten much of their clothing. Today, somewhere very near to that spot stands a blue neon sign. "Hungry?" it asks. "Visit Hanks Restaurant—Prime Rib and Lake Trout Nightly."

Forty years before Radisson, Étienne Brûlé, "the man addicted to women," passed this way. It is not known what he made of these butterflies flitting like angels down the shores of Superior, whether he so much as looked at them or just issued his curt orders in some form of proto-Ojibwa, staring bitterly at the severed stumps of his own fingers.

Now a group of young American men are standing on the shore. They are Radisson's age, barely old enough to shave, brave, inventive, playful boys smacking golf balls off the sand into the cold water of Superior. The shafts of their clubs glint in the twilight, and moments later the balls land without a sound, fifty yards offshore.

# 13

# *Neys: Captives North*

*You can't run away. I'll give you a beer, but don't run away.*
—ROBERT SCHUMACHER, CANADIAN VETERANS HOME GUARD

German prisoner-of-war orchestra at Neys camp, 1942

Situated on the North Shore of Lake Superior, Neys, Ontario, consists of a small convenience store and truck stop. Neys Lunch sells fishing lures, processed meats, bug repellant, liquor, and heart-threatening cinnamon buns. The fishing lures are big shiny spoons bearing exotic names, sometimes flecked with real gold, and said to be effective against lake trout. The processed meat comes in colourful tins. The bug repellant arrives in almost any size a person could want. The store owner is a large, bear-shaped man with a hearing problem, and if you do not speak loudly he shouts at you in a terrifying manner, though in truth he is a friendly northerner married to an equally friendly woman who smokes while she fixes the food over the grill.

Neys lies between two former towns. Port Coldwell, twelve miles east, used to be a fishing village. Trout and whitefish were caught at this village, packed in ice, and shipped by train to the grand American hotels of the eastern seaboard. Port Coldwell disappeared with the trout and is a ghost town now. On the lake proper, just beyond the rock outcroppings of Port Coldwell, is Pic Island, which Group of Seven artist Lawren Harris painted in 1924. You would never guess from this beautiful and sterile painting that the island teemed with caribou. West of here, on the other side of Neys, lies Jackfish, also a fishing village, a coaling station, and now a ghost town.

Between these two locations sit the convenience store, truck stop, and grill, which is Neys, and across the highway the gates to Neys Provincial Park. Enormous Douglas firs from British Columbia front these gates. The massive trunks of these imported giants are still to be found scattered about Superior's shores, petrifying mementos to the days of the river drives. The firs themselves were used as the log booms.

Before its incorporation into the park system, Neys was a prison camp holding German prisoners of war, and later Japanese internees. The Germans were seamen and flyers mostly who had walked or floated away from the burning wrecks of their vessels and aircraft to be captured and shipped halfway around the world to a holding station in Halifax, Nova Scotia. From there they began a sixty-four-hour train journey across a foreign country. They passed through railway sidings named Monteith or Angler, finally disembarking far away at Neys on the North Shore of Lake Superior. This was Indian country they had entered, and was likely unrecognizable from the one they had been weaned on in the stories of Karl May, one of Adolf Hitler's favourite authors and a man who popularized the "Red Indian" for three genera-tions of Europeans without ever setting foot in North America. On the cobbled beaches nearby were the strange scooped-out formations of the Pukaskwa Pits, mysterious architectural shapes from thousands of years ago. On the cliffs farther down, Native rock paintings glowered from the stone. Mishipizheu, the horned lynx with his great stickle-back, looked out across Superior from the wave-beaten surface of the Agawa Rock. These and other paintings told the stories of other wars, and other passages.

The men here were the prisoners of Superior's North Shore: of Monteith, of Heron Bay, of Angler's Camp X, of Camp 100, of Camp W, of Neys, and the other camps whose stories have faded into secrecy and the club moss of the boreal forest. For a few short years they formed a unique and temporary civilization, rivalling in size and organization anything seen before on the North Shore. Behind a triple wall of barbed wire they began a lengthy internment in a country called Canada, next to the mystifying power of what the Ojibwa are said to have called Chigaaming and what the maps termed Lake Superior.

Among themselves they did not have the faintest idea where they were. They were the new transients of war, men like Hans Krakhoffer, a seaman on a German raider, sunk off the coast of Africa, taken first to the Seychelles Islands, then to South Africa, then England, across the Atlantic to Halifax, then three days by train to the North Shore and beyond. Scattered around these men were the towns whose names they might have heard whispered by their guards, unfathomable names, linked to nothing. How were they to know that Neys was a contraction of Doheyneys, or that Selim was "miles" spelled backwards, or that cartographers spelled Nipigon at least six different ways? They knew only that they were very far away and "somewhere south of Hudson Bay."

They began their internment in blue-grey mackinaw jackets with a red circle painted on the back. At Neys these coats with their prominent targets drew complaints from German officers, who refused to wear them, claiming they contravened the Geneva Convention for the treatment of prisoners. Camp officials arranged for Canadian army greatcoats to be issued instead. Huddled in their coats, the German POWs stood together behind barbed wire on some of the oldest rock in the world, Superior pounding on the beach less than a stone's throw away. In some cases the huts were so close to the lake that prisoners felt the spray against the walls.

They had been brought here not only for the remoteness of the camps and the reduced likelihood of escaping, but to provide labour to local timber companies, whose workers were off to the war. In the tin-hulled boats of the Pigeon River Timber Company, they hugged the shores of Superior and made their way beneath the granite walls of the Little Pic River. Sometimes they steamed or rowed up the vast expanse of the Pic River through windswept Ojibwa land, alongside log cabins chinked with clay and moose hair, and finally into the bush to fell trees.

Not surprisingly, these work details proved popular with bored POWs, and were used by camp officials to discourage escape attempts. Armed guards escorted the POWs into the bush, armed, for the most part, because the prisoners were extremely nervous about black bears, with which they had no experience.

Not all prisoners were allowed out in the work crews. They had to first pass a bizarre screening test to determine the extent of their Nazi sympathies. At Neys, Canadian officials believed themselves to be confining fanatical Nazis and administered a test known as the PHERUDA rating, composed from the first letters of "Political outlook, Hitler, Education, Religion, Usefulness, Dependability, and Attitude." All POWs at Neys were rated on it; the diary entry for December 3, 1945, listed 23 "anti Nazis," 223 "rabid Nazis," and 35 "Nazi innocuous." The test was considered to be bureaucratic nonsense by German officers and camp officials alike and perhaps only served to echo the military obsessiveness exemplified in the Standing Orders at Neys, Section VII, page 7:

*2) Means of Raising an Alarm:*
*An alarm should be raised by the best and quickest means possible.*
*This may be done by:—*
    *(a) SHOUTING*
    *(b) CONTINUOUS BLOWING OF A WHISTLE*
    *(c) CONTINUOUS STRIKING OF A LOUD OBJECT TO*
        *PRODUCE A NOISE*

Some men were denied work detail for other reasons. Prisoner George Hoertz proved such a skilled watercolourist that his chief patron, the president of the Nipigon Timber Company, told him that he was not to go out into the bush and cut timber. He was to stay in the camp and paint.

The labour arrangement worked very well for the Pigeon River Timber Company. It operated seven timber camps in the surrounding bush, and its boats carried the POWs to the cutting fields; the tin-sheathed wrecks can still be found on the rocks at Neys. The prisoners received fifty cents for hewing their first cords. After that, the rate rose. All funds were held in trust and administered by a camp treasury. Of the 98,000 cords of pulpwood produced in the Neys/Angler area in 1943, German prisoners of war are estimated to have cut almost all of it.

Here in these work details in the bush, unlikely contact was made between the German military establishment and the freewheeling world of the Canadian lumber industry. It is doubtful any military hierarchy, even that of the German air force, could have proved itself immune to the bizarre frontierism that defined this trade.

Twenty years earlier the camp boss at the Pigeon River Timber Company was said to have been at his desk writing a letter when he received a surprise visit from the duke of Sutherland. When the royal visitor was ushered into his office and formally introduced, the camp boss looked up from his desk and said, "Hi, Duke, just writin' a letter to Doug. Be with you in a minute."

In this world the culture-stunned prisoners of Superior's North Shore now found themselves, axes and cant hooks in hand, breaking up jams and floating black spruce down the streams that flowed into Superior.

These exchanges worked both ways. When a Canadian guard on a work detail slipped into a crevice and broke his leg, his prisoners set the leg in a splint, hoisted him up a cliff, deposited him in a wheelbarrow, and brought both him and his rifle back to camp. At the Espanola camp, five hundred desperate men found themselves without tobacco and began shaving wood chips off a mahogany piano the YMCA had donated, and rolling that instead. When a guard demanded to know where the piano had gone, they answered gleefully, "We smoked it."

These interactions were not entirely restricted to men. At Espanola some young local women flirted with the POWs by folding their billets-doux into snowballs and tossing them over the barbed wire. "They were just like the local boys," observed one woman years later, "only more polite."

When not reading books supplied by the Imperial Order Daughters of the Empire, the men strolled around the Neys camp petting and feeding a large domesticated bear named Nellie, who wore a collar and ate out of their hand. On August afternoons they were let outside the barbed-wire fence to pick blueberries, providing they were back by four o'clock—war-tried and ruthless soldiers on their knees in the sun, picking blueberries on the North Shore. They also produced arts and crafts so exquisitely wrought that commercial distributors arrived by train to purchase them. These included models of German and British warships carved with knives, and military medallions cast from the tinfoil of cigarette packs and chocolate-bar wrappers.

They were young, athletic men with time on their hands, and they did what young men will do: they played sports. At Monteith they built a luge run, at Neys they played horseshoes, built themselves ice rinks, and learned the game of hockey. They played so much table tennis that camp officials considered it a form of madness. They secretly constructed ham radio sets, stealing the radio tubes from sets belonging to the guards, and tried to receive messages from overseas. They discovered what is true today: that reception north of Superior is extremely sketchy. They published and printed their own newspapers (the guards also published a newspaper, called *POW WOW*), formed orchestras (one is pictured at the front of this chapter), and took classes in gardening, shorthand, psychology, British history, and the Romance languages. They wrote exams that were shipped off to the University of Saskatchewan, graded, and returned. They drank beer supplied by the guards and had a preference for a brand called Kingsbeer.

Despite the food, the beer, and the activities, they also did what prisoners of war do—they attempted to escape. They attempted individually and en masse, even though they had no idea what they were up against, or even where they were. At Angler, in a fine example of German engineering, a prisoner fashioned a pair of homemade skates from the springs and fittings of his cot and set off to skate across Lake Superior. Presumably he was unaware that the lake rarely, if ever, froze over, and that it covered almost 32,000 square miles, making it slightly smaller than Portugal. He managed one mile. Prison cots also proved useful in the construction of crossbows.

At Red Rock, near Nipigon, two young sailors broke out in an effort to reach Port Arthur, seventy miles away. They returned the same day. According to a guard, "they had no way of knowing about blackflies." Prisoners built astonishing tunnels, some more than one hundred yards long. A note in the Neys official prison diary for June 1941 reads tersely, "PW's are tunneling but where?" They tunnelled endlessly, hiding the dirt in attics and under floorboards. They ventilated the shafts with tubes made from rolled oilcloths and tin cans opened at both ends and taped together. They drew up maps found to be surprisingly accurate, and made compasses by rubbing needles on silk. The map of the world that German officers painted on the wall of the Domtar plant at Espanola was not so much a way of killing time as an attempt to pinpoint themselves on the planet, and figure out a route home. At Neys, prisoners using tablespoons dug a tunnel that reached outside the wire. Two men, entirely covered in blackfly bites, made their escape as far as the Rossport train station, where they demanded, in French, to be returned to the camp.

It was on his way to Neys that "the Man Who Got Away," Franz Von Werra, made his astonishing breakout. The only German POW to escape North America and return to action in Europe leaped from a train at Smiths Falls, Ontario, and eventually dragged a rowboat for more than half a mile over the frozen sections of the St. Lawrence River before being arrested for vagrancy in Ogdensburg, New York. It is possible that with his collar up and his eyes to the ground, he passed in the street a man not much older than himself, a man lacking the fluid confidence of the fighter pilot perhaps, but showing instead the steady advance of the trained mariner. This man, Ernest Michael McSorley, would in twenty-five years command a Lake Superior freighter named the *Edmund Fitzgerald.*

Canadian officials tried desperately to have Von Werra extradited for stealing a rowboat. Von Werra, aged twenty-five, slipped away to South America, and finally flew from Rio de Janeiro back to Germany. He was killed almost immediately on a routine flight over Holland.

At Neys, Martin Mueller was shot dead while trying to escape. Mueller is often wrongly described as the 1936 Olympic gold-medal winner for the high jump. The incident was kept quiet to avoid retaliation against Allied prisoners overseas. Also at Neys, two young, lonely, and footloose prisoners made their way to the nearest dancehall and were captured there by police, who hauled them off the dance floor. Ron Samerhorn, of the Canadian Veterans Home Guard, remembered being assigned to escort a POW to a Port Arthur hospital for medical attention. When the train arrived, an astonished Samerhorn was met by the prisoner himself, who handed him a rifle, went back into the train, and returned with his two guards, both of whom were too drunk to walk.

At Angler, near Marathon, Ontario, in what remains the greatest prison break in Canadian history, the prisoners left en masse. For years the breakout remained a source of deep embarrassment to the government and saw thirty men escape into the bush after having dug a tunnel with frying pans. Outside the camp, escape plans were frustrated by the landscape and weather. A few men figured on stealing Native canoes and paddling somewhere—where would not be known. Two others built themselves collapsible kayaks with some notion of crossing Superior. They broke out into a blinding snowstorm that lasted twenty-four hours and left them staggering in waist-deep drifts.

All were caught. Two were shot while in custody, their bodies returned to Angler by dogsled. Two were wounded, and two made it as far as Medicine Hat, Alberta. One of these men had constructed a suitcase to make his appearance as a traveller more plausible. Built of bark and sheets of paper dyed with tea, this construction was strong enough to support a handle and working metal clips. It is now on display in the Thunder Bay Military Museum. Prisoner Horst Biebeck, who escaped from Angler, recalls, "After my escape [the commandant] was very pleasant to me. He said, 'As a sportsman, I must congratulate you. However . . . I have to give you twenty-eight days.' Then we shook hands."

With the arrival of fresh POWs came new information about the impending defeat of their homeland. Until then, any discussion of this sort had been dismissed as propaganda. At the Neys camp, officials screened a documentary film, *The Fall of Berlin,* but the hardliners—prisoners known as "the blacks" by Canadian military intelligence—walked out. A camp entry noted, "New arrivals tell of real horror stories from back home." On May 4, 1945, a *Globe and Mail* newspaper was passed around bearing the front-page headline "Hitler dead." The diarist at Neys wrote, "This was the first time the POWs believed the claim to be anything other than Jewish propaganda." On May 8, 1945, the Neys commandant summoned all POW senior officers and read them news of Germany's surrender. The war was over.

The process of repatriating POWs to their defeated country, half of which was occupied by Soviet forces, took two years and in some cases longer. German escape attempts actually escalated at this point, as prisoners plotted not to get back home but to remain in Canada. The pulp companies requested that the prisoners who had worked for them be permitted to stay on. An estimated 25 percent of the POWs imprisoned in Canada returned as immigrants.

Today stories are told in accented voices by old men to attentive listeners at military museums or veterans' gatherings across the country. They concern a man who slipped away beneath the barbed wire and lived on berries and moss, how he gained the friendship or pity of a Native woman and became a trapper. His name appears on no escapee lists because of the embarrassment of camp officials. He was just another man to disappear into the North, like so many before him—like Brûlé, Radisson, the voyageurs—to transform himself on the shores of Superior and never come out again.

Possibly he is still there, an old man now with his memories, his youth, his prime lived in the barbed-wire compounds of Lake Superior.

He remembers the lolling, comical approach of a black bear named Nellie, the chilling trumpet of the timber wolf or the soft thud of a snowball containing a flirtatious note from a Canadian girl. But what he remembers most is the first night when the sky dissolved into the aurora, so intense he could read a book by it. This is what sticks in his mind, looking through the windows of a camp called Neys on the brink of Superior, while that dancing horse shifted in the centre of the universe and the shafts of the northern lights spun through the darkness of a very foreign place.

# 14

# The North Shore

*I picked up so many dead and dying men from along
this track, you wouldn't believe it.*

—MUGS MCQUAIG

Main road along the Black River, north of Superior, c. 1955

The heart of Lake Superior's North Shore stretches some two hundred miles from Marathon, Ontario, to Thunder Bay. Here outcrop some of the steepest cliffs in Canada and some of the oldest rocks on the planet. This is the stretch of land that William Van Horne of the Canadian Pacific Railway meant when he described "200 miles of engineering impossibility."

The landscape is also dramatically picturesque. In 1936 a booster brochure for the Trans-Canada Highway ("the Highway of Hope") claimed not only that "the scenery [was] the finest," but also that this evaluation had been made by "authorities." Certainly the vistas are stunning; the fundamental panoramas of achingly blue water, of pitted rock faces stretching north to the tundra, of trees smeared with moss, of rock, and more rock.

The men who penetrated this armoured shore have become Canadian heroes. The section of railway line they carved through here, including the Mink Tunnel and the Red Sucker trestle, is one of the most audacious on earth. One hundred and twenty years ago sections of this line cost a million dollars a mile to lay. One hundred bridges were built through here, and an average of fifteen culverts per mile.

Between 1883 and 1885, twelve thousand men and five thousand horses pressed against the North Shore laying railway track, as the saying went, "by hand." Among train men it used to be said that no one has ever railroaded until he has worked on this division.

These men consumed twelve tons of food a day. Every month they smoked and chewed their way through four tons of tobacco. They spent their money in makeshift brothels; one of these establishments was located on what quickly became known as "Skin Island" in the centre of Peninsula Harbour off the town of Marathon. In the 1880s this place was termed "the wickedest place on earth."

A half mile away on the mainland so much blasting was taking place that, to save money, three dynamite factories were built in the short distance between Jackfish and Port Coldwell. Each turned out a ton of dynamite a day. The bill for dynamite, nitroglycerine, and black powder in this area totalled $7.5 million. The number of deaths incurred in the process has never been tallied. There are tales of Natives carrying forty-pound kegs of nitroglycerine on their backs. After one accident the remains of these men were described as a buckle and a bit of moose-skin coat. A "mishap" with nitroglycerine at one construction camp is said to have taken the life of every man in it. Workers described tubs of acid, loaded onto sleighs, inching toward the blasting grounds. So much dynamite went into this region that campers, preparing their nightly campfires, sometimes found crates of it stashed in the trees.

On these new rails came the people who were not native to the Anishnabe nation. They were immigrants, migrants, temporary railway workers, and even settlers. They brought with them the ability and the urge to tell stories, the capacity not only to write history, but to be history. Today, with Port Coldwell a single granite tombstone among white wooden crosses and the buildings of Jackfish razed to the ground, these people know that the life they lived is over, and that all but a few traces of it have disappeared for good.

The first library in the town of Dorion, east of Thunder Bay, housed a public collection of one hundred books, and opened on May 8, 1961. To borrow a book you went into Brenda Husilik's living room and signed it out. In 1963 Dorion received its first complete encyclopedia. For most of the twentieth century a fish hatchery has stood on its outskirts. In 1992 with the un-ironic candour of the local booster, an area historian, Pauline Dean, wrote, "Dorion began in the 1900s in Indian Country. It has grown over the years to become a community of friendly faces with a great deal of potential for the tourist trade. With the fish culture station, how can they lose?" Thirty years earlier, in a blizzard, dogsleds loaded with chopped liver had set out across the trails to save the brook trout at the Dorion hatcheries from starving to death.

From these sparse archives it is possible to glean some knowledge of human activity on the North Shore of Superior. Documents in the Schreiber library—once a bank, a town hall, and several other incarnations—indicate that the first bathtub reached the area in 1895. Men paid twenty-five cents to take a bath, but there is no immediate explanation as to why women were forbidden to use it.

One of the first white women to arrive in Schreiber came during the 1880s. She said of it that the surrounding blueberry patches were so thick "that you cannot see the pigs walking through them." Fifty years later, in the 1930s, the first telephones reached town. The first switchboard was in the kitchen of Helen Eddie's house. The phone company instructed her not to wear her headset during a storm, to prevent electrocution.

Although the North Shore is the history of a railway, it is equally the history of the blueberry. As passenger trains penetrated through here, blueberry camps sprang up overnight, allowing for an increasingly rare point in North America when Natives and non-Natives briefly intersected. It is said that "laughing Indians" passed enough berries through the windows of passenger trains to fill up the cars. Ageing residents from the last years of the twentieth century could still recall entire boxcars filled with baskets of blueberries. Local white women made three hundred dollars a summer picking them. Visiting Natives from the Pic River band sometimes harvested thirteen tons from the Port Coldwell area alone. Each summer tons of berries were shipped west by train to the Saskatoon Fruit Company in Saskatchewan and other firms. In a few short years German prisoners of war would comb these same hills picking blueberries. The health and size of the blueberry crop often determines the size and health of the bear population. If anything good can be said about the blackfly, it's that it pollinates the blueberry.

The berry has entered into folklore. In the Huron region south of here, Jules Couverette, a storyteller, is said to have once picked a blueberry so large he had to roll it home. A century and a half later it's no longer clear whether Jules Couverette was a man or a folk invention, an immigrant Nanabozho who cut into a blueberry with a steak knife and nearly drowned his baby in the juices that flowed out of it.

No sooner had the pigs arrived and begun tramping through the blueberry mantle of Schreiber than the cattle came. A local scribe put it this way: "Once the town had taken on a more civilized air, cows were introduced." With the introduction of cows came civilization, and even the arts. Pauline Johnson, the noted stage performer, gave a recitation here in

1895. Because the performance hall, possibly a drill shed, lacked a change room, she had to change costumes at the barbershop next door.

The town built a hockey arena but it collapsed immediately beneath the snow. A curling rink was built and also collapsed beneath the snow. A third arena burnt to the ground in 1918. Today locals say that the current hockey arena is still a bit wonky.

Following hard on the heels of pigs and cows came a type of political machinery that was put into action for the first time on June 16, 1902. On that date legislators passed a bylaw banning horses and bulls from running at large. The sound of cows rubbing against houses at night was keeping people from their sleep, and in a company rail town this was no small deal. More appalling to residents was to wake in the morning to find cows drinking from their water barrels. The CPR sold water for thirty-five cents a barrel, and folks were in no mood to be giving it away free to someone else's cattle.

In the frontier the hotel often arrives before the church. Consequently, once a month, the Schreiber Hotel was used for Protestant church services. In a lovely gesture of faith, a curtain was drawn across the bar during the service. To meet the spiritual and sometimes physical needs of the local Catholics, Father Richard Baxter himself sounded his horn and marched through the streets carrying the first vegetables to reach Schreiber. It was hoped the vegetables would help stave off a malady known as "blackleg."

In 1886 Schreiber opened its first school—in a CPR bunkhouse. It is said that over the next five years more schoolteachers came and left than there were residents in the village. According to a local author, "the wilderness that surrounded the area was imbedded in the children, causing them to act like hellions whenever a new teacher threatened to take away their freedom."

The outside world knows two things about Schreiber, and both of them are false. It is widely held that in the 1930s "Duke the Miracle Dog" saved the lives of two boys who had wandered out of town during a snowstorm. The boys that Duke rescued were students of Jackfish schoolteacher Katie Verdone, who taught, in her words, "grade one two three four five six seven eight and nine." In 1992, from her hospital bed, the white-haired, fragile, and ailing schoolteacher informed a reporter that Duke did not rescue *two* boys, but only one. "Kenny died," she said. "The dead boy was in the arms of a friend." That friend recovered but lost eight toes to frostbite. Duke, a crossbred husky, later rescued a second person by flagging down a train and guiding the crew to the lost man. Despite his best efforts, Duke the Miracle Dog could not rescue everyone who ventured out onto this line. A local engineer named Mugs McQuaig insisted that in his time the number of dead and dying men he picked up along this line was beyond belief.

Duke lived out the rest of his days in a vestibule at the local YMCA, where, according to witnesses, "he broke all leads provided by his owner and was a regular visitor on the dining car at the CPR depot." Another historical inaccuracy concerning Duke is that he was officially decorated for bravery. No such decoration was awarded. A half-century later, a Toronto newspaper posthumously presented Duke with a bronze medallion and inscribed collar. The YMCA where Duke lived out his days is gone now, torn down for lumber in 1967.

The other known fact of Schreiber is that Colonel Isbister landed his troops here on his way west to crush the Métis drive for self-government. This accounts for the town's previous name, Isbister's Landing. No book, no tourist brochure, no mention at all can be made of Schreiber without including this fact. It seems the only piece of information that makes its way into print about Schreiber.

In truth Isbister's Landing took its name from James Isbister, a construction contractor with the CPR. A document provided by Isbister's grandson and addressed to the Schreiber library practically begs that every effort be made to correct the mistake before "a corruption of historical fact becomes an accepted, even if incorrect, part of local history." This is exactly what has happened. Schreiber high school students begin their essays on local history with Colonel Isbister landing his forlorn, shivering troops here on their way to capture Louis Riel. The falsehood has been repeated so many times that it has become true.

East of Schreiber is Jackfish, one of the ghost villages of the North Shore. Jackfish was a coaling stop once, offloading coal from upbound American freighters for the steam engines of the CPR, and for the fishing tugs running out of Port Coldwell down the way. Mrs. Verdone taught school here. The foundation still stands. So does the foundation of the Jackfish hotel. At one time it was not uncommon to see a large black bear hanging by its throat from the balcony of this hotel. Members of the Group of Seven headquartered here. In *Jackfish Village,* painted in 1926, Frank Carmichael depicted the community from an oblique looming angle from behind. The town seems to drip out of the forest and into Superior. Lawren Harris found the North Shore sky possessed a "singing expansiveness" that existed nowhere else in Canada. He painted Port Coldwell, a bleak shack against black mountains, Superior rolling in, the waves rich and tangible. When he painted this canvas in 1923 people lived here, although you would never guess from the painting, which insists on an absence of life, no fishermen, no Natives, no blueberry mantle, no bears, deer, rabbits, no ancient lichens covering the rocks. Nature made smooth, tidied up for the formal needs of the artist.

By the 1940s, the Jackfish hotel had been bought by Gino Spadoni, who in a modest phrase is said to have "initiated running water." A fishing operation ran out of Jackfish, and the skeletal remains of a few drying sheds can still be seen on the cobble beach. But Jackfish existed for coal. Approximately fifteen tons of coal were required to move a locomotive the 130 miles from Jackfish to Thunder Bay. American coal freighters out of Pittsburgh were offloaded in a day and a half, with every man in Jackfish employed in the operation. As soon as the job was done, the bell rang from the schoolhouse, indicating the dance was on.

These "coal dances," as they were called, started almost the moment the freighter was unloaded, whether it was twelve noon or one o'clock in the morning. The women had been cooking since the boat arrived, although what they cooked is beginning to fall outside the ken of history. Pies certainly, blueberry pies. Fish, venison, potatoes . . . With the ringing of the bell the entire population of Jackfish began hoofing it to a guitar and fiddle on a sagging wooden floor of the schoolhouse.

The mayor did not attend because there was no mayor. No municipal infrastructure existed at all. Jackfish was a town because some two hundred people had moved there, in the manner of a Native camp, occupying the land as employees of the Canadian Pacific Railway. If people wanted an ice surface to skate on, they redirected the pipes from the steam-run coal chutes and poured Superior lake water onto a clearing in the woods and made themselves one. There were no street names and no streets. This does not mean that basic rules of civility did not apply. In 1885 a boarder bit off the nose of another man in a Jackfish boarding house. According to the *Port Arthur Herald,* he was "asked to leave."

A few decades later the coal dances were in full swing, joined by fifteen or so game American sailors who brought the coal up in the first place. These men had come from towns such as Houghton and Munising, from the Soo, Detroit, and Duluth to witness an extraordinary celebration in a foreign country, in a tiny railway town that clung to the rocks of Lake Superior. A crazy, rickety railway ran smack through the middle of town. Probably they felt right at home.

All of it came to an end in October of 1948. In that month the last cargo of coal was offloaded from the holds of the *Mantodoc.* Shortly after that, the first diesel train wound its torturous way along the North Shore. As smooth and sleek as a bullet, General Motors Diesel Ltd. No. 7001 shone a startling and very modern silver in the December cold. As it slid through the little villages of the North Shore, the people came out to greet it. Huddled in winter clothing, they can be seen in old photographs reaching for their own cameras.

They were photographing the end of their world, and they likely knew it. Ironically the North Shore itself, perhaps the coldest train route in the world, with its impossible turns and pathways, had necessitated the diesel in the first place. Steam trains attempting to negotiate this region required nearly a ton of coal per mile. More often than not the engines were doubled up.

With the coming of the diesel, the writing was on the wall, the steep rock walls of the North Shore. Mugs McQuaig described the scene as he steered the train into Jackfish—"300 feet of solid granite rising up on one side of you, and 400 feet of cold Lake Superior below you." In his opinion, he held a record among CPR railmen, "three derailments and one head-on collision in one month," January 1917. "Several times in my day," he boasted, "we would derail and go thundering through the bush."

Mugs McQuaig is a character now, along with many others, including a morose Norwegian named Rodin, who rode a bicycle and lived in Jackfish as far back as anyone can remember. He paid no taxes and was discovered by officials with Canada Pension to be single in Canada, married in Norway. At one point Rodin had made arrangements for a Native girl to come live with him as housekeeper. This young woman "arrived on one train, and left on the next." The story in one variation or another is encountered frequently on both sides of Lake Superior: the young woman, a bride or a maid, who steps off a train, a wagon, or steamboat, takes one look around, gets straight back on whatever brought her there, and goes home to where she came from. Rodin is remembered for having spread chewed tobacco on his renowned strawberry patch to discourage children from raiding it. According to one young woman who spoke from experience, Rodin was, at the age of eighty-four, "a dirty old bugger." In 1932 he fell off a roof and broke his neck.

Jackfish does not exist anymore. Katie Verdone is no longer teaching. Mugs McQuaig is no longer lifting half-dead men off the train embankment, nor is he eagerly crashing his train into the forest. Dead bears do not hang from the balcony of the Jackfish hotel. The coal dances are no longer being held. Even the Jackfish railway sign has been removed and is now nailed to the wall of someone's camp.

Today diesels roar through here without slowing down. They give off a noticeable heat as they pass through, shockingly close. When Jackfish existed, they snuck, threadlike, through the heart of town. An engineer with his elbow sticking from the train window could just about blacken the eye of a woman washing dishes in her kitchen. There are stories of trains slowing down so that the men working them could reach out and lift pies off windowsills.

Sometimes the elderly former residents of Jackfish are encountered tramping through the bush and trails with a gleeful dog and beautiful grandchildren in tow. Like most people of a certain age, they are ready to talk, and they will talk to you about a schoolteacher named Mrs. Verdone. "She was a good teacher," they say, the assumption being that teachers like her do not exist anymore. So much does not exist anymore, and that is really what they want to talk about. A woman with dark, sorrowful eyes waves her hand: "It was not like today," she says. Superior glints behind her, black with rock. For more than half her long life she lived in Jackfish, Ontario, without once seeing a police officer. "It wasn't like today!" she repeats.

Down the way the coal chutes of Jackfish press against the train embankments, virtually unrecognizable. At one time the trains stopped here six times a day, as close and regular as the beating of your own heart. People got on, got off, rode a few miles to the fishing village of Port Coldwell to visit a girlfriend, or play a card game, or babysit. The familiar faces of relatives and friends as they stepped off of trains, Natives from Pays Platt, even familiar dogs, children travelling by themselves, grandparents going just down the way to Peninsula (now Marathon), which in 1935 consisted of twenty-eight people, eleven of whom could vote. Towns this size and smaller, some of the remotest settlements in North America, received passenger train service six times a day on sections of the most breathtaking track ever laid. It was the absolute golden age of train travel, "convivial junketing," as one local woman called it. They went to other parts of the world too, west to Duluth, east to the Canadian National Exhibition at Toronto, stopping en route for passengers to pick blueberries and wildflowers. This train ride was the shared and common experience of four generations of Canadians. Now no passengers are allowed on this line. No one gets on and no one gets off. The trains don't stop anymore; they don't even slow down.

East of Jackfish lies the village of Rossport. It stretches about the length of a football field, and contains one intersection, "our intersection," as a local woman charmingly puts it. The Canadian Pacific freight trains run straight through the centre of this town, as they do any village on the North Shore. Rossport is named after a man called Ross who built the railway here, just as Schreiber is named after the man who built the railway there, just as Port Coldwell, once an unsanctioned squatters' community, is named after Robert Coldwell, who was so transfixed by the region that he had his bodily remains transported and buried in the town that had been named for him for building the railway there.

Today the trains do not slow down as they roar through Rossport and Port Coldwell. This deafening and regular onslaught has become so integrated into life on the North Shore that it's now synonymous with silence, as natural and as melodious as the cry of the white-throated sparrow.

From certain vantage points you can watch the trains creeping through the black mountains, ten or twenty minutes away. Backpackers determined to visit the old site of Jackfish must time these appearances carefully. The rock cuts are tight, and it's difficult to judge whether there's room enough for a train and a person to squeeze through at the same time. It is not the sort of thing to be wrong about.

Rossport has lately become a haven for kayakers. They rent rooms in the convivial Rossport Inn and leap out the door, striding over a patch of earth in front of the building, unaware that a locomotive lies buried beneath their feet. It sank following a mudslide in 1915 and took the engine crew with it. Clad in spandex and wrapped in all sorts of gear, these newcomers drip with health and eagerness. They are handsome, fit people, ready to paddle a lake that has become favoured worldwide by serious kayakers.

There was a time when kayaking the thirteen hundred miles of Lake Superior coastline earned a book contract. Now such expeditions are so common they warrant at best a half-page in the travel section of the *Globe and Mail* on a slow week. Still, those who make the effort are aware that they are participating in something monumental. It's not because of them and not because of the kayak, which has largely replaced the canoe on Superior. Rather, it's Superior itself, the word, and the North Shore, like some far reach of the human imagination. They are graced by it and made larger than life. They send back reports to web pages of their own design of how they landed on the pebble beach at Schreiber where the troops once landed on their way west to fight some mad Canadian visionary named Louis Riel.

Outside of these junkets, they will spend a great deal of their lives in chairs, writing software programs for large corporations. They represent a new wave of tourists, eager for health and fresh air; they have never been screened for tuberculosis and are not at risk for developing hereditary syphilis. It's difficult to connect these people to this landscape, with the reality of the mineshaft, the timber camp, or the other harsh and lost resources of the North Shore. Despite the best efforts of the tourist boards, it's still difficult to regard this region as a playground. A radio ad for a local lodge strikes the same uneasy note when it proclaims, "All the nature you need, plus the comforts of home."

Seventy years ago at a camp outside Marathon, a man named Jimmie Bell was hired to take care of the bears coming down to the meat house. A renowned World War I sniper, Bell worked from the cab of his half-ton truck and, with the headlights turned on, picked off seven bears on the first night. Lonely, brutal work performed in darkness by lonely and brutalized men.

Such characters stand in stark contrast to the blond hair and firm thighs of the Nordic newcomers and their elegant sea-kayaks. They are the financial renaissance of the North Shore, adventure-seeking tourists who have replaced the steamer-junket passengers of a century and a half earlier. People in Rossport know it; they do not smirk or look down on them. When a friendly, athletic young man from Milwaukee slaps down his map and demands to know what road he takes to drive from Rossport, Ontario, to Hudson Bay, Nunavut, people do not laugh at him. They explain that there are no roads, never have been, never will be. The young man pauses, then laughs. "I was wondering about that. I thought I just had some bad maps or something." He laughs again, for being caught so red-handed. He will head west instead, to Thunder Bay, where he imagines purple amethysts are strewn like boulders along the main street. He has read a brochure.

Thunder Bay is the only city on the North Shore, as Duluth is the only city on the South Shore. The signs today insist that Thunder Bay is "Superior by Nature." Superior or not, the region, as far as white fur traders were concerned, got off to a bad start. La Vérendrye was one of the first white men to snoop around here, trading for furs on the banks of the Kaministiquia, plucking red chokecherries that hang like shot along the banks, and searching for Cathay, which he believed lay just beyond Superior.

He brought his family of four sons, leaving his wife in Montreal, where she organized his canoe brigades. He travelled furiously, ingratiating himself with as many of the Native groups as possible, throwing feast after feast. "Without the help of the pot," he wrote, "you cannot have friendship." Following these feasts he made genial attempts to get women and boys and girls aged ten to twelve involved in trapping beaver. They were, in his opinion, "quite capable of it." In June of 1736, west of Grand Portage, a party of twenty-one Frenchmen, including La Vérendrye's young son, was attacked by a band of Dakota and killed. To demonstrate their opinion of French trading practices, the Dakota cut off the young La Vérendrye's head and wrapped it in a beaver skin. The decapitated bodies were then arranged in a council circle.

Thunder Bay is the two towns of Fort William and Port Arthur, a distinction that some stubborn locals still maintain. Collectively it is "the Lakehead." In 1867 an engineer named Dawson landed on the shores of Thunder Bay, hauled himself up on a rock, and proclaimed to several alarmed gulls, "Here will be builded a mighty city."

Dawson was perhaps only half right. A city was built, but it was built on dubious claims. At first these were the claims of exaggeration, the innocent starting point of humour found, for example, in the *Weekly Herald*'s insistence that a Lakehead potato was so big it required a shanty be built over it to protect it from snow. When a man was hungry all he need do was carve off a hunk. The same newspaper was serious when it insisted that the captain of a visiting ship had panned gold from the mud hauled up in his anchor. "Everything pans here," claimed the paper, "clear to the tops of trees."

For more than half a century these tales defined the colourful twin cities of what is now Thunder Bay. Even men of the cloth lied on her behalf. The Reverend Rufus A. Burriss, an obsessed colonization agent writing in Toronto's *Globe* in 1896, urged all doubters to simply get off the train, climb one of the hills of the North Shore, and look out across the beautiful land, which he insisted was "almost ready for the plow." He promised ten-foot stalks of corn in eleven weeks. Astonishing and shameless claims rolled off his pen: "There is not a rock not a stone even, to be seen anywhere."

As long as it brought more settlers, preferably English-speaking, from the east, there was no claim that could not be made. With the North Shore declared free of rocks, it was a small step for promoters to declare it free of mosquitoes as well. On June 16, 1900, this claim actually appeared in print in the Fort William *Weekly Times Journal*.

Fort William, it turns out, possessed "a substratum of quicksand and gravel [that] purifies and removes . . . poisonous germs." This is why fewer people died there than anywhere else in the world. This 1898 board of trade claim was backed up in a comprehensive citing of mortuary statistics. The area boasted the best "ozone" in the world, the best-looking women, and the best-looking rivers to go along with them. Nor did it lack for poets. In a line that would have made Pauline Johnson blush, the *Daily Times Journal* of Fort William crooned, "There will be smooth sailing, for we shall have passed over the corduroy roads of adversity on to the smooth bitulithic pavements of prosperity."

These claims were not offered in a vacuum. Immigration minister Clifford Sifton was making serious attempts to ban the publication abroad of Canada's winter temperatures. Potential European immigrants were told that winter temperatures on the prairies were comparable to Florida.

As the gateway to the Golden West, the Lakehead region became a virtual clearinghouse of misinformation. Agent Rufus A. Burriss measured his promotional flyers not by the number but by the weight; in 1901 he managed to ship out five tons of falsehoods. The air of the Lakehead was so pure, it turns out, that it actually cured hay fever. For that matter, it cured insomnia. And malaria. It was known for a fact that the air of Mount McKay was absolutely free of "disease germs." All that was missing was a luxury hotel on the top.

In winter, cold weather vanished. What little remained proved a cure for socialism, since socialism, according to local newspapers, can't flourish in the cold—this despite the Finnish immigrants who were turning out their own handwritten newspapers. When twelve angry Doukhobor women marched stark naked through the streets of Fort William, a journalist wanted the ensuing photographs used as proof of the mildness of the local winters.

Despite the best efforts of its boosters, the Lakehead region was not perfect. People were swearing on Brown Street, for which they spent five days in jail. The same sentence was handed out for selling rabbits without a licence. The Lakehead's first recorded murderer was a seventeen-year-old girl named Lizzie Washington. The teenager worked in her grandmother's whorehouse, in what capacity is not clear. One afternoon she was entrusted with the care of a customer's dog, which was then stolen. When the customer returned to find his dog gone, he spoke several angry words to the girl, and she shot him dead. The sensitive, unrepentant young lady received five years at Kingston, Ontario, for manslaughter.

While purporting to be the new "centre of gravity of the Dominion"— as well as the new Chicago, an inland San Francisco, and a second South Africa—the Lakehead was still a frontier region, awash in liquor and bordellos. Card players reportedly lost and won hotels in single poker hands. Whisky lubricated everything. In 1887 it was estimated that for every forty men, there was one drinking establishment. The most common local crime was being drunk and obnoxious. One of the few photographs that survive of early east-end Fort William shows beer kegs lying in the street. When Port Arthur went broke in the 1890s depression, the town's council hit upon two strategies: abolish the high school and have council borrow against unpaid liquor licences.

In 1906 ninety-eight Fort William residents died of typhoid. Every water supply in the city was found to be contaminated. For four years the Lakehead's only potable water was hauled in every morning on a wagon. Before reaching that wagon it was offloaded from a train, the notoriously slow Pee Dee rail line—Port Arthur and Duluth Railway. Some Finnish immigrants found it faster to ski forty miles than to take this train. More than once it was brought to a standstill by a swarm of caterpillars.

In the middle of these setbacks the *Daily News* of Port Arthur moaned, "How long are we to live in Mudville?" The newspapers worried that such shameful conditions would adversely affect the town's "Chicagoability." Infant mortality at the Lakehead ranked among the highest in Canada; nearly a third of Fort William's infants died at birth. According to the *Weekly Sentinel,* which was trying to convince council to spend one hundred thousand dollars on a blast furnace, the times did not warrant "that a single dollar be spent on our streets that is not absolutely necessary." When the town finally built itself a waterworks, it did so to reduce fire insurance rates.

Despite all, the Lakehead was far from a backwater. In 1892 Port Arthur built North America's first municipally constructed, owned, and operated streetcar line. Ten years later, in a referendum, the city's residents won approval to operate the line on Sunday! The Moral and Social Reform League, still reeling over the sight of Lakehead women on bicycles, predicted society's imminent collapse into "dissipation and immorality." "Hundreds of young people who attend our Sabbath schools . . . will take the streetcar to that howling wilderness, Current River Park." Toronto, the provincial capital, had to wait another half-century before it could tolerate Sunday streetcars.

Today, upriver from Fort William stands the "historical" Fort William, North America's largest reconstruction of a fur trading post. It attempts to accurately reconstruct the country's first fact, the fur trade. In 1903 the ruins of the original fort stood in the way of Canada's second fact, the transcontinental railway that was to be built across the site. The centuries-old landmark was torn down immediately.

The extensive modern reproduction sprawls over ten acres on the banks of the Kaministiquia River, "the Kam," as it is known locally. Now situated seventeen miles upriver from its original location, the fort contains forty-two "historic buildings." Young students working here dress up in period costumes and pretend to be voyageurs, bourgeois, and even Natives. Sometimes the passion of history is in their eyes. Occasionally an extroverted young man has a good time pretending to be Simon McGillivray, but he is handcuffed by the theme-park approach: the pretence that the year is 1815 and strict company rules against stepping out of character.

For five dollars it is possible to "Paddle into the Past," with a game teenager dressed as a voyageur. At the new and reconstructed "Old" Fort William, the water is now drinkable, but history has become a comedy improv, with audience participation. Here the entire family "can kick up their heels with a bunch of boisterous characters" and "become part of the fur trade fun." This fun does not include sticking your pipe into the rectum of a dead porcupine, drowning in Lake Superior, being decapitated by the Dakota, dying of a strangulated hernia, or carrying four hundred pounds on your back.

East of Thunder Bay in a filing cabinet in the Schreiber library exists an early photograph of the local women's baseball team: nine boisterous, vibrant, young women in baseball bloomers and bare arms. They look like trouble, mischievous, sharp-tongued, and capable of handling even the drunkest CPR men. They can scare off a black bear, pick a bucket of blueberries in no time, climb a rock face, paddle canoes, roll out a pastry, shoot a moose, gut a trout, break a young man's heart, and hit the cutoff man from deep right field. All nine of these young women have spread their radiance across the North Shore and lie in graveyards now. Theirs are the handsome nameless faces that make history, and they did it here, under these skies, against a body of water that its first English viewer, Jonathan Carver, called "too radiant to behold."

From a cliff in Rainbow Falls Provincial Park the storm clouds slant across Superior, sweeping west. A common view from the North Shore reveals not one, but an endless array of Sleeping Giants, their ancient backs sunk into the cold seas. It's a view that wants to turn personal problems into paltry things, vast beyond what the eye can take in. Attempts to render it end in failure. The American poet Lorraine Niedecker came close to capturing some of it when she approached Superior in stuttering, small, truncated phrases. Deliberately anti-lyrical, she constructs a world made up of rock, blood, water, freighters, iron, Jesuit, granite, death:

> *In every part of every living thing*
> *is stuff that once was rock*

According to critic Donald Davie, she was someone who painfully understood that in an epic of North America, "the heroes might be rocks and minerals instead of men."

Without the poet's understanding, the earnest highway booster from 1936 falls flat on her face attempting to turn the North Shore into a picturesque playground for "motorized America": "Every mile of the highway seems to reveal a new phase of northern scenery, graceful, curving bays, hills veined in mists of sheerest silver, vast solitudes of unexplored rock regions, cool green forests, rippling streams, placid lakes and a canopy of blue overhead." The words, chirpy and bloodless, are dead before they hit the page, concealing the region behind their own predictability.

Within that concealment are the original inhabitants. By 1936, promoters of the great Highway of Hope had recast the North Shore Native into a harmless and picturesque tourist attraction to entertain the passing motorist: "Indian camps are scattered along the Highway and many of the Indians have proved good workers. They belong to the Ojibway tribe and are a good-natured, liberty-loving and illiterate people." The intent and even the rhythm are not very different from what an ecstatic Reverend Thomas Hurlburt wrote of the North Shore a century earlier, that "a whole people are shaking off the slumber of years and casting their idols to the moles and bats."

The 1936 attempt to carve a highway across the North Shore ended in failure. Depression labourers were left on train sidings in blinding snow-storms with no idea of where they were, or where they were going. The public was indifferent to the project. The bears, wolves, and gulls had no use for a highway. It would be more than two decades before "the bitulithic pavements of prosperity" wound their swooping, torturous, and expensive way across the North Shore.

With the opening of the Trans-Canada Highway came the dreaded stranger. People whose names were not known, rootless, shadowy city people, whose gaits and voices were not immediately recognizable, could now arrive on the streets of these remote towns without having to book passage on a steamer or purchase a train ticket. For the first time, residents of the North Shore began to lock their doors.

On a bookshelf at Neys Provincial Park, at a library in Schreiber, is a book titled *A History of Jackfish*. Like all books concerning the North Shore, it is self-published, written by an amateur historian, usually a woman, and is as valuable as Hemlo gold. In it is a short poem that sounds the rhythm of rock and trees, frigid water, and the light tracings of people who, like the moss, have attempted to attach themselves to this rock. "Go to Jackfish," suggests Wilmot Hamilton,

*Look for life and find . . .*
*all the tiny specks of things*
*that coalesce a while*
*then ebb away.*

# 15

*Ships Passing*

*Here's a sigh for the* Chicora, *for the broken, sad* Chicora.
—FOLK SONG OF THE GREAT LAKES, 1890s

The *Zillah* on the verge of sinking, Lake Superior, August 1926

The tradition of feminizing the aqueous is long and complex. It includes the water itself, the ships that sail them, even the marine rule of women and children first, which does not seem to apply so rigorously in other disasters. After the *George M. Cox* ran full speed into the rocks off Isle Royale in 1933, the first mate was accused of cowardice on the grounds that his lifeboat contained only one woman. In the ensuing fistfight, which broke out in court, the first mate denied the charge and insisted his boat contained twelve women—a measure of his virility as well as bravery.

The courage and coolness of the women themselves did not go unnoticed. Chambermaids aboard the *George M. Cox* handed out aprons to freezing passengers, and when the ship's doctor ran out of bandages to wrap the wounded, it is recorded that women passengers "all hurriedly gave of their lingerie."

In 1913 the *Waldo* fetched up on a reef and broke in two off Manitou Island after being hammered by twenty- and thirty-foot waves. Hurricane conditions had existed on Superior for four days. Snow fell at speeds of sixty miles an hour. As it made its way east from Two Harbors, Minnesota, on the morning of November 7, the *Waldo*'s pilothouse and navigational compass were swept away by a wave. Using a hand-held compass balanced on a wooden stool and illuminated by a man holding a lantern over it, the crew managed to turn the immense steamer and point it at the passage between Keweenaw Point and Manitou Island, where it wrecked.

During the grounding, Alma Rice and her daughter were both paralyzed with fear and had to be carried. The group took a half-hour to reach the forward deck, less than three hundred feet away. Twenty-three men and two women scrambled into the aft quarters and got a fire burning in a bathtub to prevent themselves from freezing to death—many fires have burned in the bathtubs of Great Lakes freighters. Forty-eight hours later the captain ordered rations reduced to two cans of tomatoes, and reserved for the women. The crew apparently nodded in unanimous consent.

This unanimous consent is an old commitment to make every possible effort to save the female during a marine accident. Ensuring this safety also carries with it the tacit assumption that she is somehow to blame. The voyageurs called the wind that sweeps Superior "La Vieille"—the old woman—and offered pinches of tobacco to appease her, a trick borrowed from the Natives. The killing triplicate waves that some believe brought down the S.S. *Edmund Fitzgerald* have been called "The Three Sisters" for at least a century. Even the November wind has been feminized by singer/songwriter Gordon Lightfoot, who refers to it as a witch. With the exception of Colonel Thomas McKenney, who was wont to call it "the Father of all Lakes," Superior is widely known as "the mother" and "the mistress of all lakes."

Lake Superior has been called "the haughty queen of fresh water . . . cruel as the great court beauty in the heyday of royalty's arrogance." The marine author who penned these words, William Ratigan, also provides the ominous reminder that of the Great Lakes, "there were five sisters but only one was born queen."

Presumably the tradition of assigning gender to water and ships began with men and has been judiciously maintained by them. It's hard to see why they wouldn't womanize the wooden schooners or the huge steel structures they live in for eight months of the year, make them warm and understanding, and insist on their ability to keep a man safe. To feminize water is to admit it can revoke love, give it to someone else, and leave you to sink to the bottom.

Often a woman has the honour of christening a ship. A feminine hand holds the bottle of champagne, releasing it to smash against the steel forehead of a new vessel in a dramatic ritual of birth. In the storm of 1905, a young lady, Lau Hoxie, of Iowa, lost the opportunity to christen her own namesake when the ship sank only days before the ceremony. The ship died with a hull number, but never bore the magical name *Lau Hoxie.*

When death comes at sea, something mysterious takes place that transforms a drowning man or woman into a soul. In their final moments, they transcend the body and assume a dignity we do not grant other victims. Ships are "lost with all souls." The Morse code of distress is a cry to Save Our Souls. For their souls the brotherhood bell is rung every year at the Mariners' Cathedral in Detroit, at Whitefish Bay, and elsewhere in lonely halls around the world.

Fascination with death at sea is fascination with the passage of the human body into a soul. The process takes time; death at sea is rarely instantaneous. There is time enough for the body to thrash among the sliding dinner plates and to experience the deciding, fateful moment when the cargo shifts, time for the soul to separate from the flesh. Often there is time to write a letter and put it in a bottle, although typically these letters are discovered to be hoaxes. There is time enough to contemplate death. In the early stages of the wreck of the *Algoma,* one passenger stopped another on deck and said, "This is a terrible occurrence. It is sad to think that we will die here."

Enough time exists for sadness and terror. Various commentators on the *Edmund Fitzgerald* speculate that when the carrier began its dive to the bottom, the men, separated in two quarters fore and aft, remained alive for several minutes before the water broke in and hunted them down.

On November 7, 1885, the Canadian Pacific Railway steamship *Algoma* was blinded by a snowstorm. Like the *Edmund Fitzgerald,* the *Algoma* was the pride of a fleet, the Canadian merchant marine. After surviving the ocean voyage from Scotland's shipyards to Montreal, it was, like many vessels, cut in two and towed through the St. Lawrence River and canal systems, across Lake Ontario to Buffalo, where it was welded back together.

When it steamed into the Lakehead for the first time in 1883, with two hundred cabin passengers on board and a thousand new immigrants in steerage, the whole town came out to watch. The hull was painted with the first Plimsoll mark ever seen on the Great Lakes, the white circle and black band demarcating the level beyond which a ship should not be loaded. The blades of the propeller were detachable from the centre so that the entire screw need not be replaced after an accident.

The *Algoma* was also the first ship on the Great Lakes to be illuminated entirely by electric light; 110 bulbs cast a glow of sixteen candles each. The lighting system included a coiled flexible conductor with a watertight electric lamp attached to it. Divers used the device to conduct underwater examinations of the hull. The *Algoma* was carefully designed to prevent fire at sea. Matches were not to be struck on board; electric cigar lighters were provided instead.

On November 7 in a snowstorm, the *Algoma* ran aground on the rocks off Isle Royale in what has been called "one of the most ghastly catastrophes in the history of Lake Superior sailing." As the towering waves pounded the cabin into splinters, crushing the captain to the deck, he was heard to exclaim, "I'm done now, but what will become of these poor people?" These poor people and what becomes of them is the democratic core of shipwrecks. On Superior the outcome is predictable: they suffer a common death in a common cause, and their drowned bodies number into the thousands. It seems no one has even speculated on the number of Natives drowned in Superior.

According to marine historian Ronald Wrigley, a passenger on the *Algoma* described seeing women and children being washed over the sides. To passenger William McCarter, the sight of this was so upsetting that "a great many people grew almost crazy and jumped into the sea," to be "hurled against the rock . . . and mangled beyond recognition."

The captain, before being crushed, managed to run a lifeline along the deck for people to cling to. "In this manner," says McCarter, "we passed the night." Waves crashed over the deck and swept passengers away. McCarter describes them going to their deaths without so much as a groan. As the remaining passengers and crew waited for dawn, they huddled close together. No one felt inclined to talk. Forty-eight people died during the night; the numbers are not exact. The ship's purser was among the dead, his records lost. McCarter described seventeen people climbing up the rigging in an attempt to escape. Each new sea covered the wires, and when it passed, fewer men were there, and finally none.

Today, mounted on the wall of any of the tour boats that leave Munising, Duluth, and a half-dozen other places on the South Shore, is the United States Coast Guard's safety checklist for a PIW—person in water. Regulation Six of that checklist commands the crew to "maintain positive control of situation." It's difficult to see how anyone aboard the *Algoma* could have done that. In the saloon the first mate found a woman and her daughter, both dressed in nightgowns and crying uncontrollably. He grabbed the woman's hand, and she in turn took her daughter's hand; as the three of them tried to make it to the stern, a wave rushed into the cabin and lifted the two women into the sea. The men who saw this "lost their reason" and leaped into the water. On deck above them passengers had gone to their knees to pray and in that position were swept away.

The tug *Hattie Vinton* helped search for the dead. Aboard was a Winnipeg man named Dudgeon, come to locate the bodies of his wife and daughter. When the tug returned to Port Arthur, the man refused to leave the site of the wreck and was seen on shore scouring what was left of the *Algoma,* spread for two miles along the coast of Isle Royale.

No legendary folk ballad commemorates the loss of the *Algoma* nor the hundreds of other ships Superior has taken. The *Inkerman* and *Cerisoles* carried their names into a storm on November 24, 1918, and were never seen again. French minesweepers, built in the Lakehead shipyards, they left port under sealed orders en route to clear mines from the harbours of France. Twelve days later a vessel agent at Port Arthur received a telegram from the Soo, wanting information on the whereabouts of two ships, now a week overdue. Only the *Sebastopol,* a third minesweeper, made port.

The U.S. Coast Guard began a search off Grand Marais and found a floating pilothouse, which they determined did not belong to either the *Cerisoles* or the *Inkerman.* It belonged instead to the nameless casualties that litter the battleground of Superior.

According to float-bottle studies, the surface waters of Superior circulate counter-clockwise. In this vortex spins the tumuli of death by drowning—a flotsam of pencils, charts, cloth, sheared ropes, cushions, clothing, bottles, barrels, jars, packs of cigarettes, planks, a drowned parakeet in a cage, the commonplace debris of shipwrecks, and a dog swimming determinedly through the midst of it all. Between them, the *Inkerman* and *Cerisoles* carried crews of seventy-eight French seamen and two Canadian pilots.

On a November night in 1906, the captain of the *Hamonic* spotted what he thought was the wreck of the *Navada* breaking up on the rocks of Angus Island, where it had been for some time. While he and the first mate were examining the grounded ship, the first mate observed that it was not the *Navada* at all—but the *Leafield.* The *Hamonic* steamed into Port Arthur to report sighting the wreck, its own progress slowed by a thick sheathing of ice. Would-be rescuers were unable to locate the *Leafield;* it was never seen again. Some say it crested a giant wave and disappeared, taking its eighteen crew members with it.

Others thought the wreck the *Hamonic* officers spotted was in fact that of the *Monkshaven,* another of the ships that littered the rocks. The crew of the *Monkshaven* spent sixty hours huddled against the shore; two men went mad. An old photo shows ice draped like laundry from its rigging. The *Monkshaven,* the *Leafield,* the *Theano,* and the *Palika* were sister ships of the Algoma Steel Corporation. Three of the four sank on the underwater rocks that guard the approach to Thunder Bay. The *Hamonic,* the last ship to see the *Leafield,* burned at harbour in Sarnia, Ontario.

Ships are born on a given day, are baptized, named, and finally they die on a particular day. They resemble a community of people and, like people, become known for personal quirks and temperaments. Some are given nicknames. The whistle of a steamboat has been called as unique as the whorls of a fingerprint. The whistle of the *Noronic* was described as "deep-throated, tremulous, slighty raspy—like the voice of a big, strong man suffering from a touch of laryngitis." The *Noronic* roamed Superior and the lower lakes for thirty years, the so-called *Queen Elizabeth* of freshwater passenger ships, complete with hand-crafted oak bar, and hardwood floors laid over steel decks. It burned in a devastating fire in September 1949 while docked at Toronto. One hundred and eighteen people perished. The charred fingers that were recovered were later placed in labelled jars for purposes of identification. The entire crew of 170 made it off the ship without injury. Its captain, widely thought to be intoxicated at the time of the burning, ended his days as a desk clerk at a Sarnia hotel.

Far too often this community of ships resembles a funeral procession. Some mourners are hard and weather-beaten, and have been through this grim ritual many times before. Others are delicate and chaste, and possess unseen power. In the great storm of 1913, the wooden steamer the *Major* blew a steam pipe and dropped into the trough of Superior's seas. The ship was leaking badly, its above-deck structures blown away by wind and waves. A freighter pulled up alongside in time to rescue the crew. Abandoned, the little *Major* refused to sink. For four days the wooden ship was pounded by a hurricane. To its crew's astonishment, it showed up at Sault Ste. Marie on November 16, towed by the *George G. Barnum,* its cargo of coal intact.

In 1847 the one-hundred-foot side-wheeler *Julia Palmer,* with a weight of 240 tons, encountered a Lake Superior gale that tossed it out of control for fourteen days. The ship's owners were so traumatized by this that they promptly decommissioned the ship and turned it into a floating dock at Whitefish Bay, Michigan, the first known floating dock on Lake Superior.

Other ships, made of iron, proved less resilient. At its launch in 1882, the 286-foot *Onoko* was the design prototype for a Great Lakes freighter, and one of the largest ships on the lakes. In three decades of shipping, the fifty-thousand-dollar wheat carrier had paid for itself a dozen times over. On September 14, 1915, in perfectly calm water, an iron plate dropped away from the bottom of its hull, and the ship sank in minutes. All sixteen crew members, one passenger, and a bulldog named Rex were rescued. From a lifeboat they watched the *Onoko* settle at the stern and then explode, throwing its bow eighty feet into the air and pitching head over heels before settling for good. Divers located the ship's body seventy-four years later.

Some ships are lost in the records, such as the *Marquette,* "reduced to a barge, presumably abandoned." Others disappear from the registry, their names no longer listed. Some in this crowd live saucy and rebellious lives. The *Chicora,* a side-wheeler, was first christened the *Let Her B.* and became a notorious blockade-runner during the American Civil War. At one point it was chased fourteen hours by Union gunboats, a wild run in which the captain's wife waved a British flag through the wheelhouse window. The *Chicora* later carried mail across Superior for the Hudson's Bay Company. In 1870, it carried Wolseley's army to Thunder Bay on his way to fight Louis Riel at Red River. American authorities, aware of the *Chicora*'s sullied rebel past, refused to let it pass through the locks with foreign troops aboard. After weeks of negotiation the *Chicora* was allowed to proceed—empty. Its cargo and military men were offloaded and portaged on the Canadian side, an indignity that led to the construction of the Canadian locks.

Like the *Edmund Fitzgerald,* the storied *Chicora* would have its own song:

*Here's a sigh for the* Chicora, *for the broken, sad* Chicora
*Here's a tear for those who followed her beneath the tossing waves*

The *Chicora* perished in a storm on Lake Michigan in October 1890, taking all twenty-five souls with it. A dog, as often happens, escaped, and was found several days later on shore.

In 1734 Louis sieur de la Ronde is thought to have constructed the first decked vessel on Lake Superior—a ship that possessed sails "larger than an Indian blanket." What happened to his ship is unknown; a French vessel was discovered wrecked in Superior as early as 1763. La Ronde himself is often touted as one of Superior's first miners, but he was more likely a spy than a copper prospector. He had entered the French navy at the age of twelve, was wounded at twenty, and captured on the high seas after a seventeen-hour gun battle. He was later condemned in a Massachusetts court to hang and was finally saved by the governor of Massachusetts, who helped with his escape.

The first recorded decked vessel to wreck on Superior was the *Invincible.* The North West Company trading ship supplied goods to company headquarters at Fort William. The schooner was driven hard ashore in a storm and shattered without casualties off Whitefish Point in 1816. The first American vessel to be fully wrecked in Superior was built at Sault Ste. Marie in 1835. The American Fur Company schooner, the *John Jacob Astor,* displaced 112 tons of water and survived nine years under the command of the Stannard brothers, Charles and Benjamin.

Dr. Julius Wolff, the dean of Lake Superior shipwrecks, writes of the schooner that "on September 21, 1844, during a major equinotical storm, Captain Benjamin Stannard watched his faithful ship part her cables and go on the rocks, a shattered wreck . . ."

Here is heard the deep and subtle poetry of shipwrecks. Less knowledgeable authors would not allow a ship to "part her cables." Instead, they would be ripped dramatically apart, or snapped "like gunshots." For a ship to "go on the rocks" is the pure, measured language of the insider.

The aptly named Dr. Wolff, a native of Duluth, is said to possess an "almost hereditary" interest in Lake Superior ships. Thirty years of his adult life were spent researching, compiling, and writing *Lake Superior Shipwrecks: A Complete Reference to Maritime Accidents and Disasters.* It is impossible to write about Lake Superior shipping without opening this book.

According to Wolff, the first ship to entirely disappear on Lake Superior was the American schooner *Merchant,* on June 11, 1847, with fourteen people on board. Months later, the *Merchant's* companionway door was found on the North Shore, having floated the breadth of Lake Superior.

In modern times the Great Lakes have endured two catastrophic storms; the blow of 1905 concentrated mainly on Lake Superior, while the legendary Big Storm of 1913 was recognized at once as unparalleled in the history of all the Great Lakes. Striking over three days and nights, it shut down the Bell Telephone Company, stopped trains, stranded streetcars, and deposited drowned sailors in farmers' fields. Teams of men combed the shores of the Great Lakes collecting bodies. By the third day, 223 men and women were confirmed dead. Barely a ship on water escaped undamaged. Lost was the entire crew of the *James Carruthers,* downbound from Port Arthur, cargoed with wheat. Only seven months old, it was the largest ship on the lakes, it too a flagship and pride of the fleet.

The known list of boats wrecked, foundered, and missing includes the steamer *James Carruthers,* the steamer *Wexford,* the steamer *Charles S. Price,* the *Edwin F. Holmes,* the *Turret Chief,* the *Huronic,* the *J. G. Grammer,* the *William Nottingham,* the *G. R. Crowe,* the *Stewart,* the *Keewatin,* the *Acadia,* the *Weaver,* the *Leafield, Regina, Angus, Bridgeport*—and on it went.

On Lake Superior, ships commanded by seasoned mariners were blown longitudinally one hundred miles off course on a lake that stretches from north to south 160 miles at its widest point. Captains attempting to run their ships onto the North Shore hit bottom and found themselves on the South Shore. According to the Lake Carriers Association, "the wind and sea were frequently in conflict, the wind blowing one way and the sea running in the opposite direction, indicating a storm of cyclonic character." For sixteen hours, winds of over sixty miles an hour, gusting to seventy and more, hurled across the lakes.

On Lake Michigan the seven-man crew of the barge *Plymouth* lashed themselves to the interior and later were found frozen to death. The *Charles S. Price* rolled over, dooming twenty-eight men. In one bizarre incident, drowned crew members of the *Charles S. Price* were recovered wearing life jackets from the *Regina,* lost with all hands in the same storm. The freighter *William Nottingham,* fighting torturously across Lake Superior, ran out of fuel. Its crew brought it safely into Whitefish Bay by heaving bushels of grain into the fire boxes.

Though Superior has a reputation as one of the most ferocious seas on the planet, it is a remote body of water and, as a consequence, sees by far the least traffic of the great North American lakes. Because of this, only Lake Ontario contains fewer shipwrecks.

Nonetheless, the wrecks of Lake Superior seem cursed by an unremitting wretchedness. In 1851, with only four steamboats on the entire lake at the time, two collided off Parisienne Island. The *Manhattan* sank in shallow waters with no loss of life. The ship that hit it, the *Monticello,* later rammed a floating object and was wrecked in a storm against the beaches above Eagle River, Michigan. Ships have wrecked in Lake Superior when their crews, blinded by smoke from forest fires, have crashed their vessels into the jagged shores.

The first steamboat to ply Superior had to be dragged agonizingly over greased-log rollers up the main street of Sault Ste. Marie prior to the building of the Soo Locks. This procedure took seven weeks. For eight years the 260-ton *Independence* catered to the needs of miners and settlers until it blew up in 1853, becoming Superior's first boiler explosion. The *Independence,* a coal-fired "black tub" with one mast, frequently left the Keweenaw Peninsula cargoed with a single piece of copper weighing as much as two thousand pounds. Aboard this ship worked "a Negro cook" with a quick wit. He once packed a shipment of new butter in with the old, producing "a curious mixture of pale and yellow." A passenger, alarmed by the mixture, demanded to know what kind of butter he was eating. In the mining lingo of the day, the cook answered, "Boss, that's conglomerate butter with spar veins."

The *Independence* blew up near Sault Ste. Marie, killing only four people. Survivors hung on to bales of hay destined for horse fodder at the copper camps on the Keweenaw Peninsula. The explosion damaged a facial nerve of crew member Amos Stiles, causing him to frown for the rest of his life and earning him the nickname "the man who never smiled." The captain of the *Independence* survived to later clasp the face of Bishop Baraga and spoonfeed him his soup. In command of the *Manistee,* he went down with his ship after writing a memorable note and placing it in a bottle. Some later claimed this letter to be a cruel hoax. The *Manistee* was never found, but a spoon bearing its name was later discovered in the belly of a large fish.

Fifteen-year-old George Perry McKay, the son of the captain, also survived the sinking of the *Independence.* He was *born* on a ship, and began sailing on the *Algonquin* under his father's command when the *Algonquin* was the only vessel on Superior. At twenty-six he was in command of the *Pewabic,* downbound from Superior when it collided with the *Meteor* in Lake Huron. The twenty-seven-year-old commander of the *Meteor* and young McKay promptly got into a fight over who would be in charge following the accident. The ships collided in a fog, although even without fog, danger existed. Vessels commonly passed close enough to each other to exchange newspapers. An estimated 125 people died on the *Pewabic.* The *Meteor,* only slightly damaged, continued on to Lake Superior, where it burst into flames and was scuttled. The first mate of the *Pewabic* was convicted of manslaughter and later exonerated.

Three hundred, perhaps four hundred, dead ships lie on the bottom of Superior. An equal number collided with the shore, crashed into piers, or each other, and have been salvaged. At one time it seems that every ship on Superior has come to grief, often more than once. In some shipping seasons in the mid-1800s, one in three Great Lakes vessels was wrecked in any given year. For decades these ships had only the basic charts compiled by Bayfield and manoeuvred without the aid of lighthouses or navigational beams. In the middle of the lake, the still uncharted Superior Shoal jutted up from 720 feet to less than twenty feet below the surface. This massive reef, the cause of an unknown number of wrecks, was not discovered until 1930 when it was actually struck by a survey ship taking depth soundings. Along with the wreckages of steel and hewn timber, untold numbers of Ojibwa canoes have swamped or splintered against the shores. Ships without names found dead, or not found at all.

Numbering these casualties is a vague process involving shoddy records, interpretations of when a vessel can be classed a ship, whether it can be salvaged, and whether a stranding constitutes a lost ship. Sometimes the back half of a sunken vessel was brought to the surface and welded to the front half of another one, as happened with the 580-foot *William Moreland*. The freighter sank near the tip of the Keweenaw Peninsula in 1910, and broke in half. The salvaged stern was welded to a new bow section and sailed for sixty more years under various names.

Frequent name changes add to the difficulty in recording the birth and death of ships. So do ships with the same name. The *Algoma* that transported the wives and children of Silver Islet miners into a northwest gale was not the same *Algoma* that wrecked against Isle Royale in 1883. The *Merchant* that vanished on Lake Superior on June 11, 1847, was not the same *Merchant* that sank in Lake Erie in 1875. Typical estimates of shipwrecks in the Great Lakes range from 6,000 to 25,000, with the number 30,000 confidently tossed about.

What distinguishes Superior's wrecks is not their quantity but the ferocity, the well-known refusal of Superior to give up her dead: the cold water prevents putrification of the body, keeping it submerged. There is also the quick, determined disappearance of the wrecks themselves, followed by the scarcity of survivors. During the November storm of 1905, winds of eighty miles an hour whipped the lake for three days, driving fourteen carriers ashore. The *Western Star* struck the Keweenaw Peninsula with such force that people could walk all the way around the ship without getting their feet wet.

On Superior the life jacket has been described as a device for helping the Coast Guard locate your body. When the *St. Clair* burned to the waterline off Fourteen Mile Point, twenty-six people were lost. According to the shipping news of 1876, "most of the passengers put on life preservers, but the water was extremely cold and they soon perished." These twenty-six men and women died of hypothermia on a summer day in July. In 1919 the lumber freighter *Myron* took a mauling from the waves and sank. Most of its crew of sixteen donned life jackets and gathered into two lifeboats. A vessel got close enough to toss lifelines to the crew, but the men were too weakened by cold to reach for them, and all perished. The 1917 spring breakup in the Duluth harbour took place in June, with icebergs bulking seventy feet beneath the water.

In the killer storm of November 1905 the *Mataafa* tried to make its way through the two long concrete piers that frame the entrance to Duluth. To residents living in the houses up and down the steep hills, it was clear it was not going to make it. Like players in an ancient tragedy, they made their way to the piers. An estimated ten thousand people were soon gathered to watch the *Mataafa* lift high in the channel and smash against the concrete. A second collision sheared off the propeller. After spinning 180 degrees it was stranded six hundred feet from the shores of Duluth.

Isolated in the flooding stern, twelve crew members were forced out onto the open main deck, where they avoided being washed overboard by crouching behind the smokestacks and ventilators. Another eleven were relatively safe in the raised bow section, and several more who managed to make it up on deck joined them. At 4:00 p.m. the *Mataafa* snapped in half amidships. The captain came on deck with a megaphone and began addressing the crowds. They could not hear a word but knew he was pleading to be saved.

The Duluth lifesaving team, busy on another rescue, arrived back in Duluth at five o'clock, set up a Lyle gun on a tugboat, and fired a series of lines out to the *Mataafa*. By then the crew was too lifeless to rig up a breeches buoy. A day later the waters calmed enough to send out a rescue tug, and fifteen men were taken alive off the bow. Of the eleven men in the stern, only four were left—all frozen, lying on the deck behind the smokestack. Several of the bodies had to be chopped free with axes. Six hundred feet away, ten thousand people kept vigil as bonfires burned the length of the Duluth shoreline.

The cruelty of the lake is not confined to the killing month of November. In June 1953 visibility was down to several feet when the chief engineer of the *Scotiadoc* saw "something like a huge black shadow coming at us." Moments later his vessel was rammed by the S.S. *Burlington,* the chief engineer's third wreck. The steel plates of the *Scotiadoc* were ripped open, and a quarter million bushels of wheat poured into Superior. The *Burlington* circled in a rescue, and with the exception of one man, the crew, including two women who worked in the galley, were saved. That man, the night cook, had suffered polio earlier in life. The brace on his leg dragged him under before rescuers reached him.

The side-wheel steamer *Superior* sank with an estimated fifty lives, the largest maritime loss of life on Lake Superior. In a gale in 1856, the ship first lost its rudder. Its stacks went over the side near Pictured Rocks, Michigan, and it crashed broadside west of Cascade, and broke up in fifteen minutes. The Pictured Rocks are fifteen miles of sheer coloured sandstone, with nothing to get a hand on.

On December 6, 1927, the large package freighter the *Kamloops* sailed out of the Soo into a blizzard. Encumbered by tons of ice, it wrecked under mysterious circumstances, and the crew was lost. The night the freighter sank, the mercury showed eighteen degrees below zero. Six months later nine bodies were discovered on the rocks at Isle Royale. A sport fisherman found two more, and these were wrapped in sailcloth, placed on the deck of a United States Coast Guard cutter, and taken to Port Arthur for burial in plots paid for by the Canadian Steamship Lines.

The following spring after unsuccessful searches by a Canadian hydroplane, six more bodies, one of them a woman, were found on the shores of Isle Royale and carried away in stretchers made of fishing net and tree branches. The woman was Alice Betridge of Southampton, Ontario, a stewardess. In June the brother of the *Kamloops* captain undertook his own search and concluded that the entire crew had got away safely and lived on shore for several days before they perished. Crude shelters were found along the water's edge with a man's body in one of them, as well as a large quantity of peppermint lozenges, spread out on the shore to dry. Persistent rumour had the first mate of the *Kamloops* found sitting on a rock, frozen solid, with a pipe in his mouth.

The *Henry B. Smith* cast off into a storm with many of its thirty-two hatches still open and deckhands, in towering waves, desperately trying to close them. Like the *Edmund Fitzgerald,* the *Kamloops,* and others, this 525-foot ore-carrier was one of the biggest on the Great Lakes and the reigning flagship of the Acme Transit Company. The night the *Henry B. Smith* disappeared, the captain was said to be so drunk that it took two men to carry him on board. Two weeks after it left port a body was discovered in the water fifty miles west of Whitefish Point. This body and debris streaming across Superior were wrongly thought to belong to the *Waldo,* stuck on the rocks sixty miles to the northwest, one of the many ships in trouble during that storm. The following May, eighty miles across the lake at Michipicoten Island, two Natives found the body of the *Henry B. Smith*'s engineer, John Gallagher. In June on the Canadian side, someone found a bottle containing a letter addressed to the Hawgood Company in the Rockefeller Building at Cleveland. The letter claimed that the *Henry B. Smith* split in two at the Number 5 hatch just east of Marquette. The note was thought to be a fraud.

In September 1848 the *Goliah* was seen north of the Soo. Its smokestack and mast were gone and it was on fire. In the hold were two thousand barrels of mining supplies including two hundred kegs of blasting powder. The ship exploded off the coast; none of the bodies were found.

Some of the cargo washed up on the shores—of Lake Huron, echoing old sailors' yarns of enormous winds that blow a ship off one lake and put it down on another.

Other vessels die less dramatically. After long, useful lives they are scuttled in the sand or disappear riding the crest of a wave. The *Gunilda,* an exquisite steel yacht, perished because its owner, millionaire W. L. Harkness of Cleveland, was unwilling to pay a Canadian pilot fifteen dollars to guide it through the rocks at Rossport. "Come now, Captain, you have your charts, and you have been in this country before," said Harkness. After a failed salvage operation, the *Gunilda* sank off the McGarvey Reef. Mr. Harkness had to sail to Cleveland as a passenger aboard the *Huronic.*

In 1863 the *Sunbeam* died a slow death in a sudden summer storm off the Keweenaw Peninsula. Its engine had quit; the ship, listing badly, began to sink. One man survived the experience. His name is given as John Frazier or Charles Fregeu, a wheelsman who surrendered his seat in a lifeboat to a chambermaid who had nearly been left behind.

Fregeu withdrew from the lifeboat and, using signal halyards from the flag mast, tied himself onto a floating piece of deck. He also lashed on a five-gallon keg of port. For thirty hours he washed down the coast of the Keweenaw Peninsula and was finally hurled against the sandstone cliffs. The waves shattered his craft against the rocks, and he was cut badly at the forehead, crippled at the knees, and injured at the shoulders. Another wave hurled him out of the lake and onto a rock ledge, where he survived thirty more hours before being rescued by a rafting party.

Charles Fregeu, or John Frazier, had obeyed an old law, written in cold water, that a woman's survival was more valuable than his own. For this, his life was spared. The *Sunbeam*'s lifeboats capsized at once and the twenty-eight men and women were lost.

One of the most recent major vessels to perish in Superior was the *Mesquite,* a United States Coast Guard vessel that grounded in difficult seas while retrieving signal buoys in the pitch dark of December 4, 1989. The *Mesquite* had been rescuing distressed vessels on Lake Superior since the 1950s.

Its wrecking, the only U.S. Coast Guard vessel ever lost on Lake Superior, re-examines an old inclination to feminize water and the crafts that ride on her. When the *Mesquite* ran aground off Keweenaw Point, it was in command of a young ensign, Susan Subocz. The wreck was attributed to a series of small navigational errors made over time by several people. The fifty-three crew members donned inflatable suits, entered three life rafts, and were picked up by the Indian freighter *Magai Desai*.

By the mid-twentieth century, the convention of feminizing the waters, once steeped in reverence, had decayed. With the era of the passenger fleet quickly coming to an end, marine authors began to describe these storied lake ships as "old girls" and "aging duchesses." Of the "queen" of this fleet, the *Noronic,* it was whispered, "As the years went by, it became ever a little harder to keep the aging lady looking jaunty and gay. There were inevitably sags and wrinkles that could only be erased by increasing cosmetic care."

The imagery will not give in without a struggle. The *William F. Sauber,* weighed down by tons of ice, foundered in a gale off Whitefish Point, Michigan, in 1903. Its captain, William Morris, refused to take the final seat in a lifeboat. When urged to do so by his chief engineer, it seems he instructed his rescuers to "Fuck off!" He was thrown a line but refused to reach for it. "The old girl had been good to him," concludes William Ratigan; "he could not bear to turn his back and leave her to die alone."

# 16

*Big Fitz*

*There must have been some hellish kind of chaos going on.*
—CAPTAIN DUDLEY PAQUETTE

"The largest man-made object ever to be dropped into fresh water"

*O*n a June morning in 1958, ten thousand people gathered in Detroit's Rouge River shipyard and watched a woman standing on top of a platform. Her name was Elizabeth Fitzgerald, and she wore a dark blue skirt and a white pillbox hat with a short net veil. With her hands sheathed in white gloves, she stepped to the microphone and spoke five nervous words, "I christen thee *Edmund Fitzgerald*." With that she swung a bottle of champagne against the hull and the S.S. *Edmund Fitzgerald* was ushered into Christian life, fully baptized.

The name belonged to the man beside her, her husband, the chief officer and president of Northwestern Mutual Life Insurance, the ship's owners. A Detroit newspaper photo shows the couple standing on the main deck; she holding down her pillbox against the wind, Edmund's boater pulled tight on his head, his hands in his pockets. He has just had named after him what writers were calling "the largest man-made object ever to be dropped into fresh water," to which he could only respond, "It is almost embarrassing to have such a magnificent vessel as a namesake." Behind the couple, in black letters across the facing of the aft quarters, the words *Edmund Fitzgerald* show like markings on a headstone.

For the first few years of its life, until larger vessels edged it out, the S.S. *Edmund Fitzgerald* was a phenomenon. People travelled for miles to have their photographs snapped with the ship moored behind them. These photographs belong to an era of men who wore suits on weekends and pinned their hopes on large machines. The women in these photographs wear dresses fitted at the waist, flaring below the knee, pumps on their feet and hats on their heads. Arms are uplifted against the wind to keep their hats from blowing off. Sometimes a camera can be seen. Typically the man holds it. He is the one photographing the *Edmund Fitzgerald*.

Other visitors stand about and gaze at the ship with reverence. They stare at a future based on progress and immense technology. The ship dwarfs them; the rudder alone weighs twenty-three tons. Each of its twenty-one hatch covers weighs seven tons. Men and women stand like specks against its rust-red side. They have come to photograph their own smallness pitted against the huge, unstoppable future that has pulled up alongside them.

Forty times a year the great freighter came up from the lower lakes, usually from Toledo, Ohio, and passed through the Soo Locks. There it ascended the nineteen feet that spread out along the St. Marys River and separate lakes Superior from Huron. This troublesome climb constitutes the *up* in "up north," and was solved by American engineer Charles Harvey in 1855. Like many Americans, Harvey first encountered Sault Ste. Marie, Michigan, after his doctor sent him there to recuperate from an attack of typhoid fever.

The construction of the Soo Locks is one of the great success stories of U.S. engineering. Charles Harvey was twenty-four when he undertook the assignment. Competing with the railways for a labour force, he hired immigrant workers *before* they stepped off the boats at New York. When workers died of cholera, he had them replaced. Living and operating out of Henry Schoolcraft's old white house, he arranged to cut a channel through the heart of a Chippewa graveyard. When horrified Natives assembled in numbers to watch his workers shovel the bones of their relatives into a muddy heap, the young engineer did not flinch.

In 1953, 129 million tons of cargo passed through the locks at Sault Ste. Marie—more than the tonnage of the Panama, the Suez, the Manchester, and the Kiel canal systems combined.

Having cleared "the Miracle Mile," as it was called, the *Edmund Fitzgerald* steamed west, 460 miles across the length of Lake Superior. Finally it put in at the Burlington Northern docks at the town of Superior, Wisconsin, next to the shoreline city of Duluth, three miles deep, twenty-six miles long. The old Lake Superior sandstone buildings shone red on the steep hills.

More cargo passes through the ports of Duluth and Superior than through the San Francisco harbour. Twenty-five different kinds of grain are siloed here. Once docked the *Edmund Fitzgerald* loaded up with taconite pellets. Predictably, it made the same round-trip journey every four or five days for seventeen years.

The tedium of the ship's circuit was accompanied by the tedium of modern shipping, in which men labour aboard floating factories. For the most part they fasten and unfasten clamps. They are also subject to a substantial range of industrial accidents. They fall over steel combings, slip on taconite pellets, trip down stairwells, are concussed against steel doorways, burned in diesel fires, deafened by the engine room, and slashed by the cables and mooring lines that coil like snakes around the ship. They also face the possibility of drowning.

On November 9, 1975, the *Edmund Fitzgerald,* loaded with 26,116 long tons of taconite pellets, pulled away from the Burlington Northern Dock No.1 at Superior, Wisconsin, and proceeded east into a brilliant autumn day. Shortly after 4:00 p.m., near Two Harbors, Minnesota, it was far enough from shore that off-duty crew members watching Channel 10 out of Duluth lost reception and saw their television screens become awash with snow and interference.

The *Arthur M. Anderson* was sighted up ahead. Between them the two carriers were hauling some 60,000 tons of ore pellets into the heart of the United States steel industry. Separated by ten or twenty miles, the two "straight deckers" followed an eastern course for Detroit. By the time darkness fell, they had passed north of the Apostle Islands; the *Ira H. Owen* and a crew of nineteen had vanished here in the storm of 1905. Their course, as it had so many times before, would see the *Big Fitz* and the *Anderson,* the next day, "lock down" at the Soo.

In the afternoon the United States National Weather Service issued gale warnings for Superior. By 7:00 a.m., a storm was menacing the western region of the lake, blowing for several hours out of the northeast and depositing two inches of snow on the shores. By 1:00 a.m., the *Edmund Fitzgerald* was twenty miles off Isle Royale; skies were overcast, winds were up to 52 knots, and visibility was down to two to five miles in a heavy, continuous rain. An hour later, the weather advisory escalated to a storm warning.

The *Fitzgerald*'s captain, Ernest McSorley, concluded a radio conversation with his counterpart on the *Arthur M. Anderson,* Bernie Cooper. The two agreed to take the longer but safer "fall north route" northeast, seeking protection in the lee of the Canadian North Shore.

By early morning, November 10, the *Edmund Fitzgerald* informed head office that its arrival at the Soo Locks would be delayed by weather. With the wind and seas rising, the *Big Fitz* and the *Anderson* sailed similar routes for six hours. By noon the *Edmund Fitzgerald* had entered the eye of the storm, a twenty-mile zone of calm situated in a wall of wind. At 1:00 p.m. the *Anderson* altered course to clear Michipicoten Island. The *Edmund Fitzgerald* was eight miles in front of the ship. At 1:40 p.m. McSorley advised the *Anderson* he had just cleared Michipicoten Island and that his ship was "rolling some." An hour later the *Anderson* cleared the Six Fathom Shoal area and had the lights of the *Edmund Fitzgerald* in view, sixteen miles ahead. The winds were blowing now at 42 knots. The barometric pressure had dropped to 28.56 inches, the lowest reading any officer on either bridge had ever seen. A snow came on and the lights of the *Edmund Fitzgerald* disappeared from view. At 3:30 p.m. the *Anderson* received a radio message from McSorley, who said the *Edmund Fitzgerald* had been damaged topside: a rail fence was down, two vent covers were lost or damaged, and the ship was listing. McSorley slowed down to allow the *Anderson* to catch up and keep a watch. Radar aboard the *Anderson* showed the *Big Fitz* seventeen miles ahead and to starboard. Several minutes later the United States Coast Guard broadcast an emergency warning, instructing all vessels to seek safe harbour. At Sault Ste. Marie, the winds were gusting to 96 miles an hour. Water was coming in over the lock gates, and the Mackinac Bridge had been closed to traffic.

At nearly five o'clock that evening the *Anderson* logged northwest winds of 58 knots. Waves mounted to eighteen feet as snow continued to fall. At this point the *Edmund Fitzgerald* was thirty-five miles away from the shelter of Whitefish Point. At 5:30 a Swedish saltwater vessel in the vicinity, the *Avafors,* contacted the *Edmund Fitzgerald* and informed McSorley that the radio beacon at Whitefish Point had failed. The same beacon had been malfunctioning for three years. During the conversation the pilot heard McSorley shout, "Don't let nobody on deck!" The captain then told the pilot that the *Fitzgerald* "had a bad list, had lost both radars, and was taking heavy seas over the deck." In McSorley's words, it was one of the worst seas he had ever been in.

At 6:00 p.m. the *Anderson* pulled out from the southeast lee of Caribou Island and met waves of twenty-five feet. At 7:10 p.m. the *Anderson* again contacted the *Edmund Fitzgerald* to warn of a vessel approaching it nine miles ahead.

"Well, am I going to clear?" demanded McSorley.

"Yes, he is going to pass to the west of you," said the *Anderson* mate.

"Well, fine."

Before signing off, the *Anderson* mate asked, "Oh, by the way, how are you making out with your problem?"

"We are holding our own," answered McSorley. In fact, his ship was listing badly. His pumps were sucking out 32,000 gallons of Lake Superior per minute, to no avail. In all likelihood water was flooding his cargo holds where the pumps couldn't reach it. He had no radar. Waves as tall as three-storey houses, weighing hundreds of tons, had been smashing against his ship for hours. "We are holding our own," he said. This phrase, mute with the machismo of seafaring and the guarded conduct of on-air ship-to-ship communication, were the last words ever heard from the *Edmund Fitzgerald*.

At 8:32, the *Anderson*'s captain repeated his worries to the Coast Guard: "I am very concerned with the welfare of the steamer *Edmund Fitzgerald*. He was right in front of us experiencing a little difficulty. He was taking on a small amount of water and none of the upbound ships have passed him. I can see no light as before, and don't have him on radar. I just hope he didn't take a nose-dive."

At the request of the Coast Guard, Cooper agreed to turn about in the harrowing seas and search for survivors. None was ever found.

The inquiry that followed the loss of the *Edmund Fitzgerald* has been called the largest and most detailed casualty investigation in all of American maritime history. When it was over the United States Marine Board concluded that the probable cause of the sinking of the S.S. *Edmund Fitzgerald* was "loss of buoyancy and stability which resulted from massive flooding of the cargo hold [that] took place through ineffective hatch closures as boarding seas rolled along the Spar Deck."

The spar deck of the *Edmund Fitzgerald* was punctuated by twenty-one hatch covers, lifted and replaced by a mounted rolling crane. Each of the covers was held in place by sixty-eight manually operated steel clamps positioned on two-foot centres. Each of these clamps took two crew members wielding a clamp wrench about thirty seconds to fasten or unfasten.

Despite the investigators' report and the solidity of steel clamps and immense hatch covers, there seems to be nothing that did not sink the *Edmund Fitzgerald*. Jacques Cousteau, the French underwater explorer, postulated that the massive carrier broke up on the surface; the two sections, colliding with each other, went down in pieces. To most experts, the big ship went down in one piece; it entered a "wall of water," took "a nose-dive," and broke in two after hitting bottom five hundred feet below.

The Coast Guard blamed improperly closed hatches. Sailors blamed the Coast Guard for being unwilling to stand up to ship owners. To the owners, desperate to avoid costly safety modifications, the ship simply struck a reef off Caribou Island and sank. The Lake Carriers Association, the owners' lobby, insisted that "reduced professionalism in today's seaman" played a role in the tragedy.

Some blame the Three Sisters trolling their deadly path across Superior, hitting hard twice, then, as the *Big Fitz* foundered, coming in brutally with the third wave that finished it off, depositing five thousand tons of water onto its deck. Other people believe the ship was overloaded. It sank because the compartments between its holds were not watertight. It sank because of a faulty keel. It sank after being struck topside by an unknown object in a freshwater hurricane, or it foundered because of a rare Great Lakes phenomenon known as a "seiche" that sucked a vast quantity of water out of Lake Superior, then slammed it back all at once. It sank because of an incompetent captain, because of "the Great Lakes Triangle," the crew whisked away by extraterrestrials. It sank from a stress fracture, as cheap and suspect steel shattered like glass in the frigidity of Superior, and because its owners were too stingy to keep it in decent repair.

No single cause has ever been convincingly attributed to the sinking. Instead there are constellations of guilt, a wide net in which the cause is contained. One *Fitzgerald* expert and writer, Frederick Stonehouse, while supporting the findings of the Coast Guard, attributes its sinking to a massive "conspiracy of ineptitude."

This conspiracy began centuries earlier in the casual and widespread indifference to safety that characterized the shipping trade throughout the world. In 1876, after a long campaign by an Englishman, Samuel Plimsoll, the British Parliament agreed to institute laws requiring a load line to be painted on the hulls of British cargo vessels. An estimated two thousand shipwrecks occurred each year in British waters and, according to Plimsoll's research, almost all of these were due to overloading. His Plimsoll mark appeared in 1876 and produced immediate reductions in British casualties.

Thirteen years later the United States Congress introduced similar legislation. Shipowners, a wealthy, powerful group with influence that reached deep into the country's banks and railway establishments, responded by forming the Lake Carriers Association, defeating the load-line bill without difficulty. Decade after decade the law was kept off the books while casualties mounted in men, women, and ships.

In 1914 an estimated 875 ships sailed the Great Lakes. Of these a staggering 702 were involved in "vessel casualties." Sixteen were total losses. In 1903 the J. C. Gilchrist fleet alone lost seven ships. Not until as recently as 1936 did the Coast Guard finally require load lines on American vessels on the Great Lakes.

The introduction of wireless radio encountered the same resistance. Bulk-shipping companies belonging to the Lake Carriers Association instigated an aggressive campaign against any laws that required radios on their ships. Until 1934 cargo vessels remained legally exempt. When the change was finally made, small, more vulnerable vessels were excluded from the legislation.

This indifference to safety has been blamed on shipping companies, insurance underwriters, bureaucrats from the Steamboat Inspection Service, and even the Coast Guard. However, Mark Thompson, a naval historian, singles out one group for particular responsibility: "In the ongoing cycle of shipwrecks and death on the Great Lakes there is no group that must bear more of the blame than the generation of captains who have commanded ships on North America's freshwater seas."

Whether they like it or not, captains are the focal point in the some-times deadly tug of war between safety and profits. Ernest McSorley was a company man first. In his three years in command of the *Big Fitz*, he was said to "beat hell out of her," rarely slowing down for bad weather. Like other captains, he sailed without the hatch covers being securely clamped. A year before his retirement, and several months before his ship sank, he was overheard arguing with a crew member who insisted the keel was loose again. McSorley replied, "All this son of a bitch has to do is stay together for one more year. After that, I don't care what happens to it."

Not surprisingly, morale among the *Edmund Fitzgerald*'s crew has been described as extremely low. McSorley's career was winding down, and he was concerned for the health of his ailing wife. Seemingly he failed to ensure that his crew kept up even routine maintenance. Taconite pellets rolled around the spar deck. These dense iron marbles, treacherous to anyone who trod on them, spilled around the hatch coamings during loadings and unloadings. To slip on a taconite pellet could mean a wrenched back and two weeks in bed. Workers aboard the *Edmund Fitzgerald* found it prudent to travel down below in side tunnels. A deep structural problem involving the keel was repeatedly ignored.

According to testimony from a former *Edmund Fitzgerald* cook, the ship "groaned more than most" and made a sound he'd never heard on any other vessel. He was convinced the *Fitzgerald* had a loose keel, and he had seen a workman shove a crowbar right under it: "What he pushed out of there was welding rods and everything else from when the ship was built," he testified. The welding rods had been thrown in as shims, to help the hull plates meet solidly.

At seventeen years of age, the *Edmund Fitzgerald* was a neglected and ailing vessel. It had also taken its blows. In 1969, in a serious grounding, the ship suffered damage to its bottom and internal superstructure. A year later, it collided with the S.S. *Hochelaga* and sustained damage above the waterline. Three times the ship suffered injury above the waterline in collisions with the lock walls at Sault Ste. Marie. Welding cracks in the ship's keel area were discovered in 1969 and again in 1973. The *Fitz* also had an unusual bow action, what McSorley called "that wiggly thing"— in hard weather the bow of his carrier flipped to one side and took forever to return. "If she starts to do the wiggling thing, let me know. This thing scares me sometimes," he told a mate. His stated opinion of his own ship was that it was "not as great as you might think."

In five years its hull had been damaged five times. In that condition, bruised, possibly sailing with a loose keel and its twenty-one hatch covers held down by a minimum of clamps, it headed full speed into the worst storm to strike Lake Superior in more than half a century.

At the time, the relatively new science of meteorology was also viewed as an unwelcome intrusion on the Great Lakes. Captain Dudley Paquette, captain of the S.S. *Wilfred Sykes* on that night of November 10, suggested to marine author Hugh Bishop that skippers like McSorley had little training in predicting and outmanoeuvring weather. "Most of the old-time captains wouldn't know the difference between an isobar and a soda bar." In his opinion, the *Fitzgerald* sank partly because its captain "didn't have enough training in weather forecasting to use common sense and pick a route out of the worst of the wind and seas." Even the Lake Carriers Association concluded in its self-serving report that "improved meteorological training of deck officers will further enhance safety of Lake Shipping."

The intensity of a Great Lakes storm can be difficult to imagine. In 1965 an engineer aboard the *Joseph Block* found it necessary to tie himself to his chair to stay at the controls. On the night of November 10, 1975, wind-driven water was clearing the pilothouse of the *Wilfred Sykes,* thirty-five feet above the deck. Its captain described a phenomenon known as "beam seas," the wind and the water driving directly at the side of the vessel. These conditions, Paquette explains, "create almost pure confusion." This is in the minds of people who have spent their adult lives at sea and goes well beyond the cook's dampening down tablecloths to prevent cutlery and plates from sliding off the table.

Despite the circumstances on that dreadful night, of all the ships on Superior only one sank, the relatively young *Edmund Fitzgerald.* It is possible this massive carrier had been sinking for hours, that as its captain ploughed hard into the mounting waves, it was sinking. With every nautical mile, the ship slipped another degree below the surface. Even with pumps spewing thousands of gallons per minute, the ship was sinking. Inch by inch the distance between Superior and the spar deck decreased. What had once been compartments filled with air were now filling with water, tons and tons of water, coming from the top, perhaps from below. "Don't let nobody on deck!" snarled the captain. His ship was sinking. He might have known it.

"How are you doing with your problem?"

McSorley answers in the code of marine masculinity. He's not like the ship's former captain Pete Pulcher, a whimsical, bratty man who once arrived at the Soo Locks with himself and his entire deck crew dressed in orange fluorescent wigs and who guided the *Edmund Fitzgerald* up and down the Detroit River, blaring Mozart from the ship's speakers.

This is a different man. McSorley did not get to be the youngest master on the Great Lakes by dressing up like a clown, playing Mozart, or insisting on expensive repairs. The unthinkable is about to happen. His ship is sinking. His heart pounds.

"We are holding our own," he says.

The S.S. *Edmund Fitzgerald* was sinking. Conceivably it had been doing so from the first days in the shipyard, when workers tossed in welding rods as shims to plug up hull plates that did not fit flush. As each week passed without the mandatory safety drills being conducted, the ship was sinking. Each time a taconite pellet was allowed to roll around on deck and every time an engineer was told to keep quiet about the problems he'd seen on board, the ship was sinking.

It was also sinking at the hands of the Coast Guard, who on a yearly basis lowered the amount of legal freeboard required for a Great Lakes cargo carrier. From the time the ship was built in 1958 to the time it disappeared in 1975, the United States Coast Guard allowed the *Edmund Fitzgerald* to load an extra three more feet of cargo. A single inch of increased draft on a ship that size meant an extra 130 long tons per trip. Multiplied by forty-five trips per year and then the ship's lifetime of perhaps fifty years, that inch translates into millions of dollars.

Year by year the *Edmund Fitzgerald* was riding lower in the water. In 1958 nautical engineers had concluded this ship could be safely loaded in winter to 24 feet 6 inches. In 1973 the *Fitzgerald's* load line for the critical late-fall sailing season was increased a full 20 inches. Fully loaded, it now floated closer to the bottom of Lake Superior than it had the year before. When the *Fitzgerald* left Wisconsin for the last time on November 9, it was cargoed to a draft of 27 feet 2 inches forward, and 27 feet 6 inches aft, low enough that a twelve-foot wave would board it. A fifteen-foot wave hurled three feet of water across the deck. A thirty-five-foot wave like the ones encountered on November 10 put the deck nearly twenty-five feet beneath the surface of Superior.

After the investigation the Coast Guard's first recommendation was to rescind its own reduction in freeboard brought about by changes in 1969, 1971, and 1973. The Lake Carriers Association issued its own report in which it complimented itself on its safety record through the years, and demanded that no changes be made to current load-line regulations: the *Edmund Fitzgerald* had struck a shoal and sunk.

The Coast Guard prevailed. In response, the shipping industry began construction of the new breed of 1,100-foot-long supertankers. Some of these vessels, "super carriers" like the *Walter J. McCarthy,* are self-unloading, and capable of removing 10,000 tons of cargo from their own bellies every hour. They are also lake-locked. Too big to pass through the Welland Canal, they will never leave the Great Lakes. The spar deck of the *Walter J. McCarthy* is one-fifth of a mile long. Sailors move back and forth along it on bicycles. Some say these ships are so big that there is no place for them to find shelter during a storm.

More than a quarter of a century later, the *Edmund Fitzgerald* has become one of the most marketed shipwrecks in the world. The head office of this industry is the Great Lakes Shipwreck Museum Gift Shop in Michigan's Upper Peninsula. Situated at Whitefish Point, just north of Paradise and some seventeen miles south of where the *Big Fitz* sank, the shop is staffed by helpful, polite sales clerks run off their feet by wave after wave of eager visitors.

They are eager to buy anything with the words *"Edmund Fitzgerald"* on it or any conceivable image of its red hull and white forecastle. They've come to the right place: *Edmund Fitzgerald* mouse pads are available here for $8.95. So are *Edmund Fitzgerald* picture frames, scale-model *Edmund Fitzgerald* savings banks, playing cards, fridge magnets, key chains, and paperweights. Clothing designers are also in on the craze; a Gear brand *Edmund Fitzgerald* "25 Years a Legend" golf shirt sells for $42.95. An *Edmund Fitzgerald* sweatshirt can be had for half that. David Conkin's prints of the *Edmund Fitzgerald* are available signed and unframed for $150. The same print double-signed by Conkin and Gordon Lightfoot, the Canadian singer/songwriter, sells for just under three hundred dollars. The twenty-inch model of the *Edmund Fitzgerald* comes with a "beautiful mahogany display case," while the commemorative *Fitz* mug is a "Museum Store exclusive."

For those who can't make the drive to Whitefish Point, the museum's website offers a range of *Edmund Fitzgerald* memorabilia, collectibles, and books, which can be purchased online. They include Robert Hemming's *The Gales of November,* "a total *you are there* experience." Also Frederick Stonehouse's now classic *The Wreck of the* Edmund Fitzgerald— reprinted twenty-one times. This portable library of information includes a chapter on "The Ever Ready Bunny," explaining how interest in the *Edmund Fitzgerald* "just keeps going and going and going." To make sure children do not miss out on the *Edmund Fitzgerald* "adventure," books have been published for them: Tres Seymour's *The Gulls of the* Edmund Fitzgerald and *The* Edmund Fitzgerald *Lost with All Hands.* This book of fifty pages, "a must for every young reader," contains "actual photos." For older readers there is *29 Missing: The True and Tragic Story of the Disappearance of the SS* Edmund Fitzgerald. Described as a work of "juvenile literature," this small volume contains no photos, actual or otherwise, and is derived almost entirely from previous books.

For those who have read them all, Hugh E. Bishop's *The Night the Fitz Went Down* represents the newest addition to the library, a fascinating look at Great Lakes shipping. Bishop reminds us that "interest in the *Fitzgerald* has not diminished."

It seems the only book not widely advertised on the museum's website is one by a Canadian, Dr. Joseph MacInnis's *Fitzgerald's Storm,* published in 1997. The author is openly contemptuous of not only the museum's director, Tom Farnquist, but also of "the great American free-enterprise machine that slices and dices violence and tragedy into books, movies, talk shows, and whatever else might make a buck."

To distinguish himself from these slicing and dicing Americans, MacInnis had his book published in Canada. Prominently displayed on the back cover is the statement that "a portion of the author's royalties will be donated to the families of the *Edmund Fitzgerald* crew."

At the gift shop in Michigan's Upper Peninsula, the sales clerk explains that "if it costs between three dollars and sixty dollars and it's got the *Edmund Fitzgerald* on it, we can't keep it on the shelf." In fact, *Edmund*

*Fitzgerald* trinkets are flying off the shelf as we speak. Asked to account for this interest, she answers without hesitation, "Because it was the last one, because it was 1975, because it was the biggest, because of the twenty-nine men, and because it shouldn't have happened. We also work very hard around here to let the people know about it," she adds.

Because of that hard work a crowd has gathered at this small museum and gift shop. In some way we are here to grieve for the men of the *Edmund Fitzgerald* who perished in cold water amid the rending of metal, the screams of men, and the relentless rush of wind. We are here to brush a little closer to death by drowning. To help with this, a song plays softly in the background. Gordon Lightfoot's "The Wreck of the *Edmund Fitzgerald*" is on a loop and will play some forty times a day, seven days a week, interspersed periodically with several minutes of dreamy underwater-sounding, New Age music.

It is almost not possible to write about the *Edmund Fitzgerald* without bringing up "the song." Typically any of the growing number of authors who take on the doomed freighter will devote a chapter to it. A convention observed by nearly all is that each chapter begins with a quote from "the song" and includes, as a separate chapter or appendix, the lyrics in full. Today we know as much about the song as we do about the *Edmund Fitzgerald*.

According to MacInnis, the song "poured in profusion from [Gordon Lightfoot's] brain to his muscular arm," after drinking gallons of Irish coffee. To Robert Hemming, the mournful whine of Lightfoot's voice sounds "like the wind whistling through a ship's rigging." Another *Fitzgerald* writer calls the song not only a national hit recording, but a geological ambassador that introduces "the power and the fury of Lake Superior's legendary storms to the rest of the world." Less than a year after the *Fitzgerald*'s sinking, relatives of the twenty-nine dead men could sit in their living rooms and watch a TV ad for the album. As "The Wreck of the *Edmund Fitzgerald*" played, a cartoon body, perhaps a boyfriend or father or son, floated across the television screen, waving at them while the ship sank. In his chapter titled simply "The Song," Dr. MacInnis closes with the statement that "as the years passed the song and the shipwreck . . . became one." On November 10, when the media conducts its *Edmund*

*Fitzgerald* resurrection, journalists refer to the doomed freighter as "a pop culture legend."

In the homeland of Gordon Lightfoot there is barely a soul over the age of forty who cannot sing or at least hum a verse from "The Wreck of the *Edmund Fitzgerald*." Because of this song, it comes as a surprise to many Canadians to learn that the *Edmund Fitzgerald* was not a Canadian freighter and that the men who died on it were Americans. It did sink in Canadian waters, however, and because of this Canadian taxpayers would soon shell out nearly half a million dollars so the *Big Fitz's* bell could be placed in the Great Lakes Shipwreck Museum in Michigan.

MacInnis attributes this Canadian generosity to an incident in Somalia on March 16, 1993, when members of the now disbanded Canadian Airborne Regiment tortured, raped, and murdered a Somali teenager, Shidane Arone. The incident so tarnished the military that when Tom Farnquist concocted his scheme to remove the bell off the wreck, the Department of National Defence offered the services of the H.M.C.S. *Cormorant,* a crew of ninety, and two deepwater submersibles, free of charge for ten days.

Probably the Canadian military was unaware that Farnquist had what MacInnis calls "a long history of illegally removing archeologically significant objects from shipwrecks," or that the United States Department of Natural Resources on at least one occasion had entered his museum and seized the contents. It is unlikely the Canadians were aware of the copyright concerns over the Lightfoot song, today tinkling endlessly from the speakers in the museum.

The Canadian Armed Forces were not the only ones to be sucked deep into the vortex of the *Edmund Fitzgerald* industry. The Sony Corporation donated underwater video cameras that produced the high-resolution images in videos sold at trade shows, on websites, and at lectures. The National Geographic Society commissioned Tom Farnquist to write the article. The Sault Tribe of the Chippewa helped finance the bell's recovery with an interest-free loan. National Car Rental provided a courtesy van to transport the two-hundred-pound bell to the museum at Whitefish Point.

Before this could happen, the business had to be resolved in court. On the Ontario side, the government agreed to issue an archeological licence so that the bell could be removed. Tom Farnquist would also have to overcome his rival, former private eye, fellow diver, and *Edmund Fitzgerald* enthusiast Frederick Shannon.

In July 1994, Shannon spent seventy-five thousand dollars on Expedition '94 Ltd., which included renting a submarine and filming forty-two hours of videotape of the broken wreck of the *Edmund Fitzgerald*. Believing that Farnquist's scheme to remove the *Big Fitz*'s bell would cut into profits from this dive, Shannon sued Farnquist. When asked how the removal of the *Edmund Fitzgerald*'s bell could possibly affect the financial prospects of his client's enterprise, Shannon's lawyer answered, "He may not sell as many books." Shannon's case to stop the removal of the bell was dismissed.

Mr. Shannon finally screened his controversial video at forty dollars a ticket—controversial in that it contained images of a man's body face down in the mud. During the screening he also berated the Farnquist-initiated salvage effort that, in his words, had "raped the soul of a ship."

While Farnquist might have raped the soul of a ship, Shannon had videotaped the remains of a human corpse. In response, Michigan legislators in 1997 passed a law making it illegal to do so. "Based on the current state of American society," wrote Frederick Stonehouse, this attempt to legislate good taste was "a doomed effort."

Doomed or not, Michigan congressman Bart Stupak said of Shannon that "his intentions are immoral and tasteless. It appears his only motive to display these pictures is to make a profit." Ontario's chief coroner stated that with the discovery of the body, Ontario considered the wreck a natural gravesite. Under Ontario law these wreck sites can be visited, but no artifacts may be removed. In the United States these sites are called Submerged Cultural Resources.

Frederick Stonehouse has since offered the intriguing theory that the body found face down outside the bow of the *Big Fitz* was not one of *her* crewmen at all. In his opinion, signs of decay on the life jacket indicate the sailor came from a much older wreck, perhaps the *Inkerman* or the

*Cerisoles* that disappeared in November 1918. The body, suggests Stonehouse, is "a 'floater.'"

With a corpse on videotape and the soul of the *Edmund Fitzgerald* mounted front and centre in a tiny museum, the museum owners did the only logical thing—they built a bigger gift shop.

Today these intrigues are compounded by the swirling Babylon of the internet, on which can be found a dozen websites and some seven thousand listings for the *Edmund Fitzgerald,* interactive CD-ROMs, line-by-line "explanations of Gordon Lightfoot's legendary ballad," and downloadable MIDI files of the song itself. It is possible to read interviews with family members of crewmen who lost their lives on the doomed carrier, and to read interviews with *friends* of family members of the drowned crewmen, even with the actors who played the doomed men in the theatrical production *Holdin' Our Own.* An internet rumour has the movie in the works.

It is also possible to hear in Real Audio the captain of the *Arthur M. Anderson* reporting tensely through a wall of static the suspected loss of the *Big Fitz* to the United States Coast Guard. You can ponder the ruminations of a thirty-three-year-old *Fitzgerald* gadfly who, when asked if the wreck is becoming too commercial, answers, "Not until it becomes a child's toy at Wal-Mart."

Those saddened by the commercialization of this tragedy can cry into their beer. *The Edmund Fitzgerald* Porter, brewed by the Great Lakes Brewing Company of Cleveland, is said to produce "a nice smooth tan head, and leaves a small degree of lacework on the glass." Apparently the "deep qualification" of this beer cannot be overemphasized.

For novel readers, there is Joan Skelton's *The Survivor of the* Edmund Fitzgerald, perhaps the only attempt by a woman writer to piggyback onto the *Big Fitz* action. Those still fed up can escape to the theatre and enjoy the *Edmund Fitzgerald* opera, *Ten November,* with libretto by Eric Peltoniemi and Steven Dietz. The score was written by a self-confessed "land-locked lake stupid Denverite," after hearing the Gordon Lightfoot song and drinking large amounts of "exceptional coffee"—perhaps the same coffee said to have caused the song to pour forth in such profusion in the first place.

At the gift shop another wave of tourists is pouring through the aisles, unravelling T-shirts and wrongly reshelving *Edmund Fitzgerald* paper-weights among the *Edmund Fitzgerald* playing cards. The sales clerk is at the far end of the store arranging a cluster of pale, innocuous objects that resemble shortbread cookies. Like the *Edmund Fitzgerald,* they could be anything. In its celebrated death, the *Edmund Fitzgerald* has become a legendary folk song, a good beer, an image embossed on trinkets. It has been heralded as proof of humanity's arrogance, of the failure of science and the limits of technology.

Now, in the corner of a large gift shop a new incarnation has been brought to market. Laid out on a white tablecloth lie a row of *Edmund Fitzgerald* heart-shaped Christmas-tree decorations.

Across the lawn from the gift shop, visitors stand in line waiting to see a bell that once was mounted on the S.S. *Edmund Fitzgerald.* A song composed by a Canadian singer/songwriter plays continually in the back-ground. It is an eerie, affecting song and will play for a long time yet. Trinkets can be had, among them a T-shirt with the U.S. and Canadian flags joined with the words "Voices Silent Not Forgotten."

Inside the museum a sign reads, "Let them rest in peace." The words belong to Ruth Hudson, mother of Bruce Hudson, a deckhand lost November 10, 1975, at the age of twenty-two. Her son wore flared pants and denim jackets, was crazy for motorcycles and martial arts. He died with watchman Ransom Cundy, who couldn't swim and wore a baseball cap to cover his bald head. People called him Handsome Ransom. He carried a heavy grief over the *Fitz*'s 26,000 tons of taconite pellets; his son-in-law had shot and killed his eldest daughter, then shot himself. Ray Cundy died November 10, 1975. So did Jack McCarthy, the first mate. He wore steel-rimmed glasses and lost his own captaincy twenty-five years earlier when he grounded his vessel, the *Ben E. Tate,* in Lake Erie. He had ambitions to become a writer. Third Mate Mike Armagost weighed 230 pounds and had once ridden a horse into a bar in Iron River, Wisconsin. He died with Bob Rafferty, steward. Rafferty's wife said of her husband, "If I threw water on the house and shook it, maybe he would have stayed home more."

Twenty-four others died that night. They hailed from common places: Milwaukee, Houghton, Toledo, Washburn, Moquah, Ashtabula . . . Their names were Oliver, Russ, Dave, Blaine, Gordon, Ernest, John, Jim, Nolan, Tom, Mark, Joe, and many others.

The common names of men. The voices made silent.

# 17

# *Calling the Wolf by Name*

*As for Madeline Island, the Chippewas called
it a long Indian name meaning woodpecker.*

—GUY M. BURNHAM

View from Neys, a contraction of Doheyneys

*O*n a summer day many years ago a woman sat in a canoe in the mouth
of a river, eating from a bowl. She didn't know the lake in front of her
was Lake Superior. To her it was perhaps Kitche Gami, or Chigaaming.
She did not know that the birchbark vessel she floated in was a "canoe"—
a corruption of a Spanish word or Portuguese, *canoa*, which dates back to
Columbus, and made its way into the French as *canot*, and English as

*canoe.* She didn't know the bowl she was eating from was a "bowl." To her it was *Ontoga,* or something similar to that.

She ate leisurely, feeling the steady lap of the river against the boat, the rise and fall of the vessel. The sun scattered across the water and warmed her eyes. Several baited lines trailed in the water.

As she put her fingers to the bowl and then to her mouth, a cloud of pigeons broke from behind the trees on the riverbank, startling her. In that moment the bowl slipped from her hand. She reached for it, but too late. The bowl disappeared into the river. Peering over the side she saw her own reflection in the water.

*"Ontonagon,"* she cried sadly—"my bowl is gone."

This, reportedly, is how Michigan's Ontonagon River got its name. Today it sounds as if a committee of poets had deliberately made it up, so that centuries later we might get a glimpse of the people who lived and died here and whose descendants still live here. In this little story is sounded a people's stoicism, the play of irony and self-mockery, the dance of humour and the quietude of wisdom.

It is not much different from other northern stories of equally questionable origin. When the duke of Windsor paid his first visit to the Canadian North, he sat down to a restaurant meal *à la façon du pays.* When he was finished, he laid his fork across his plate, at which a sharp-eyed waitress reportedly sang out, "Keep your fork, Duke. There's pie!"

This doubtful vignette cuts to the heart of the North. It speaks of common sense, common folk, and a shortage of cutlery. More important, it speaks of pie.

The role of pie in the overall history of North America has been grossly overlooked. In a land that teems with berries, it's inevitable that this food would take on a wide significance. When it came time to set the dessert menu for the extravagant CPR dining cars, William Van Horne made it clear "that deep apple, peach and etc. pie should be the standard." On the maps of Superior the great Groseilliers himself exists only once—as *pie filling.* The Gooseberry River as it appears on most modern maps of Minnesota was once the Groseilliers River, Lake Superior's only physical reference to Radisson's quiet and epileptic companion. Perhaps, as one historian has suggested, "pioneers and lumberjacks, uninspired by the name of a great explorer, preferred the shorter name." Or maybe an over-worked typesetter changed it on a whim. Until very recently, the river had a tendency to wander up and down the shoreline with each new map.

For Canadians the ascendency of pie is taken for granted. It does not surprise us to find Pie Island on the map of Lake Superior. The American traveller Morris Longstreth was not so understanding. In his opinion, "only a Pudding-Head would call a place Pie Island."

This remark aside, the naming of places is held to be an extremely serious business. Scholars insist it is how men appropriate land; our fierce nomenclature marches in front of us like Cortez's soldiers, raping, pillaging, taking what belongs to others and claiming it for our own. In this way we render the foreign familiar. According to Professor W. H. New, at the very least it involves "the map-making metaphor—the collocation of images that connects explorer with map-maker with claimer and namer." The professor goes on to explain that fortunately modern scholarship is about to change all this, and one day soon we will be able to "reject in short the maleness, the implication of sexual conquest, claim, proprietorship, that is implicit in the explorer image of empire and penetration (of continent of body) . . . [so that] an image of landscape in motion replaces the image of land-as-a-static-territory-to-be-named-into-compliance, and so confined."

In fairness to the professor, some names *are* imposed in the official and ponderous way he describes. Henry Rowe Schoolcraft worked day after day inventing names. A solemn, self-important figure at his desk, he received a salary from the United States government to attach names to a land mass recently divided into parcels. Married to a half-Native woman whose own name sounded the beauty of a starry night, Schoolcraft chose to improve on the Native names by using his linguistic knowledge to concoct Native-*sounding* names. His attempt to have Lake Superior renamed "Algoma" was not successful, although the word has since been sucked deep into the region's nomenclature. In Sault Ste. Marie, Ontario, it is possible to find Algoma Septic and Algoma Fingerprint Specialists, among others.

Through the power of their names, Native cultures are presumed to enter the magic of place and legend. By ours we are said to stabilize the unknown, make the New World rigid enough to support the assumptions of the Old one. When this gridlock has been imposed on the New World we may, like the settler Susanna Moodie, announce triumphantly, "The rough has been made smooth, the crooked has been made straight."

Thankfully not all namings carry with them the oppressiveness that so intrigues Professor New. Travellers on the crooked highway across the top of Lake Superior have no choice but to pass over Missing Horse Creek, a trickle of water in a deep wooded gorge. The name conjures a hardier day of prospectors and miners, of large loads strapped to the backs of uncomplaining horses. Conjured also is the catastrophic moment when the horse goes missing, the grubstake is lost, and lives ruined. A family's destiny is contained in Missing Horse Creek. A few miles later as the traveller hurtles across Dead Horse Creek, the story is complete: a horse goes missing at one creek, is found dead at another. Here is a brief, no-nonsense northern narrative with a beginning and end. Like many northern stories it has no middle. Between the start and finish exist a region's history and a glimpse at the people who lived in it.

In territory evoked by such names it is inevitable that a member of the royal family would be told to keep his fork because of pie. Here an unnamed bay can be called Noname Bay. Train men in a hurry designate one place Miles, and spell the next place backwards to make Selim. This intriguing dyslexia was common during the building of the railway, and speaks of the back and forth of trains, the sudden imposition of history that, like so much history, consists of a couple of guys horsing around. The Canadian last spike was driven in at Noslo on the North Shore, near Jackfish. Noslo is neither a town nor a village, nor even a train stop, just a name invented to provide a tag by which to remember a ceremony. Noslo. Presumably the job of creating this place was given to a man named Olson.

Lake Superior exists in three major languages. Each of them has laid a patina of names over the region, creating a world and a portrait of the people who inhabit it. The French came to Superior enthralled by the story of a virgin birth. The long waterway that brought them to the eastern tip of Superior they called "Sainte Marie." The local people were content with Kitchi Gami Ssebi, which is taken to mean "the River of the Great Lake." The rapids where the Natives gathered each year to harvest the whitefish also fall within the ken of a Catholic narrative. In faraway places the young mother of Christ had her name supplanting the names of a people whose language she could not speak, and whose own god-like entity had also sprung from a virgin birth.

The Jesuits believed the islands off the Bayfield Peninsula were twelve in number and named them the Twelve Apostles. When it was understood that these islands numbered more than twenty, the Twelve was deleted. Today of those twenty-two islands, one maintains an aboriginal name—Manitou Island.

The interplay of Ojibwa, French, and English is the epic poem of this region. French and English words, like the strangers who spoke them, were invited into local Native communities, into homes, and into wedlock and onto rush mats. From these unions they gave birth to new and delightful children. Bishop Baraga ushered curious Ojibwa into his church with a simple "boo zhoo." This greeting, widely used by Natives throughout the South Shore, is believed to be a corruption of the French *bonjour*. A French voyageur and an Ojibwa hunter could meet on a path, greet each other with a "boo zhoo," and continue on, convinced that each of them had said hello in the other person's language.

Chequamegon, Wisconsin, the site of some of the first Jesuit arrivals on Superior, has been spelled an estimated forty different ways. By examining Schoolcraft's explanations of the Native syllables, *Kaw* and *gon*, historian Guy Burnham explains its meaning as "the Bay of the Long Point." William Warren, the American historian whose mother was Ojibwa, records a story that Nanabozho cornered the Great Beaver here, but that it escaped by crashing out through the soft mud; hence Changouamig ("Soft Beaver Dam") or Shagawamik ("At the Soft Beaver Dam"). Johann Kohl spelled the word "Shaguamikon" and was confident it meant "something gnawed on all sides." There is some suggestion that Chequamegon, in fact, is entirely of French origin and has no Native roots whatsoever. A voyageur once saw a yellow dog on a South Shore riverbank and named the place Rivière Chien Jaune. When English traders came by a century later they heard not "Chien Jaune," but "St. John" and labelled it that way on their maps. When Louis Agassiz's party went looking for a stream called Flea River in the mid-1800s, they had to content themselves with the Rivière aux Crapauds—"Toad River." Some of Agassiz's men ascended a mountain and christened it Mount Cambridge—in case it had not yet been named.

According to Johann Kohl, the Ojibwa made few distinctions between sun and moon. The moon was the "night sun," and the full moon was the "round night sun." He soon discovered they divided the year into twelve moons, and February was "the moon of the suckers," because in that month the fish started upriver. March was "the moon of the snow crust," June "the strawberry moon," September "the moon of the wild rice," and so on. Kohl describes watching two old men argue heatedly about which month they were in.

In these namings are displayed the basic practicality of Ojibwa speech. In each name exists a small library of information about place. Anyone wishing to spear fish by torchlight might consider going to Wauswaugoning, "The Bay Where They Spear Fish by Torchlight." The present-day Reservation River tells a predictable story about the relation between Natives and white administrators. Its earlier name told about Natives and their relationship to the region, Mawskiquawcawnawsebi—"High Bush Cranberry Marsh River."

One of the earliest written names for Lake Superior was Lac des Nadouessioux, referring to the Dakota people living on the western shore. The name Lac Superieur is prosaic and means "the lake at the top," or "the upper one," to distinguish it from "the lower lakes." In the 1600s the Jesuit Claude-Jean Allouez changed the name to Lac Tracy, to honour a Quebec nobleman and official. This marked perhaps the first regional use of naming to pay homage to a benefactor or patron. Louis sieur de la Ronde honoured two wealthy men by naming Lake Superior islands after them. Isle Philippeaux he named to appease Jean-Frederic Phelpeaux, an opponent of his mining schemes. He named another Pontchartrain to celebrate Phelpeaux's father. That neither of these islands existed did not bother La Ronde. He made them up because he found them useful. Cartographers so commonly inked them onto maps that Benjamin Franklin claimed half of Isle Philippeaux for the United States during negotiations of the Treaty of Paris in 1783.

In "The Wreck of the *Edmund Fitzgerald*," Gordon Lightfoot sings of a big lake that "they" call by the name of Gitchee Gumee. "They" here are meant to be the Ojibwa. For the last century almost all non-Native commentators on Lake Superior have taken it for granted that the Native people universally referred to Lake Superior as Gitche Gumee. What they mean is that the non-Native Henry Wadsworth Longfellow called it that in his 1855 classic, *The Song of Hiawatha*.

This poem became so famous that it made living Natives unnecessary. White visitors were soon voicing their disappointment in the American Indian for not living up to Longfellow's descriptions. They found the living Natives dirty, unromantic, and reluctant to speak in the odd trochaic tetrameter of the celebrated poem. Writing in 1929, Guy Burnham informs his readers that "the simple Chippewa still reverence the squirrel, which *remembering the words of Hiawatha* they call a-jetamo." It seems that without *Hiawatha*, the locals would have had no name for "squirrel." A CPR brochure distributed to its North-seeking clientele stated confidently that "the legend of Hiawatha was taught to all

Ojibway children, as soon as they can lisp." What the brochure means is that the poem was taught to all *white* children the moment they could read.

On the South Shore in 1855, Johann Kohl found Kitchi Gami the prevalent descriptive for Lake Superior, and so used it to title his book. Publications by the Pukaskwa National Park on the Canadian side suggest that the Anishnabe translation for Lake Superior is Chegaming, "the Spirit Ocean," and that area Natives have known it by that name for centuries. Those same officials are less confident when it comes to translating Pukaskwa (pronounced "Puckasaw" or "Puckasu"), a word they suggest means "Place of Safe Harbour," "Place of Evil," or "Eater of the Marrow of Bones." Here, according to one legend, Joe Pukaskwa killed his wife, Sarah, and threw her burnt bones into the river.

Tentativeness regarding Native names is apparent on both sides of Superior. Lake Gogebic lies some twenty miles inland from Silver City, Michigan. Not many years ago it was known as Agogebic, which, according to a sign posted there, means "Smooth Rock" or "Little Fish" or "Nest of Porcupines" or "Rocky Shore" or "Place of Diving" or "Porcupine Lake." The sign concedes that perhaps "the true meaning has been obscured by the years." Another sign nearby explains more confidently that the frogs on the shores of this lake employ the backs of their eyeballs to push food down their throats.

Some names seem to sound the rhythm and pitch of Lake Superior, such as Manitou Shainse, who signed the Robinson Superior Treaty in 1850. Today his *X* on that document is considered a mark of illiteracy, but it could point equally to his humility. Kohl was repeatedly frustrated when he attempted to determine a Native's name. Even to get it from someone else was a difficult task. According to him, "If you ask an Ojibwe woman 'To whom does the gun belong?' and it is her husband's gun, she will say, 'It belongs to *him*.' If you ask, further, who she means by *him,* she will reply, 'The man who has a seat there,' and point with her hand to her husband's seat."

For whatever reason, Kohl could not persuade locals to speak their names. He once confronted an Ojibwa man and demanded he identify himself. The fellow considered the request, turned to a friend, and said, "*You* tell him my name."

It did not take long for the Natives along the shores of Superior to learn the language brought to them by voyageur French Canadians and English-speaking traders. With it they freely communicated to highly educated ethnographers, geologists, authors, art critics, aristocrats, and bored middle-aged men and women showing up on the South Shore, eager to put some spice into their lives and write yet another book about the "Indian." These men and women, fluent in French, English, German, Italian, and Latin, were desperate to record what they could about a people they passionately believed to be on the verge of extinction.

At some point the Germans even invented a word for this. They called it *Europamudigkeit,* "a weariness or sickness with Europe." Out of this weariness was born the desire to experience Wilderness and to know the North American Native—in many European publications the Native and the Wilderness were the same thing. It was a weariness that blew Radisson across the Atlantic Ocean twenty-four times. It drove Étienne Brûlé through his life and his death. Weariness with Europe fascinated two generations of Europeans with the "Indian" writings of the German author Karl May, and made him fabulously successful. It hurried Anna Jameson down the Soo rapids in a canoe, a must-do tourist activity for which local Ojibwa would soon charge five dollars a trip. It caused a British orphan named Archie Belaney to re-invent himself as Grey Owl and roll a spoon back and forth over his nose to flatten it.

Today Lake Superior is still marketed this way: "Superior by nature." "The call of the wild." "A wild and unpopulated region . . . sought out by those who seek nature in its rawest form." As that nature becomes less raw and the wilderness less wild, the nomenclature is forced into increasingly bizarre contortions to cover for it. In Houghton, Michigan, it is possible to clean your car at the Wilderness Car Wash.

Names in their diversity constitute the flesh and blood of a place. They become embedded in its history until they are its history. In 1936 the Marathon Paper Mills Company of Wisconsin built a paper mill on the Canadian shore and thus created the town of Marathon. The hotel, the Everest, was named after a mill official. Locals to this day still call it the "Never Rest," a once reliable source of gossip and scandal. According to the billboards, Marathon is "Superior in the Long Run." People who live in the Goulais River region of Lake Superior call themselves Gooligans. A northern chip-truck operation has painted on its side "Lord of the Fries." The Bite Me Bait and Tackle shop offers "24 hour emergency service."

History, or at least down-home pride, is read in these signs. A plaque near the St. Marys River proudly announces that Sault Ste. Marie is the home of Canada's "largest backlit mural." Another sign reminds visitors that the Soo is home to Canada's first woman astronaut, Dr. Roberta Bondar, who rode the space shuttle in 1992. Other signs advertise the Canadian Bush Plane Museum. The science of fighting forest fires from the sky was pioneered here at the Soo. Some stories suggest that pilots first developed their techniques by water-bombing a young woman as she lay sunbathing in a green bikini on the south side of Queen Street.

The *Chief Shingwauk* pulls out of Sault Ste. Marie, Ontario, three times daily, taking visitors on a tour of the Soo Locks. According to tour handouts, the *Chief Shingwauk* is named after "a very popular local Ojibway chief." The handouts neglect to mention that a Chief Shingwauk was popular largely for leading an armed attack against a local mine in 1848. That mine was located in a place called Mica Bay, north of Coppermine Point and south of Silver Islet. These names indicate a vision of Superior as burned into the minds of engineers and businessmen, a place from which wealth can be taken and transported somewhere else.

Along the North Shore place names pay tribute to the ascendancy of the engineer. Nearly every town is named after the engineering contractor who laid in the rails there. Rossport, in memory of Walter Ross, a naming that reflects an Anglo-Saxon ideal of effort and honour. Unfortunately, Rossport leads us back only to Mr. Ross, an interesting subject no doubt, but one that ultimately shuts out the nuances that define a place. If Rossport had retained its Native name, perhaps the American yacht *Gunilda* might not have sunk here: Bawgawashinge— "Shallow Water Over the Bar."

The changing of names is usually catastrophic to our comprehension of place, reflecting the intrusion of another forceful culture with its own understanding of what's real and what matters. When a religious revival meeting took place on Lake Herbert, near Mellen, Wisconsin, in the 1920s, an overflowing of enthusiasm caused locals to rename the lake Lake Galilee. While such a name celebrates an event that took place here, it also obliterates the existence of pioneer William Herbert. Mrs. William Herbert is said to have been a sister of Mr. Tom Martin's father, who for many years ran an Ashland sawmill. And on it goes, the commonplace threads of local history that finally form the entire garment. All of these interconnections are lost forever behind Lake Galilee.

Rossport, Port Coldwell, Mica Bay: the names stand in sharp contrast to Monigwanekaning on the American side, translated as "Place of the Golden-Breasted Woodpecker" or "Place Where There Are Many Lapwings." These creatures are integral to place. They utter sounds by which a place is recognized, sounds that start and reverberate through childhood and life. Animal sounds are interpreted by the people who live among them. To the Ojibwa the cry of the squirrel was once, some say, a portent of death. Selwyn Dewdney, the author of *Indian Rock Painting of the Great Lakes*, spent so much time deciphering the cries of the loon that he claimed to be able to distinguish seven different calls. The seventh, he said, was the cry the loon makes when it spots an eagle, "You are the king!" Two hundred years ago voyageurs on Superior could make loons circle about their heads by shouting "oory oory," a term thought to be Native for "hurrah." Today, the cry of the loon is rare on Superior's South Shore. The guttural song of the Personal Water Craft has replaced it, as they roar back and forth all day on the same crucial bays where the loons would otherwise nest.

Little Girl Point in Michigan is such a place. The scenic road leading to it is lined with modern pictographs. Unlike the older ones that fascinated Dewdney, painted in ochre and congealed with sturgeon oil, these have a meaning that is undeniably clear: "KEEP OUT" . . . "NO TRESPASSING" . . . "PRIVATE PROPERTY." These signs intone a relatively recent language of exclusion and ownership. No whisper of a genial "boo zhoo" can be heard in them.

Colonel Thomas McKenney noted of this spot that a little girl had drowned here. She was Ojibwa, presumably, her father a French Canadian. The name is still found on maps. Typographical inconsistencies sometimes make it "Little Girls Point," commemorating, on this spot, the grief for every girl child drowned in Superior. On sunny days brave children try to immerse themselves in the water on this shore. They stand sometimes knee deep but no farther. Little Girl Point is now a boat launch and kayak put-in place. Sea-Doos keen endlessly.

Of the names that make up the roll call of Lake Superior the names of ships must be included: from the *Manhattan* to the *Benjamin Noble,* from the *Pitz* to the *Grandpa Woo,* which foundered in 1996. With these names go a muster roll of drowned sailors and even airmen, men such as Pilot Bakla Jr. and his radarman, Lieutenant Nelson, who scrambled a Scorpion jet fighter from the Kincheloe Air Force base and disappeared forever over Superior in November 1953 while tracking a UFO.

To name Lake Superior means to name settlers such as Mrs. Tilley of Goulais River, who, during a spring flood, paddled a canoe out to her marooned cows to milk them. A doctor named Charles Smellie on more than one occasion hopped a westbound freight train to treat patients along the North Shore. Another man, Charlie Carlson, had three children who rode ice floes across Mamainse Harbour, to go to school. His name sounds the Scandinavian presence, the private and public saunas in Duluth, Thunder Bay, and many other towns. Finns and Ojibwa who intermarried in the Keweenaw area were called Finndians. The Hoito rooming house in Thunder Bay mounts a monumental breakfast that routinely sees people lining up in the street. The Hoito was once run by the residents who lived in it, a taste of Finnish labour relations. Across the lake a large banner hangs from a building in Marquette: "American Unions—The People Who Brought You the Weekend."

Down the way on Highway 61 a storm is blowing over the Minnesota coast of Lake Superior. Cars pull over, men get out to check ropes and hitches. Inside their vehicles people watch a brutal wind skid a full garbage can across the asphalt. As quickly as it comes, the storm is gone, the sky opens and a double rainbow arcs through the turquoise and plunks one end of itself down on the surface of the lake. A swollen Temperance River staggers drunkenly beneath the highway. "Cutface Creek" and "Devil Track River" race down the gorges on their way to the water. "Danger: Extremely Cold Water" . . . "Taconite" . . . "Beaver Bay" . . . "Duluth." Signs are everywhere, for whitefish, for dew worms, for something called a hush puppy. In the Great Lakes Aquarium at Duluth a sign warns ominously, "Lake Superior encompasses one tenth of all there is."

Early in the twentieth century, loggers came through the Bayfield Peninsula, cursing, spitting, swapping swamp tales, and cutting pine boards wider than the length of a man's arm. When they left people called what they left behind the Bayfield Barrens. Thirty years later it was still called the Bayfield Barrens.

Today Lucky Highway 13 traces the length of the peninsula to the Red Cliff Indian Reservation. Here at the Isle Vista Casino, a Native American Music Festival is drawing sparse crowds under cover of a tent. In the casino next door men with long plaited hair and bolo ties nod quietly at complete strangers and call them "brother."

According to a legend that is centuries old, the world will be healed near to this spot. A boy will come. He will uncover the scroll of the Seventh Council Fire composed long ago before the Ojibwa dispersal and buried in the walls of the South Shore, here on Superior at "the Place Where Food Grows on Water"—that food being wild rice. Through this child with peculiar shining eyes, a lasting peace will come upon the earth.

Beneath the tent the bands mount and dismount the stage: the Black Bear Band, the Wolf River Band, Frank Anakwad Montano, the No Reservations Band. A song starts up, a lonesome dirge of men, women, cigarettes, trains, trucks, and liquor. "Hurting time," proclaims one singer, stepping back to reveal a smiling three-hundred-pound drummer wearing a T-shirt that states, "No One Knows I'm Elvis."

The band plays. A white, full moon dangles over Superior. Two lovers sit off in the darkness between the wigwams and medicine tents. In the parking lot gleaming cars proclaim the plates of Wisconsin, Michigan, Minnesota. Here and there a bumper sticker reads, "LAKE SUPERIOR: THE FIFTY-FIRST STATE."

# Bibliography

**BOOKS**

Adam, Arthur T., ed. *The Explorations of Pierre Esprit Radisson.* Loren Kallsen, modernizer. Minneapolis, Minn.: Ross & Haines, 1961.

Agassiz, Louis. *Lake Superior, with a Narrative of the Tour by J. Elliot Cabot.* 1850. Facsimile, Huntington, N.Y.: Robert E. Kreiger Publishing Co., 1974.

American History Class of L'Anse High School, *History of L'Anse Township.* Chapbook. L'Anse, Mich.: L'Anse Sentinel, 1922.

Baraga, Rev. Frederic. *Chippewa Indians as Recorded by Rev. Frederic Baraga in 1847.* No. 10. New York: Studia Slovenica, 1976.

Barr, Elinor. *Silver Islet: Striking It Rich in Lake Superior.* Toronto: Natural Heritage/Natural History Inc., 1988.

Baxter, T. S. H. *Quiet Coves and Rocky Highlands: Exploring Lake Superior.* Wawa, Ont.: Superior Lore, 1985.

Berlo, Jane Catherine, ed. *The Early Years of Native American Art History.* Seattle: University of Washington Press, 1992.

Bertrand, J. P. *Timber Wolves: Greed and Corruption in Northwestern Ontario's Timber Industry, 1875–1960.* Thunder Bay, Ont.: Thunder Bay Historical Museum Society, 1997.

Bigsby, John J. *The Shoe and Canoe; or, Pictures of Travel in the Canadas.* 2 vols. London: Chapman & Hall, 1850.

Bishop, Hugh E., in cooperation with Dudley Paquette. *The Night the Fitz Went Down.* Duluth, Minn.: Lake Superior Port Cities, Inc., 2000.

Bogue, Margaret Beattie, and Virginia A. Palmer. *Around the Shores of Lake Superior: A Guide to Historic Sites.* Madison: University of Wisconsin Sea Grant College Program, 1979.

Boultbee, Jean. *Pic, Pulp and People: A History of the Marathon District.* Marathon, Ont.: Township of Marathon, 1981.

Bowen, Dana Thomas. *Lore of the Lakes.* Cleveland, Ohio: Freshwater Press, 1940.

Brehm, Victoria, ed. *The Women's Great Lakes Reader.* Duluth, Minn.: Holy Cow Press, 1998.

Bremer, Richard G. *Indian Agent and Wilderness Scholar: The Life of Henry Rowe Schoolcraft.* Mount Pleasant, Mich.: Clarke Historical Library, Central Michigan University, 1987.

Burnham, Guy M. *The Lake Superior Country in History and in Story.* 1929. Reprint, Park Falls, Wis.: Paradigm Press, 1996.

Butterfield, Consul Willshire. *History of Brûlé's Discoveries and Explorations.* Cleveland, Ohio: Helman-Taylor Co., 1898.

Campbell, Marjorie Wilkins. *The North West Company.* Toronto: Macmillan, 1957.

Carter, James L., and Ernest H. Ranking, eds. *North to Lake Superior: The Journal of Charles W. Penny, 1840.* Marquette, Mich.: John M. Longyear Research Library, 1970.

Carver, Jonathan. *The Journals of Jonathan Carver and Related Documents, 1766–1770.* Ed. John Parker. St. Paul: Minnesota Historical Society Press, 1976.

Charlevoix, Pierre François-Xavier de. *Journal of a Voyage to North America.* London: R. and J. Dodsley, 1761.

Chisholm, Barbara, and Andrea Gutsche. *Under the Shadow of the Gods.* Toronto: Lynx Images Inc., 1999.

Chute, Janet. *The Legacy of Shingwaukonse: A Century of Native Leadership.* Toronto: University of Toronto Press, 1998.

Craig, John. *The Noronic Is Burning.* Toronto: General Publishing, 1976.

Cujes, Rudolph P. *Ninidjanissidog Saiagiinagog: Contribution of the Slovenes to the Socio-cultural Development of the Canadian Indians.* Antigonish, N.S.: St. Francis Xavier University, 1968.

Danzinger, Edmund Jefferson, Jr. *The Chippewas of Lake Superior.* Norman: University of Oklahoma Press, 1979.

Dean, Pauline. *Sagas of Superior: The Inland Sea and Its Canadian Shore.* Manitowadge, Ont.: Great Spirit Writers, 1992.

Davie, Donald. *Two Ways Out of Whitman.* Manchester, U.K.: Carcanet Press, 2000.

Devens, Carol. *Countering Colonization: Native American Women and Great Lakes Missions, 1630–1900.* Berkeley: University of California Press, 1992.

Dewdney, Selwyn. *Indian Rock Painting of the Great Lakes.* Toronto: University of Toronto Press, 1967.

*Dictionary of Canadian Biography,* vols. 1, 2, 8, 9, 10. Toronto: University of Toronto Press, 1969.

Donnelly, Joseph P. *Jacques Marquette S. J., 1637–1675.* Chicago: Loyola University Press, 1968.

Douglas, Dan. *Northern Algoma: A People's History.* Toronto: Dundurn Press, 1995.

Drew, Wayland. *Superior: The Haunted Shore*. Toronto: Gage Publishing, 1975.

Drier, Roy Ward, and Octave Joseph DuTemple. *Prehistoric Mining in the Lake Superior Region*. Calumet, Mich.: private publication, 1961.

Fahlstrom, Paul Gerin. *The Great Copper Boulder of Ontonagon*. Tracys Landing, Md.: self-published, 1994.

Gilman, Carolyn. *The Grand Portage Story*. St. Paul: Minnesota Historical Society Press, 1992.

Gray, Charlotte. *Flint & Feather: The Life and Times of E. Pauline Johnson, Tekahionwake*. Toronto: Harper Flamingo Canada, 2002.

Gutsche, Andrea, and Cindy Bisaillon. *Mysterious Islands*. Toronto: Lynx Images, 1999.

Hale, Horatio, ed. *Iroquois Book of Rites*. Philadelphia, Penn.: D. G. Brinton, 1883.

Hall, Charlotte, M.D. *A Journey to the Western Islands, Samuel Johnson and James Boswell*. Camp Hill, Penn.: Recorded Books, 1988.

Harmon, Daniel Williams. *Sixteen Years in the Indian Country: The Journal of Daniel Williams Harmon, 1800–1816*. Ed. W. Kaye Lamb. Toronto: Macmillan, 1957.

Hatcher, Harlan, and Erich A. Walter. *A Pictorial History of the Great Lakes*. New York: American Legacy Press, 1958.

Hemingway, Ernest. "The Big Two-Hearted River: Part I." In *The Short Stories of Ernest Hemingway*. New York: Charles Scribner's Sons, 1953.

Hemming, Robert J. *The Gales of November*. Chicago: Contemporary Books, 1981.

Hogan, John Sheridan. *Canada: An Essay*. Montreal: B. Dawson, 1855.

Holling, Holling Clancy. *Paddle-to-the-Sea*. New York: Houghton Mifflin, 1941.

James, Edwin, M.D. *A Narrative of the Captivity and Adventures of John Tanner During Thirty Years Residence Among the Indians in the Interior of North America*. New York: G. & C. & H. Carvill, 1830. Reprint, Minneapolis, Minn.: Ross & Haines, 1956.

Jameson, Anna. *Winter Studies and Summer Rambles in Canada*. Toronto: McClelland & Stewart, 1923.

Jamison, James K. *By Cross and Anchor: The Story of Frederic Baraga on Lake Superior*. Paterson, N.J.: St. Anthony Guild Press, 1946.

Jamison, Knox. *The History of Ontonagon County Towns*. Ontonagon County, Mich.: self-published, 1967.

Jasen, Patricia. *Wild Things, Nature, Culture, and Tourism in Ontario, 1790–1914*. Toronto: University of Toronto Press, 1995.

Johnston, Patricia Condon. *Eastman Johnson's Lake Superior Indians*. Afton, Minn.: Johnston Publishing, 1983.

Kantar, Andrew. *Twenty-Nine Missing: The True and Tragic Story of the Disappearance of the SS* Edmund Fitzgerald. East Lansing: Michigan State University Press, 1998.

Kennedy, J. H. *Jesuit and Savage in New France.* New Haven, Conn.: Yale University Press, 1950.

Kenton, Edna, ed. *The Jesuit Relations and Allied Documents.* New York: Albert & Charles Boni, 1925.

Kinietz, W. Vernon. *The Indians of the Western Great Lakes 1615–1760.* Ann Arbour: University of Michigan Press, 1965.

Knight, James. *The Founding of Churchill: Being the journal of Captain James Knight, governor-in-chief in Hudson Bay from the 14th of July to the 13th of September, 1717.* Ed. James F. Kenny. Toronto: Dent, 1932.

Kohl, Johann Georg. *Kitchi-Gami: Life among the Lake Superior Ojibway.* 1860. Reprint, St. Paul: Minnesota Historical Society Press, 1985.

Lambert, Bernard. *Shepherd of the Wilderness: A Biography of Bishop Frederic Baraga.* Sydney, Australia: Business Offset Service, 1968.

Lewis, Janet. *The Invasion: A Narrative of Events Concerning the Johnston Family of St. Mary.* New York: Harcourt Brace, 1932.

Longfellow, Henry Wadsworth. *The Song of Hiawatha.* 1855. Reprint, New York: Bounty Books, 1968.

Longstreth, T. Morris. *The Lake Superior Country.* Toronto: McClelland & Stewart, 1924.

MacDonald, Bill. *Emanations of Silver Islet.* Thunder Bay, Ont.: Porphry Press, 1995.

MacInnis, Joseph. *Fitzgerald's Storm.* Toronto: Macmillan, 1997.

Marcella, Jeanne, ed. *A History of Jackfish.* Terrace Bay, Ont.: Terrace Bay Public Library, 1986.

Marshal, Jim. *Lake Superior Journal: Jim Marshall's Views from the Bridge.* Duluth, Minn.: Lake Superior Port Cities, Inc., 1999.

Mason, Philip P. Introduction to *Copper Country Journal: The Diary of Schoolmaster Henry Hobart, 1863–1864.* Detroit, Mich.: Wayne State University Press, 1991.

Mason, Roger Burford. *Travels in the Shining Island: The Story of James Evans and the Invention of the Cree Syllabary Alphabet.* Toronto: Natural Heritage/Natural History, 1996.

Mason, Ronald J. *Great Lakes Archaeology.* New York and Toronto: Academic Press, 1981.

McKay, H. H. *Fishes of Ontario.* Toronto: Ontario Department of Lands and Forests, 1963.

McKenney, Thomas L. *Sketches of a Tour to the Lakes: of the Character and Customs of the Chippeway Indians and of Incidents connected with the Treaty of Fond du Lac.* 1826. Reprint, Minneapolis, Minn.: Ross & Haines, 1959.

McNeice, Gladys. *The Ermatinger Family of Sault Ste. Marie.* Sault Ste. Marie, Mich.: Creative Printing House, 1984.

Murdoch, Angus. *Boom Copper: The Story of the First U.S. Mining Boom.* New York: Macmillan, 1960.

New, W. H. *Land Sliding: Imagining Space, Presence, and Power in Canadian Writing.* Toronto: University of Toronto Press, 1997.

Niedecker, Lorraine. "Lake Superior." In Donald Davie, *Two Ways Out of Whitman.* Manchester, U.K.: Carcanet Press, 2000.

Nute, Grace Lee. *Lake Superior.* New York and Indianapolis: Bobbs Merrill, 1944.

———. *The Voyageur.* New York: D. Appleton & Co., 1931.

Osborn, C. S. *The Soo.* 1887. Reprint, Grand Rapids, Mich.: Black Letter Press, 1983.

Osborn, Chase, and Stellanova Osborn. *Schoolcraft, Longfellow, Hiawatha.* Lancaster, Penn.: Jacques Cattell Press, 1942.

Parkman, Francis. *LaSalle and the Discovery of the Great West.* New York: Signet Classics, 1963.

Perrot, Nicolas. "Memoir on the Manners, Customs, and Religion of the Savages of North America." In *The Indian Tribes of the Upper Mississippi Valley and Region of the Great Lakes.* Trans. and ed. Emma Helen Blair. Cleveland, Ohio: Arthur H. Clark Co., 1911.

Pratt, E. J. "Brébeuf and his Brethren." In *Collected Works.* Toronto: Macmillan, 1944.

Radisson, Pierre Esprit. *The Voyages of Peter Esprit Radisson.* New York: Publication of the Prince Society, 1885.

Rajnovich, Grace. *Reading Rock Art.* Toronto: Natural Heritage/Natural History, 1994.

Ratigan, William. *Great Lakes Shipwrecks & Survivors.* Grand Rapids, Mich.: W. M. B. Eerdmans Publishing, 1960.

*Rossport Ontario Canada.* Chapbook. Rossport Historical Society, Box 57, Rossport, Ont. P0T 2R0, n.d.

Shelley, Mary Wollstonecraft. *Frankenstein.* London: Penguin Books, 1992.

Smith, Derek G. *Canadian Indians and the Law: Selected Documents, 1663–1972.* Toronto: McClelland & Stewart, 1975.

Stonehouse, Frederick. *The Wreck of the* Edmund Fitzgerald. Gwinn, Mich.: Avrey Color Studios, Inc., 1977.

Strickland, Helen Moore. *Silver Under the Sea*. Cobalt, Ont.: Highway Book Shop, 1979.

Thompson, Mark. *Graveyard of the Lakes*. Detroit, Mich.: Wayne State University Press, 2000.

*Trading and Shipping on the Great Lakes*. Toronto: J. H. Beers, 1899. Reprint, Toronto: Coles Publishing Company Limited, 1980.

Tronrud, Thorold J. *Guardians of Progress: Boosters & Boosterism in Thunder Bay, 1870–1914*. Thunder Bay, Ont.: Thunder Bay Historical Museum Society, 1993.

Vecsey, Christopher. *Traditional Ojibwa Religion*. Philadelphia, Penn.: American Philosophical Society, 1983.

Verwyst, Chrysostom. *Missionary Labors of Fathers Marquette, Ménard and Allouez*. Milwaukee, Wis.: Hoffman Brothers, 1886.

Walling, Regis M., and Rev. N. Daniel Rupp, eds. *The Diary of Bishop Frederic Baraga*. Detroit, Mich.: Wayne State University Press, 1990.

Warkentin, Germaine. *Canadian Exploration Literature*. Toronto: Oxford University Press, 1993.

Wolff, Julius F., Jr. *Lake Superior Shipwrecks: A Complete Reference to Maritime Accidents and Disasters*. Duluth, Minn.: Lake Superior Port Cities, Inc., 1990.

Wrigley, Ronald. *Shipwrecked; Vessels That Met Tragedy on Northern Lake Superior*. Cobalt, Ont.: Highway Book Shop, 1958.

JOURNALS AND OTHER SOURCES

Auer, Nancy A., ed. *A Lake Sturgeon Rehabilitation Plan for Lake Superior*. Houghton: Department of Biological Sciences, Michigan Technological University, Michigan 49931, July 2, 2001.

*The Beaver*. Oct./Nov. 1940; Oct./Nov. 2001.

Great Lakes Commission. *Lake Superior: A Case History of the Lake and Its Fisheries*. Great Lakes Fishery Commission, Ann Arbour, Mich., 1973.

Great Lakes Basin Commission. *Great Lakes Basin Framework Study, Appendix C9 Commercial Navigation*. Public Information Office, Ann Arbour, Mich., 1975.

Hybels, Robert James. "Lake Superior Copper Fever," *Michigan History*. June 17, 1950.

International Association for Great Lakes Research. *Journal of Great Lakes Research*, vol. 13, no. 2 (1987), and vol. 14, no. 1 (1988).

*Journey to Yesteryear: A History of Schreiber*. Schreiber, Ont.: Memorabilia Program, Schreiber Public Library, 1974.

Keweenaw County Historical Society. *10 Lights: The Lighthouses of the Keweenaw Peninsula*. Eagle Harbor, Mich. 49950, n.d.

Mountain, James A. *The Inhospitable Shore: An Historical Resources Study of Neys Provincial Park—Port Coldwell, Ontario*. Toronto: Ministry of Natural Resources, Division of Parks, Historical Sites Branch, 1983.

Parini, Jay. "The Tide Falls, Longfellow's Neglected Virtues," *Times Literary Supplement*. May 25, 2001.

Thunder Bay Historical Museum Society. *Papers & Records*, vol. XX, 1992. Re German prisoners of war in WWII.

Thunder Bay Museum Historical Society, *Papers & Records*, vol. XXVII, 1999.

# Acknowledgments

For all of its hardness and brutality, for all the killed animals, felled forests, blasted rock faces, hard-rock miners, and drowned sailors, Lake Superior is essentially a story told by women. It is to these women I am massively indebted, to the stately Grace Lee Nute whose writings have assumed almost biblical proportions in the Superior canon. I am indebted as well to the other women who have written Superior: Elinor Barr, Marjorie Wilkins Campbell, Helen Moore Strickland, Janet Lewis and her remarkable novel, *The Invasion,* and Lorraine Niedecker, who attempted Lake Superior in verse and came closer than anyone has the right to expect. I am indebted to Carolyn Gilman and her thoroughly engrossing history of Grand Portage, in particular her depiction of the transformation of fur trader Daniel Harmon, which was too rich not to be told again in this book.

I am also indebted to the unheralded women who run the libraries and local historical centres—at least one of which operates in the dark to save on electricity bills. These abandoned cabooses and former pool halls shine like beacons on both sides of Superior. My thanks to Rosemary Comeau of the Marathon Historical Society, to Jeanne Marcella of the Terrace Bay Public Library, to the helpful staff of the Schreiber Public Library, and to Laura Jacobs of the University of Wisconsin-Superior.

My gratitude and indebtedness extends south of Superior to Hilary McMahon, my agent at Westwood Creative Artists, always cheerful, helpful, and remarkably efficient. To all at Penguin Canada I am deeply grateful—to my editor Andrea Crozier, to Sandra Tooze, to Maria Scala and to Mary Opper—for their hard work on both the inside and outside of this book. Finally I wish to thank my long-time partner/research assistant, Deborah Clipperton, for the joy and the beauty that she brought to this project and to me. Thanks also to Margaret Clipperton for her help and her anecdotes.

I am indebted as well to a number of men. Angel Guerra's initial enthusiasm caused this journey to be undertaken in the first place. Donald Bastian's scrutiny of my original draft was a great help. Matthew Harvey and Percy Toop contributed rare and useful documents during the research phases. Thanks to Thorold J. Tronrud for writing his wonderfully scandalous *Guardians of Progress: Boosters & Boosterism in Thunder Bay 1870–1914*.

I am pleased to thank as well the Ontario Ministry of Natural Resources, Parks Branch, and the Ontario Arts Council and Canada Council for their crucial support over the years.

*Source Notes*

Permission granted to reprint quotations from Johann Georg Kohl, *Kitchi-Gami: Life among the Lake Superior Ojibway* (London: Chapman and Hall, 1860; St. Paul, Minn.: Minnesota Historical Society Press, 1985).

Quotations from *Silver Under the Sea* by Helen Moore Strickland used with permission of the publisher, Highway Book Shop, Cobalt, Ontario.

Wilmot Hamilton's poem in *A History of Jackfish* used with permission of the author.

Quotations from *The Diary of Bishop Frederic Baraga,* edited by Regis M. Walling and Rev. N. Daniel Rupp, used with permission of the Diocese of Marquette.

# Illustration Credits

The publisher gratefully acknowledges permission to use the following images:

| CHAPTER | SOURCE |
|---|---|
| 1 | John Foster/Masterfile |
| 2 | Buffalo Bill Historical Center, Cody, WY; Gift of Mrs. Karl Frank; 14.86 |
| 3 | *Indians of the United States, Volume 1,* by Henry Rowe Schoolcraft |
| 4 | C. W. Jefferys/National Archives of Canada/ C-070268 |
| 5 | *The Voyageur* by Grace Lee Nute, Minnesota Historical Society Press, 1987 |
| 6 | The Library of Congress, Washington, D.C. |
| 7 | Wisconsin Historical Society, WHi-4953 |
| 8 | Tanner: Edwin James, ed., *A Narrative of the Captivity and Adventures of John Tanner* (New York: G. & C. & H. Carvill, 1830). Dechert Collection, Annenberg Rare Book & Manuscript Library, University of Pennsylvania. |
| | Schoolcraft: Francis S. Drake, ed., *Indians of the United States, Volume 1: The Work of Henry Rowe Schoolcraft, 1883–1884.* |
| 9 | Peter Unwin |
| 10 | Mr. T. L. Tanton, National Archives of Canada, #PA 15956 |
| 11 | Queen's Printer for Ontario, 1963. Reproduced with permission. |
| 12 | Peter Unwin |
| 13 | Thunder Bay Historical Museum Society, 974.2.4B |
| 14 | Marathon & District Historical Society |
| 15 | Julius F. Wolff collection, Lake Superior Marine Museum Archives; Lake Superior Maritime Collections, UW-Superior |
| 16 | Historical Collections of the Great Lakes, Bowling Green State University |
| 17 | Deborah Clipperton |

# Index

Abanel, Father, 33
Abenaki language, 27
aboriginals. *See* Natives
Acme Transit Company, 195
Agassiz, Louis, 124, 137, 223
agates, 138
Agawa Rock, 22, 153
alcohol
    *Edmund Fitzgerald* beer, 215
    Lakehead and, 175–76
    Silver Islet and, 109, 117
Algoma, 220–21
*Algoma,* 106, 183–85, 192
Algoma Steel Corporation, 186
Algonkian language, 8–9
*Algonquin,* 62, 63, 191
Algonquins, 42
Allouez, Claude-Jean, 5, 19, 26–29, 32,
    85–86, 224
American Fur Company, 40, 42, 49, 125,
    188
Anishnabe, 18
Aqua Plano Indians, 112
Arctic, 2, 3
Armagost, Mike, 217
Arone, Shidane, 213
*Arthur M. Anderson,* 201–3, 215
ascendentalism, 2–3
Ashland, Wisconsin, 13
Astor, John Jacob, 40
*Augusta,* 97
*Avafors,* 202

Baraga, Frederic, 18, 19, 83–101, 94–95,
    191
    language ability of, 87–90
    Natives and, 90–93, 222
    statue of, 83–84, 100–191

Baxter, Richard, 116, 165
Baxter, T. S. H., 7, 20
Bayfield, Henry, 119–20, 192
Bayfield, Wisconsin, 119, 120
Bear tribe, Brûlé and, 10, 11
bears, 135–36, 172
    blueberries and, 164
    Jackfish and, 167, 169
    POWs and, 156, 160
beaver
    as food, 13, 14, 39
    Natives and, 47–48, 222–23
Belaney, Archie, 226
Bell, Jimmie, 172
*Ben E. Tate,* 217
Bendry, Captain James, 143–44
Betridge, Alice, 195
Biebeck, Horst, 158
*Big Fitz. See Edmund Fitzgerald*
Biggar (cook), 116
Bigsby, John J., 41
Bingham, Abel, 75–76
Bishop, Hugh, 207
blackflies, 30, 33, 157, 164
blueberries, 163–64
Bondar, Roberta, 227
*Boom Copper,* 64
Brébeuf, Jean de, 10, 30
Bremer, Richard, 80
brothels, 162, 175
Brown, William "Uncle Billy," 126
Brûlé, Étienne, 8–11, 20, 150, 226
*Burlington,* 194
Burnham, Guy, 2, 222, 224
Burriss, Rufus A., 174, 175
Butterfield, Consul Willshire, 10
*By Cross and Anchor,* 96

Cabot, J. Elliot, 124, 137
Campbell, Marjorie Wilkins, 36, 37, 38
*Canada: An Essay,* 5
Canadian Airborne Regiment, 213
Canadian Armed Forces, 213
Canadian Pacific Railway, 16, 127
    Jackfish and, 167, 168
    North Shore and, 161–62, 171
    pies and, 219
    steamships, 183
    water sales and, 165
cannibalism, 3, 11, 12, 18
canoes, 192
    etymology of word, 218–19
Carlson, Charlie, 229
Carmichael, Jack, 167
*Carte de Jesuits,* 26
Carver, Jonathan, 7, 57, 178
Cass, Lewis, 46, 57–60, 63, 122
cattle, 164, 165
caviar, 131
*Cerisoles,* 185, 214
Champlain, Samuel de, 8, 9, 10
Charlevoix, Pierre-François-Xavier de, 7, 57
Chebul, Father, 88, 99
*Cheluyskin,* 2
Chequamegon, 13, 222–23
*Chicora,* 187–88
China, route to, 9, 10, 173
Chippewa, 18, 31. *See also* Ojibwa
    ceremonies of, 48–49
    Charles Harvey and, 200
    copper and (*see under* copper)
    Frederic Baraga and, 86–87, 89–90
    fur traders and, 36
    Ontonagon Boulder and (*see* Onton-
        agon Boulder)
    treaty with U.S. and, 45–55, 58, 60,
        63
    women, 26, 28, 40, 53
Chippeway, 18
cholera, 200
Christianity. *See also* Baraga, Frederic;
    Jesuits
    Natives and, 27, 38
Clement XIV, Pope, 32
coal, 167–68, 170

coal dances, 167–68, 169
Coast Guard, 193, 195, 196, 197
    *Edmund Fitzgerald* and, 202–6, 209–10
Coldwell, Robert, 171
Conkin, David, 210
Contoui, Charlotte, 143
Cooper, Astley P., 113
Cooper, Bernie, 202
copper
    Chippewa and, 51, 57–58, 60, 61, 63
    first mining rush and, 64, 66
    *Independence* and, 191
    Keweenaw Peninsula and, 145, 146, 147
    mining, 88, 146
    Mishipizheu and, 20, 23
    Natives and, 57–58
    Ontonagon Boulder and (*see* Ontana-
        gon Boulder)
    prospecting for, 31, 58
    Radisson and, 12
    Thomas Macfarlane and, 104
Copper Harbor, 62, 63
Copper Rock. *See* Ontonagon Boulder
*Cormorant,* 213
*coureurs de bois,* 35, 38
Cousteau, Jacques, 204
Couverette, Jules, 164
Cowper, William, 46, 54, 55
Cree, language of, 21
Cross, J. W. and Helen, 109
Cross, Maggie, 109
Cundy, Ransom, 216
Cunningham, General, 63, 64

Dablon, Claude, 26, 28
Dakotas, 173, 223
Danzinger, Edmund, 18
Daumont, sieur de Saint-Lusson, 26
Davie, Donald, 178
Dawson, Simon, 173
Dead Horse Creek, 221
Dean, Pauline, 18, 163
deer, stuffed, 50–51
Dene, 18
Dewdney, Selwyn, 19, 228
*Dictionary of the Otchipwe Language,* 87
Dietz, Steven, 215

Donnelly, Joseph P., 31
Dorion, 163
Doukhobors, 175
Doyle, Arthur Conan, 105
drownings, 17, 20, 106, 139, 182–85
drugs, Johnston family and, 70, 71, 72
Druillettes, Gabriel, 27
Dudgeon, Mr., *Hattie Vinton* and, 185
Dudouyt, Abbé, 29
"Duke of Miracle Dog," 165–66
Duluth, 173
    Brûlé and, 9
    harbour, ships and, 193–94
Duluth, Daniel Greyson, 5
dynamite, 162

Eagle River, 145
Eddie, Helen, 164
*Edmund Fitzgerald,* 7, 19, 23, 120, 157,
    183, 198–217
    bell of, 213–14, 216
    cargo load and waves, 209
    inquiry, 204–5
    internet and, 215
    keel of, 206–7
    memorabilia, 137, 210–17
    size of, 199
    storm and, 201–3
Edmund Fitzgerald *Lost with All Hands,*
    *The,* 211
education
    Natives and, 76, 89, 90
    in Schreiber, 165
Eldred, Julius, 61, 62–64, 65
engineers, 227
Evans, James, 20–21, 80
Everett, Philo M., 143
Evergreen Cemetery, 148
Expedition '94 Ltd., 214
*Explorations of Pierre Esprit Radisson, The,*
    11

*Fall of Berlin, The,* 159
Farnquist, Tom, 211, 213, 214
Finnish immigrants, 175, 176, 229
firearms. *See* weapons
fire-eaters, 49

fish/fishing, 119–34
    Bayfield, Wisconsin, and, 120–21
    catch rates, 124, 125, 126
    CPR and, 127–28
    dams and, 128, 131, 132
    decline of (greed and), 124–28
    Great Lakes cisco and, 128
    hatchery, 163
    lampracide and, 128
    lamprey and, 125–26, 128–29, 134
    Native "spirits" as, 21, 22
    nets and, 123, 126–27
    pickerel, 4
    pollution and, 4, 129
    Radisson and, 12
    Sault Ste. Marie and, 121, 123–24
    siskowet, 129–30
    slimy sculpin, 128
    spears and, 123
    sportsmen and, 134
    sturgeon, 129–32
    treaties and, 125
    "trout, fat," 129–30
    trout, lake, 126, 127, 128
    trout, rainbow, 125
    walleye, 128
    whitefish, 120–28, 133–34, 222
    in winter, 127
Fitzgerald, Edmund, 199
Fitzgerald, Elizabeth, 198
*Fitzgerald's Storm,* 211
Fond du Lac, 45, 49, 52, 63
    treaty at, 45–55, 58, 60, 63
food. *See also* cannibalism; fish/fishing;
    starvation
    beaver as, 13, 14
    Natives and, 10
forests/forestry, 5, 230
    banning of log drives and, 124
    Douglas firs and, 152
    Europen artists and, 28
    POWs and, 154, 155, 159
    Silver Islet and, 108
    storms and, 145
Fort William, 89, 173–77
    "historical," 176–77
*Fort William Journal,* 4

*Frankenstein,* 3
Franklin, Benjamin, 224
Frazier, John, 196
Fregeu, Charles, 196
Fresnel, Jean Augustin, 146
Frue, Helen Adams, 105, 106
Frue, William Bell, 104, 107, 108, 110, 117
Frue Vanner, 117
fur trading, 5. *See also* Hudson's Bay Company; North West Company; voyageurs
    decline of, 42, 124–25
    Fort William and, 176–77
    Grand Portage and, 36
    Native culture and, 37–38
    Radisson, Groseillers, and, 14–15
    Scotsmen and, 43
    voyageurs and, 41

*Gales of November, The,* 211
Gallagher, John, 195
Gaudin, Louis, 94, 95
George, Benjamin, 144
*George G. Barnum,* 187
*George M. Cox,* 180, 181
Gesick, Marji, 143
Gilchrist, J. C., 205
Gitchee Gumee, 224. *See also* Kitche Gami
Gladstone, William, 39
gold, 5, 174
*Goliah,* 195
Gordon, Charles George, 39, 40
Grand Island, 139
Grand Portage, 34, 36, 38
Great Lakes, 182
    ship casualties in 1914, 205
    ships' lights and, 183
    shipwrecks and, 192
Great Lakes Aquarium, 128, 132, 230
Great Lakes Shipwreck Museum, 210, 213
Greeley, Horace, 144
*Grey Hawk: Life and Adventures,* 74
Groseilliers, Médard Chouart, sieur de, 11–15, 150, 219–20
Group of Seven, 167
*Gulls of the* Edmund Fitzgerald, *The,* 211

*Gunilda,* 196, 228
guns. *See* weapons

Hale, Horatio, 140
Hamilton, Wilmot, 179
Hammond, Colonel, 61–62
*Hamonic,* 185, 186
Harkness, W. L., 196
Harmon, David, 38, 41, 44
Harris, Lawren, 152, 167
Harvey, Charles, 200
Hascall, John, 101
Hassell, Thomas, 21
Hatch, Ida, 144
*Hattie Vinton,* 185
hawks, sparrow, 136–37
Hemingway, Ernest, 142
Hemming, Robert, 212
Henry, Alexander, 3, 57
*Henry B. Smith,* 195
Herbert, William, 228
Hiawatha, 70, 112
Hiawatha National Forest, 139, 140
Highway of Hope, 178
*Historical and Statistical Information . . . United States,* 81
*History of Jackfish, A,* 179
Hobart, Henry, 107, 145, 147
Hochelaga, 207
Hoertz, George, 155
Hogan, John Sheridan, 5
*Holdin' Our Own,* 215
Holmes, Oliver Wendell, 141
hotel(s)
    Eagle River, 143, 144
    Jackfish, 167, 169
    moving a, 143, 144
    Schreiber, 165
Houghton, 106
Houghton, Douglass, 39, 106
Houghton Point, 144
Hoxie, Lau, 182
Hudson, Bruce, 216
Hudson, Ruth, 216
Hudson's Bay Company, 4
    fish and, 125
    James Evans and, 80

North West Company and, 39
    Radisson, Groseillers, and, 15
Hurlburt, Thomas, 179
Huron country, 9
*Huronic,* 189, 196
Hurons, Brûlé and, 9–10, 11
Husilik, Brenda, 163
Hybels, Robert James, 66

icebergs, 193
Ignatius of Loyola, 30
*Illinois,* 139
immigration. *See* settlers
*Independence,* 143, 144, 190–91
Indian Civilization Act, 49
Indian Removal Act, 54
*Indian Rock Painting of the Great Lakes,* 228
infant mortality, 176
*Inkerman,* 185, 213
*Instructions on the Sacraments,* 89
*Invincible,* 188
*Ira H. Owen,* 201
iron, 143. *See also* taconite
Ironside, George, 113
Iroquois
    Brûlé and, 9, 10, 30
    Jesuits and, 30
    Radisson and, 11–12, 15, 21
*Iroquois Book of Rites,* 140
Isbister, Jam*es, 166*
isinglass, 131
Isle Royale, 180, 183, 192, 194, 195, 201

Jacker, Edward, 88, 97, 100
Jackfish, 152, 162, 163, 167–71
*Jackfish Village,* 167
Jackson, Andrew, 55
Jackson Mine, 143
*Jacques Marquette,* 31
jails
    Lakehead, 175
    Silver Islet, 109–10
James, Edwin, 23, 73, 74
Jameson, Anna, 5, 70–71, 73, 115, 121, 226
    fish/fishing and, 122, 124, 129
Jamison, James K., 96

jasper, 138
Jefferys, C. W., 28
*Jesuit Relations,* 10, 19, 20, 30, 130
    editor of, 21
Jesuits, 10
    character of, 32
    Natives and, 26–33
    Ontonagon Boulder and, 57
    Sault Ste. Marie mission and, 25–28
    as *Wametigoshe,* 28
Jogues, Isaac, 30
*John Jacob Astor,* 188
*John Tanner . . . ,* 74
Johnson, Pauline, 6, 164, 174
Johnston, Anne Marie, 67, 72, 80
Johnston, Charlotte, 67, 69, 71, 72
Johnston, Eastman, 133
Johnston, Eliza, 71–72, 79
Johnston, George, 80, 112
Johnston, Jane. *See* Schoolcraft, Jane
Johnston, John, 68–69, 79
    fishing and, 124
    Lake Superior and, 6
Johnston, Susan, 68
Johnston, William, 81
*Joseph Block,* 208
*Julia Palmer,* 187

*Kalveda,* 141
Kaministiquia, 115, 173, 177
*Kamloops,* 194, 195
Kane, Paul, 18
Kawbawgam, Charlotte, 143
kayaks, 158, 171–72
Kellog, Francis, 22
Kennicott, Robert, 39
Keweenaw Peninsula, 47–48, 66, 83, 88, 136, 146–47
Kirke brothers, 9
Kitche Gami, 218, 222, 225
Knight, James, 4–5
Kohl, Johann, 31, 48, 90, 91, 95, 223, 225
    fish/fishing and, 123, 125, 129
Krakhoffer, Hans, 153

La Hontan, Louis-Armand, baron de, 57
La Pointe, 42, 85, 86

la Ronde, sieur de, 188, 224
La Salle, Robert Cavelier, sieur de, 5, 29
La Vérendrye, Pierre Gaultier, 173
Lacomb, Mrs., 86
*Lady Elgin,* 97
Lake Carriers Association, 204, 205, 207, 209
Lake Galilee, 228
Lake Gogebic, 225
Lake Superior
    float-bottle studies of, 185
    greatest depth, 139
    names and, 222–29
    reef, 192
    tributaries of, 132
    width of, 189–90
*Lake Superior,* 36, 124
*Lake Superior Country,* 3
*Lake Superior News and Miner's Journal,* 145
*Lake Superior Shipwrecks,* 189
Lake Tracy, 27, 224
Lakehead, 173, 174, 175
Lambert, Bernard, 84
lamprey. *See under* fish/fishing
L'Anse, 143
    cemetery, 135, 148–49
Laughing Whitefish, 143
Lautischat, Laurence, 97–98
Le Jeune, Paul, 21, 27
*Leafield,* 185, 186, 189
*Let Her B.,* 187
Lewis, Winslow, 146
libraries, 163, 177, 179, 211
life jackets, 193
Lightfoot, Gordon, 181, 210, 212, 213, 224
lighthouses, 139, 140, 146–47, 192
    sperm whale oil and, 147
Little Girl Point, 228–29
Livingstone, Jane, 115
Longboat, Tom, 76
Longfellow, Henry Wadsworth, 2, 70, 78, 112, 115, 140–41, 142, 224
Longstreth, T. Morris, 2, 3, 5, 6, 104, 220
loons, 228
Louis XIV, 26
Lount, Samuel, 114

Macfarlane, Thomas, 104, 117
MacInnis, Joseph, 211, 212, 213
Mackenzie, Alexander, 41, 57, 58
Mackinac Indian Agency, 81
Madeline Island, 42, 85
*Magai Desai,* 197
*Major,* 186
*Manhattan,* 190, 229
*Manistee,* 191
manitou, 19, 21, 23
Manitou Island, 181, 222
*Mantodoc,* 168
maps, names and, 219–29
Marathon, 170, 172, 227
Marquette, 98, 100, 139
*Marquette,* 187
Marquette, Jacques, 5, 30
Marvin, John, 105
*Mataafa,* 193–94
Mather, William, 139
May, Karl, 152, 226
McCarter, William, 184
McCarthy, Jack, 217
McGillivray, Simon, 177
McGillivray, William, 34–35, 38
McKay, George Perry, 191
McKay, John, 99
McKenney, Thomas, 40, 41, 182
    fish/fishing and, 121, 122, 123–24, 133
    Jane Schoolcraft and, 70, 71, 72
    Native women and, 53–54, 229
    Natives and, 45–55, 65, 142
    Ontonagon Boulder and, 47, 54, 57–60, 63
McMurray, Charlotte. *See* Johnston, Charlotte
McMurray, William, 72, 122
McQuaig, Mugs, 166, 169
McSorley, Ernest Michael, 7, 157, 202–3, 206–8
Melville, Herman, 137
Ménard, Pierre, 30–31, 100
*Merchant,* 192
mercury, 4, 129
*Mesquite,* 196–97
Messiah, John, 115
*Meteor,* 191

meteorology, 207
Mica Bay, 227, 228
Mica Bay War, 113
Michamakila, 20
Michigan Territory, 46
Michipicoten Island, 20, 202
Miller, Charlie, 144
*Mineral Rock,* 99
miners
    first, 188
    Silver Islet, 105–11
mining
    copper (*see* copper)
    dangers of, 110–11, 148
    fuses and, 145
    permits, 113
    Sault Ste. Marie and, 78
    silver (*see* silver)
    surveying and, 103
    treaties and, 113
Mink Tunnel, 162
Mishipizeu, 19–24, 153
Missing Horse Creek, 221
Mitchell, Esther, 149
Mohawks, 12, 27
*Monkshaven,* 186
Montreal Mining Company, 103, 104
Moodie, Susanna, 5, 221
Moral and Social Reform League, 176
Morris, William, 197
mosquitoes, 30, 120, 174
Mount McKay, 175
Mountain, James, 127
Mueller, Martin, 158
Munising, Michigan, 136, 139, 140
Murdoch, Angus, 64
*Myron,* 193

names
    maps and, 219–29
    ships and, 192, 229
Nanabozho, 19, 22, 102, 129, 130, 134, 222
*Narrative of . . . John Tanner, A,* 73
National Geographic Society, 213
Natives. *See also various aboriginal nations and tribes*
    art and (*see* pictograms)

Brûlé and, 10–11
Christianity and, 27 (*see also* Baraga, Frederic; Jesuits)
copper and, 20, 57–58, 60
education system and, 76, 89, 90
European weapons and, 12–13
fishing and (*see* fish/fishing)
Fond du Lac treaty and, 45–55, 58, 60, 63
fur traders and (*see* fur trading)
hospitality of, 31
Jesuit attitudes to, 26–33
La Vérendrye and, 173
languages, Frederic Baraga and, 87–90
as literary exotics, 2
map names and, 219, 220–24
medicine and, 50
moon and, 223
the North and, 4
as people to be taught, 5, 51
Radisson, Groseillers, and, 11–15
reserves, royalty payments and, 114
Robinson Superior Treaty and, 112–13, 125
romanticism of, 671
Silver Islet and, 112–13, 114–16
"spirits" and, 17–24, 47–48, 65
spirituality of, 32–33
"Trail of Tears" and, 54
white men as, 8–9, 37–38, 42, 226 (*see also* Tanner, John)
women (*see* women, Native)
*Navada,* 185
Nazis, test for, 154
New, W. H., 220, 221
New France
    Radisson, Groseillers, and, 15
    Sault Ste. Marie and, 25–29
    territorial claims of, 26, 28
Neys, Ontario, 151–54, 179, 218
Niedecker, Lorraine, 178
*Night the Fitz Went Down, The,* 211
Nile River, 40
nitroglycerine, 162
Noronic, 186, 197
North, the
    ascendentalism and, 2–3
    beauty of, 3, 5

good *vs.* evil and, 3–4
healing power of, 2–3, 4, 6
Natives and, 4
wilderness and, 4
North West Company, 22, 34
Chippewa and, 36
Hudson's Bay Company and, 39
Scotsmen and, 43
ships, 188
*North West Company, The,* 36
Noslo, 221
Nute, Grace Lee, 36, 37, 43

Ojibwa. *See also* Chippewa
canoes, 192
cemeteries, 149
Finns and, 229
fish and, 121, 123, 130. 133
Grand Island, treaties and, 139
Henry Schoolcraft and, 74, 80–82
Highway of Hope and, 178–79
historians and, 115
John Tanner and (*see* Tanner, John)
Johnston family and, 68–69
language, 87, 225–26
legends, 19, 22, 48, 130, 230
Longstreth and, 6
meaning of name, 18
Mishipizeu and, 22
siskowet and, 129
sturgeon and, 130
treaties and (*see* Robinson Superior Treaty)
Okondokon, 61, 63
Oly (fish seller), 120–21, 134
Onodogas, 140
*Onoka,* 187
Ontonagon, 144, 145
Ontonagon Boulder, 47, 54, 56–66
Ontonagon River, 60, 61, 219
opera house, 143
*Oriole,* 139
Osborn, C. S., 4, 122
Ottawa tribe, 127

Palika, 186
Paquette, Dudley, 207
Parkman, Francis, 11, 26, 29

Paul, James, 61, 62
Pays Platt, 170
Peltoniemi, Eric, 215
pemmican, 39
Peninsula Harbour, 162
Penny, Charles, 35, 42, 59, 64
fish/fishing and, 122, 124, 125
Native women and, 53
Pepys, Samuel, 11
Perrot, Nicolas, 19, 26, 29
*Pewabic,* 191
Phelpeaux, Jean-Frederic, 224
Pic Island, 152
pictograms, 16, 19, 20, 22–23, 153
Pictured Rocks, 194
pie, 219–20
Pigeon River Timber Company, 154, 155
Pinery Indian Cemetery, 149
Plimsoll, Samuel, 205
Point au Chapeau, 35
pollution, 4, 129, 131, 132
porcupines, 39
Port Arthur, 173, 176
Port Arthur and Duluth Railway, 176
Port Coldwell, 152, 162, 163, 167, 170, 171, 228
portaging. *See under* voyageurs
Porter, George F., 47, 59
POW camps, 151–60
escapes from, 156–59
Pratt, E. J., 32
Pukaskwa National Park, 15–16
Pukaskwa Pits, 153
Pulcher, Pete, 208

Quebec Mining Company, 113, 114
*Quiet Coves and Rocky Highlands,* 7

racoons, 125
Radisson, Pierre Esprit, 11–15, 150, 220, 226
Native "spirits" and, 21
Rafferty, Bob, 217
railways, 176. *See also* Canadian Pacific Railway
blueberries and, 164
building of, 162–63
caterpillars and, 176

first diesel trains and, 168
Jackfish and, 167–71
L'Anse and, 143
map names and, 221
mudslides and, 171
Rainbow Falls Provincial Park, 178
Rathbone, Justus H., 136
Ratigan, William, 182, 197
Raudot, Antoine Denis, 4, 19, 33, 123
Raudot, Jacques, 5
*Recovery,* 119
Red Sucker trestle, 162
Rice, Alma, 181
Riel, Louis, 172, 187
Robinson, Benjamin, 113–14
Robinson Superior Treaty, 112–13, 125, 225
rock art paintings. *See* pictograms
Rodin (Norwegian), 169
Ross, Walter, 227
Rossport, 171, 172, 196, 227–28
Rossport Fishing Derby, 126
Ryerson, John, 5

*sagamite,* 10, 38
Saint-Lusson, Daumont, sieur de, 26, 28, 29, 33, 103
Samerhorn, Ron, 158
Sault, 18–19, 213
Sault Ste. Marie, 227
    Jesuit mission at, 25–28, 33
    locks at (*see* Soo Locks)
    mining and, 78
    naming of, 222
    rapids, 121
    Windigo and, 3
Sayre, Esther, 114
Schoolcraft, Anne Marie. *See* Johnston, Anne Marie
Schoolcraft, Henry Rowe, 46, 56, 60, 63, 64
    Jane Johnston and, 67, 68, 69, 70, 72
    John Tanner and, 73–74, 75
    map names and, 220, 222
    Natives and, 79–82, 115, 140, 142, 220
Schoolcraft, James, 68, 72, 73–74, 76, 81
Schoolcraft, Jane, 53–54, 69–72, 80, 81
Schoolcraft, Johnston, 82
*Schoolcraft, Longfellow, Hiawatha,* 69

Schreiber, 163–66, 177, 179
*Scotiadoc,* 194
sea lamprey. *See* fish/fishing, lamprey
*Sebastopol,* 185
Seneca, 29
settlers, 5, 114–15
    *Algoma* and, 183
    Lakehead and, 174–76
Seven Oaks massacre, 39, 43
Shannon, Frederick, 214
Shelley, Mary, 3
*Shepherd of the Wilderness, The,* 84
Sheridan, Robert, 53, 54
Shingwauk, 113
ships, 180–97. *See also Edmund Fitzgerald; individual ships*
    building and towing of, 183
    captains of, 206
    casualties in 1914, 205
    Civil War and, 187
    coal and, 167
    collisions of, 139, 194
    decked, first, 188
    drownings and (*see* drownings)
    fires and, 183, 193, 194
    as floating docks, 187
    Keweenaw Peninsula and, 145, 146, 191, 192, 196, 197
    La Salle and, 29
    load lines on, 205, 209
    names of, 192, 229
    1905 storm and, 193
    1913 storm and, 189–90
    overloading of, 205, 209
    Silver Islet sightseers and, 112
    steam, first, 143, 190
    storms and, 19, 23, 99, 106, 145, 181, 183–90, 192–97, 208 (*see also Edmund Fitzgerald*)
    supertankers, 210
    wireless radio and, 205–6
    women and, 180–82
    wrecks, 192–93, 214
shipyards
    Lakehead, 185
    Sault Ste. Marie, 188
Sibley, Alexander, 102, 104, 107, 117
    Natives and, 115

Sibley Peninsula, 102, 112
Sifton, Clifford, 174
silver
    Silver Islet and, 102–18
    stock prices, 116
    value of, at Silver Islet, 111, 117
Silver City, 144, 145
Silver Islet, 102–18
    explosions at, 110–11
    mine shafts at, 103, 117, 118
    miners, 105–11
    Natives and, 112–13, 114–16
Silver Islet Employees Benefit Society, 110
*Silver Under the Sea,* 103, 111
Sioux, 12, 18–19
*Siskiwit,* 129
siskowet, 129–30
Skelton, Joan, 215
*Sketches of a Tour . . . ,* 46
"Skin Island," 162
Sleeping Giant, 102, 178
Slovenia, 84
Smellie, Charles, 229
Snowshoe Priest. *See* Baraga, Frederic
*Song of Hiawatha, The,* 2, 70, 78, 115,
    140, 141, 142, 224
Soo Locks, 187, 190, 200
    *Edmund Fitzgerald* and, 207
    tonnage through, 200
    whitefish at, 121
Spadoni, Gino, 167
*St. Clair,* 193
St. Germain, Vincent, 22
St. Marys River, 200, 227
Standard Iron Bar, 103
Stannard, Benjamin and Charles, 188
starvation
    Gabriel Druillettes and, 27
    Radisson, Groseillers, and, 13–14, 150
    wolves and, 17
Steamboat Inspection Service, 206
Stiles, Amos, 191
Stonehouse, Frederick, 205, 211, 214
storms
    ships and (*see under* ships)
    Silver Islet and, 107–8
    telephones and, 164
streetcars, 176

Strickland, Helen Moore, 103, 104, 105,
    108, 110, 115
Stupak, Bart, 214
sturgeon. *See under* fish/fishing
Sturgeon Rehabilitation Plan, 132
Subocz, Susan, 197
Sudan, 39
*Sunbeam,* 196
*Superior,* 194
Superior, Wisconsin, 200, 201
Superior Shoal, 192
surveys
    hydrographic, 119–20, 192
    Silver Islet, 103
*Survivor of the* Edmund Fitzgerald, *The,*
    215
Sutherland, duke of, 155

taconite, 23, 112, 200, 201, 206
Tanner, John, 67, 73–78
    U.S. legislation and, 75
telephones, 164
*Ten November,* 215
*Theano,* 186
Thiele, Henry Louis, 97
Thompson, Mark, 206
Thunder Bay, 173–74
Tilden, Bryand, Jr., 76, 77
Toynbee, Arnold, 40
Tracy, marquis de, 27
"Trail of Tears," 54
Trans-Canada Highway, 16, 162, 179
treaties. *See under* Natives
Tresize, Jemmis, 145
trout. *See under* fish/fishing
Twelve Apostles, 222
*29 Missing,* 211
typhoid fever, 176

UFOs, 229
United States
    army, 47
    Civil War, 82, 187
    government, Henry Schoolcraft and, 81
    government, Natives and, 46, 49,
        51–52, 55, 60
    government, Ontonagon Boulder and,
        47, 59, 63, 65

Van Horne, William, 161, 219
Vecsey, Christopher, 19
Verdone, Katie, 165, 167, 169, 170
Verwyst, Chrysostom, 89, 94, 98
Voelker, John D., 143
*Voyageur, The,* 36
voyageurs, 35–44
    ageing of, 42
    character of, 39–44
    diet of, 38–39
    fishing and, 124
    fur trading and (*see* fur trading)
    historians and, 36
    loons and, 228
    Nile River expedition and, 39–40
    paddling rate of, 35, 40
    portaging and, 37, 40–41 (*see also* Grand Portage)
    strength of, 40–41, 43–44

Wabishkeepenas, 57
*Waldo,* 181, 195
*Walter J. McCarthy,* 210
*Wametigoshe,* 28
Warren, William, 18, 222
Washington, Lizzie, 175
water
    contaminated, Fort William and, 176
    sales, CPR and, 165
weapons, Natives and, 12–13, 23
Wells, Charles, 144
Werra, Franz von, 157–58
*Western Star,* 193
White, Colonel, 61–62
whitefish, 120–28
    Natives and, 121, 122–23, 124, 222

Whitefish Bay, 10
Whitefish Point, 202, 210, 213
Whitman, Walt, 2
Whittier, John Greenleaf, 2
wigwams, 36
wilderness. *See under* North, the
*Wilfred Sykes,* 207
*William F. Sauber,* 197
*William Moreland,* 192
Windigo, 3, 14
Windigo cabbage, 31
Windsor, duke of, 219
*Winter Studies and Summer Rambles in Canada,* 121
Wolff, Julius, 188–89
Wolseley, Garnet Joseph, 187
women
    baseball and, 177
    bicycles and, 176
    ships and, 180–82, 196, 197
    Silver Islet saga and, 105
women, Native
    Charles Penny and, 53
    David Harmon and, 38
    fishing nets and, 123
    Thomas McKenny and, 53–54
    voyageurs and, 36, 40
World War II, prison camps and, 151–60
Wraxall, Lascelles, 31
*Wreck of the* Edmund Fitzgerald, *The,* 211
"Wreck of the *Edmund Fitzgerald,* The," 212, 213, 224
Wrigley, Ronald, 184

Zeba, 144
*Zillah,* 180